Fragile Moments

When God Speaks in Whispers

This book belongs to:

_____

Fragile Moments

When God Speaks in Whispers

Edited by
Phyllis Hobe

Fleming H. Revell Company
Old Tappan, New Jersey

IV

Printed in the United States of America
ISBN 0-8007-1176-9

ACKNOWLEDGMENTS

Grateful acknowledgment is hereby expressed to all who have contributed to this volume. Any inadvertent omissions of credit will be gladly corrected in future editions./ "Meet the Master" and "The Greatness of God" are from THE CHARLES L. ALLEN TREASURY, Edited by Charles L. Wallis, © 1970 by Fleming H. Revell Company. Used by permission./ "Christmas Day in the Morning" by Pearl S. Buck, reprinted by permission of Harold Ober Associates, Inc. Copyright © 1955 by Pearl S. Buck./ "Death and the Dawn" by Pearl S. Buck, reprinted by permission of Harold Ober Associates, Inc. Copyright © 1956 by Pearl S. Buck./ "A Family for Freddie," by Abbie Blair. Reprinted with permission from the December 1964 *Reader's Digest*. Copyright © 1964 by The Reader's Digest Assn., Inc./ "Sunday Best" by Dorothy Canfield. Copyright 1939 by Dorothy Canfield; renewed 1967 by Sarah Fisher Scott. Abridged from "Nothing Ever Happens" in A HARVEST OF STORIES by Dorothy Canfield, by permission of Harcourt Brace Jovanovich, Inc./An excerpt from FUNERAL SERVICES by James L. Christensen, published by Fleming H. Revell./ "The Ancient Cry" and "Strangers in a Strange Land" are from LET THE SUN SHINE IN by Grace Noll Crowell, published by Fleming H. Revell./ "On Suffering" is abridged from "The Suffering Women" from A NEW JOY by Colleen Townsend Evans, © 1973 by Fleming H. Revell Company. Used by permission./ "Snowflake" by Paul Gallico. Reprinted by permission of Harold Ober Associates, Inc. Copyright © 1952 by Pauline Gallico./ "Lent for Awhile," "The Mother's Question" and "How Do You Tackle Your Work?" by Edgar A. Guest. Reprinted from COLLECTED VERSE OF EDGAR A. GUEST by Edgar A. Guest, © 1934, with the permission of Contemporary Books, Inc., Chicago./ "A Sharing of Wonder," "Interview With an Immortal," and "Wedding By the Sea" are from A TOUCH OF WONDER by Arthur Gordon. Copyright © 1974 by Fleming H. Revell Company. Used by permission. Arthur Gordon for "The Search." Used by permission./Excerpt from "Be bold . . . and mighty forces will come to your aid" by Arthur Gordon which appeared in GUIDEPOSTS TREASURY OF FAITH by Guideposts Associates. Copyright © 1970 by Guideposts Associates, Inc. Reprinted by permission of Doubleday & Company, Inc./O. Henry. "The Gift of the Magi" from THE COMPLETE WORKS OF O. HENRY. Reprinted by permission of Doubleday & Company, Inc./Marjorie Holmes, "The Artist in Every Child" and "Enough Stars to Go Around." Excerpted from AS TALL AS MY HEART, © 1974 by Marjorie Holmes Mighell, EPM Publications, Inc., 1003 Turkey Run Road, McLean, VA 22101./An excerpt from Chapter Six of TWO FROM GALILEE by Marjorie Holmes, © 1972 by Marjorie Holmes Mighell, published by Fleming H. Revell Company. Used by permission./ "Daddy Can Fix It" first appeared in *The Evening Star*, June 15, 1958, "Children's Hands" first appeared in *The Evening Star*, May 21, 1961, and "Swan Lake" © 1964 by The Evening Star Newspaper Co. All from the book LOVE AND LAUGHTER by Marjorie Holmes. Reprinted by permission of Doubleday & Company./An excerpt from CHRIST AT THE ROUND TABLE by E. Stanley Jones. Copyright renewal © 1955 by E. Stanley Jones. Used by the permission of the publisher, Abingdon Press./An excerpt from SOMETHING MORE by Catherine Marshall. Copyright © 1974 by Catherine Marshall LeSourd. Published by Chosen Books, Lincoln, VA 22078. Used by permission./An excerpt from TO LIVE AGAIN. Copyright © 1957 by Catherine Marshall. Published by Chosen Books, Lincoln, VA 22078./An excerpt from THE PRAYERS OF PETER MARSHALL. Copyright © 1954 by Catherine Marshall. Published by Chosen Books, Lincoln, VA 22078. Used by permission./ "It Can Be Done" and an excerpt from "How to Achieve Your Goals" are from NORMAN VINCENT PEALE'S TREASURY OF COURAGE AND CONFIDENCE by Norman Vincent Peale, © 1970 by Norman Vincent Peale. Reprinted by permission of The Foundation for Christian Living./Excerpts from "The Power and the Joy" and "Excitement and the Power" are from THE POSITIVE POWER OF JESUS CHRIST by Norman Vincent Peale, published by Tyndale House Publishers, Inc. Copyright 1980 by Norman Vincent Peale./ "Good Evening, Professor" and "How to Be Happy" are from the book THE ADVENTURE OF BEING A WIFE by Mrs. Norman Vincent Peale. © 1971 by Ruth S. Peale and Arthur Gordon. Published by Prentice-Hall, Inc., Englewood Cliffs, New Jersey 07632./ "Anna" by Eugenia Price is from THE UNIQUE WORLD OF WOMEN, by Eugenia Price. Copyright 1969 by Zondervan Publishing House. Used by permission./ "The Freedom of Love" by Eugenia Price. Used by permission of Zondervan Publishing House./ "The Windows of Gold," "The Legend of the Wingless Birds," "What Is Love?" "The Seasons of the Soul," "If We Put Our Problems in God's Hand," "The Legend of the Spider and the Silken Strand Held in God's Hand," "The End of the Road Is But a Bend in the Road," and "Help Yourself to Happiness" are reprinted by the kind and generous permission of Helen Steiner Rice./ "The Flood" by Conrad Richter. Copyright 1945 by The Curtis Publishing Co. from THE RAWHIDE KNOT AND OTHER STORIES by Conrad Richter. Reprinted by permission of Alfred A. Knopf, Inc. Copyright © 1978 by Harvena Richter. Reprinted by permission of Paul R. Reynolds, Inc., 12 East 41st Street, New York, N.Y., 10017/ "A Christmas Tree in Brooklyn." Abridged and adapted from pages 179-187 in A TREE GROWS IN BROOKLYN by Betty Smith. Copyright 1943 by Betty Smith./ "Annie Sullivan, A Friend" and "Dolly Madison" are from GALLANT WOMEN by Senator Margaret Chase Smith and H. Paul Jeffers. Copyright 1968 by Margaret Chase Smith and H. Paul Jeffers. Used with permission of McGraw-Hill Book Company./ "Read All About It!" is excerpted from THE SUCCESS SYSTEM THAT NEVER FAILS by W. Clement Stone, © 1962, by Prentice-Hall, Inc. Published by Prentice-Hall, Inc., Englewood Cliffs, New Jersey 07632./ An excerpt from "Spring" by Gladys Tabor. Copyright © 1959 by Gladys Tabor. Reprinted by permission of Brandt & Brandt./ "Truce in the Forest" by Fritz Vincken. Reprinted with permission from the January 1973 *Reader's Digest*. Copyright © 1973 by The Reader's Digest Assn., Inc./ "Lead Her Like a Pigeon," by Jessamyn West. Copyright 1944, 1972 by Jessamyn West. Reprinted from her volume THE FRIENDLY PERSUASION by permission of Harcourt Brace Jovanovich, Inc./ Verses from the Holy Bible: New International Version. Copyright © 1978 by the New York International Bible Society. Used by permission of Zondervan Bible Publishers./ Verses from The Living Bible, copyright 1971 by Tyndale House Publishers, Wheaton, Ill. Used by permission.

We also wish to thank the following contributors and sources for their permission to reprint selections in this book: Marie Curling, Mildred Brown Duncan, Faye Field, Arve Hatcher, Robin James, E. Stanley Jones, Sue Kidd, C. J. Papara and Eleanor V. Sass./We also wish to thank those contributors and sources from whom we were unable to obtain a response prior to publication: Donna Geyer, Margaret Sangster, D. Carl Yoder, and John V. A. Weaver.

Diligent effort has been made to locate and secure permission for the inclusion of all copyrighted material in this book. If any such acknowledgments have been inadvertently omitted, the compiler and publishers would appreciate receiving full information so that proper credit may be given in future editions.

Photographic Credits Cover Art: "Cobweb at Dawn" by Robert Walsh; also pages 191 and 210. Larry G. McKee, pages 11, 12, 29, 30, 47, 48, 65, 66, 83, 84, 101, 102, 119, 120, 137, 138, 155, 156, 173, 174, 192, and 209.

TABLE OF CONTENTS

When God Speaks in Whispers

Sometimes we might envy the men and women who walked this earth long, long before us. Their lives were simple, their distractions few. And in our Bibles we read of how God Himself communicated with them—in His own voice. To His people, in those far-off days, God was truly "Closer . . . than breathing, and nearer than hands and feet." (Tennyson)

Do we not today yearn for that relationship? To hear the voice of God—His words wafting through the breeze blowing across the waters . . . roaring like thunder that shakes the skies . . . cutting so sharply through the darkness that it startles us from sleep . . . crackling in the burning bush, aglow with His divine fire.

Well, make no mistake about it. God *does* still speak to you today. And—wonder of wonders—His voice is often just a whisper. A moment when He quietly touches your heart. Listen for it. There is no din that can drown out the sweet sound of His voice as He leads you, encourages you, instructs you, inspires you.

The selections in this book are about those moments, fragile moments, as experienced by some of the finest inspirational writers of all times. Let God speak to you through them . . . in the thoughts of a woman contemplating the simple oak table around which her family dined . . . in the journey of a snowflake searching for meaning in its life . . . in the joy of a son giving his father a gift money could never buy . . . in the quiet courage of two impoverished children who wanted a Christmas tree . . . in the prayers of a father at the seaside wedding of his daughter . . . in the years-long search of a man who only wished to find the King of Kings and worship Him . . . and in the spirit-touched events in the lives of men and women just like you and me.

Read them. And listen. It is my prayer that this collection of fragile moments in the lives of others will help you discover them in your own life—that you will hear God's whispers to you.

Phyllis Hobe

CHILDHOOD

A FRAGILE MOMENT...

Whenever I'm disappointed with my lot in life, I stop and think about little Jamie Scott. Jamie was trying out for a part in his school play. His mother told me that he'd set his heart on being in it, though she feared he would not be chosen. On the day the parts were awarded, I went with her to collect him after school. Jamie rushed up to her, eyes shining with pride and excitement. "Guess what, Mum," he shouted, and then said those words that remain a lesson to me: "I've been chosen to clap and cheer."

Marie Curling

I love little children, and it is not a slight thing when they, who are fresh from God, love us.

Charles Dickens

PAUL BUNYAN'S CRADLE

Esther Shephard

If what they say is true Paul Bunyan was born down in Maine. And he must of been a pretty husky baby too, just like you'd expect him to be, from knowin' him afterwards.

When he was only three weeks old he rolled around so much in his sleep that he knocked down four square miles of standin' timber and the government got after his folks and told 'em they'd have to move him away.

So then they got some timbers together and made a floatin' cradle for Paul and anchored it off Eastport, but every time Paul rocked in his cradle, if he rocked shoreward, it made such a swell it come near drownin' out all the villages on the coast of Maine, and the waves was so high Nova Scotia come pretty near becomin' an island instead of a peninsula.

And so that wouldn't do, of course, and the government got after 'em again and told 'em they'd have to do somethin' about it. They'd have to move him out of there and put him somewheres else, they was told, and so they figured they'd better take him home again and keep him in the house for a spell.

But it happened Paul was asleep in his cradle when they went to get him, and they had to send for the British navy and it took seven hours of bombardin' to wake him up. And then when Paul stepped out of his cradle it made such a swell it caused a seventy-five foot tide in the Bay of Fundy and several villages was swept away and

seven of the invincible English warships was sunk to the bottom of the sea.

Well, Paul got out of his cradle then, and that saved Nova Scotia from becomin' an island, but the tides in the Bay of Fundy is just as high as they ever was.

And so I guess the old folks must of had their hands full with him all right. And I ought to say, the king of England sent over and confiscated the timbers in Paul's cradle and built seven new warships to take the place of the ones he'd lost.

When Paul was only seven months old he sawed off the legs from under his dad's bed one night.

The old man noticed when he woke up in the mornin' that his bed seemed considerable lower than it used to be, and so he got up and investigated, and sure enough, there was the legs all sawed off from under it and the pieces layin' out on the floor.

And then he remembered he'd felt somethin' the night before, but he'd thought he must be dreamin'—the way you do dream that you're fallin' down sometimes when you first go off to sleep.

And he looked around to see who could of done it and there was Paul layin' there sound asleep with his dad's cross-cut saw still held tight in his fist and smilin' in his sleep as pretty as anythin'.

And he called his wife and when she come in he says to her:

"Did you feel anythin' in the night?" he says.

"No," she says. "Is anythin' wrong?"

"Well, just look here," he says. And he showed her the four-by-eights layin' there on the floor and the saw in the kid's hand.

"I didn't light the lamp when I went to get up this mornin'," she says, "and I guess I didn't notice it."

"Well, he's done it anyway," says the old man. "And I'll bet that boy of ourn is goin' to be a great logger some day. If he lives to grow up he's goin' to do some great loggin' by and by, you just see—a whole lot bigger than any of the men around here has ever done."

And they was right, all right. There ain't never been loggin' before nor since like Paul Bunyan done.

THE MOTHER'S QUESTION

When I was a boy, and it chanced to rain,
   Mother would always watch for me;
She used to stand by the window pane,
   Worried and troubled as she could be.
And this was the question I used to hear,
The very minute that I drew near;
The words she used, I can't forget:
"Tell me, my boy, if your feet are wet."

Worried about me was mother dear,
   As healthy a lad as ever strolled
Over a turnpike, far or near,
   'Fraid to death that I'd take a cold.
Always stood by the window pane,
Watching for me in the pouring rain;
And her words in my ears are ringing yet:
"Tell me, my boy, if your feet are wet."

Stockings warmed by the kitchen fire,
   And slippers ready for me to wear;
Seemed that mother would never tire,
   Giving her boy the best of care.
Thinking of him the long day through,
In the worried way that all mothers do;
Whenever it rained she'd start to fret,
Always fearing my feet were wet.

And now, whenever it rains, I see
   A vision of mother in days of yore,
Still waiting there to welcome me,
   As she used to do by the open door.
And always I think as I enter there
Of mother's love and a mother's care;
Her words in my ears are ringing yet:
"Tell me, my boy, if your feet are wet."

Edgar Guest

CHILDREN'S HANDS

Marjorie Holmes

Children's hands . . .

First they are but tiny tendrils, gripping your finger, brushing at your breast . . .

Next they are plump and dimpled, getting into things so that you must say, "No, no!" continually. Or, "Mustn't touch, naughty hands." . . .

Then, still small and grubby, they are clutching crayons, scribbling. Or groping awkwardly with pencils, learning to print their names . . .

Then soon, so soon, they are lengthening—catching baseballs, swinging ropes for jumping, playing jacks . . .

And a little longer still, anxiously struggling to tie a necktie for a party, or applying a first excited touch of lipstick . . .

And now, longer and stronger yet, they are being fitted for class rings, adjusting the unfamiliar robes and tasseled hats for Commencement, reaching out to take diplomas from older, surer hands . . .

And after that outstretched so eagerly and confidently for engagement rings, and wedding rings, and jobs . . .

And then, completed, they take up the new, the just beginning, with wonder and pride. Lifting her own child, the new mother marvels, "Isn't he beautiful? Just look at those tiny hands!"

THE CHILDREN'S HOUR

Between the dark and the daylight,
    When the night is beginning to lower,
Comes a pause in the day's occupations,
    That is known as the Children's Hour.

I hear in the chamber above me
    The patter of little feet,
The sound of a door that is opened
    And voices soft and sweet.

From my study I see in the lamplight,
    Descending the broad hall stair,
Grave Alice, and laughing Allegra
    And Edith with golden hair.

A whisper, and then a silence:
    Yet I know by their merry eyes
They are plotting and planning together
    To take me by surprise.

A sudden rush from the stairway,
    A sudden raid from the hall!
By three doors left unguarded
    They enter my castle wall!

Do you think, O blue-eyed banditti,
    Because you have scaled the wall,
Such an old moustache as I am
    Is not a match for you all!

I have you fast in my fortress,
    And will not let you depart,
But put you down into the dungeon
    In the round-tower of my heart.

And there will I keep you forever.
    Yes, forever and a day,
Till the wall shall crumble to ruin,
    And moulder in dust away!

Henry Wadsworth Longfellow

GENTLE JESUS

Gentle Jesus, meek and mild,
Look upon a little child!

Make me gentle as Thou art,
Come and live within my heart.

Take my childish hand in Thine,
Guide these little feet of mine.

So shall all my happy days
Sing their pleasant song of praise;

And the world shall always see
Christ, the Holy Child, in me.

Charles Wesley

CHILDHOOD

CRADLE HYMN

Away in a manger, no crib for a bed,
The little Lord Jesus laid down His sweet
　head.
The stars in the bright sky looked down
　where He lay—
The little Lord Jesus, asleep on the hay.

The cattle are lowing, the baby awakes,
But little Lord Jesus, no crying He makes.
I love Thee, Lord Jesus! Look down from
　the sky,
And stay by my cradle till morning is nigh.

Be near me, Lord Jesus, I ask Thee to stay
Close by me forever, and love me, I pray.
Bless all the dear children, in Thy tender
　care,
And take us to heaven to live with Thee there.

Martin Luther

MOLLY COTTON-TAIL

Erskine Caldwell

My aunt had come down South to visit us
and we were all sitting around the fireplace
talking. Aunt Nellie did most of the talking
and my mother the rest of it. My father
came in occasionally for a few minutes at a
time and then went out again to walk
around the house and sit in the barnyard.
He and Aunt Nellie did not get along
together at all. Aunt Nellie was sure she was
smarter than anybody else and my father
did not want to get into an argument with
her and lose his temper.

Aunt Nellie's husband had gone down to
Florida on a hunting trip and she came as
far as Carolina to see us while he was away.
My uncle was crazy about hunting and
spent all his spare time away from home
gunning for game.

"Bess," Aunt Nellie asked my mother,
"does Johnny like to hunt?" She nodded
impersonally toward me where I sat by the
fireplace.

My mother said I did not. And that was
true. I liked to catch rabbits and squirrels
for pets but I did not want to kill them. I
had a pet hen right then; she had been run
over by a buggy wheel when she was growing
up and one of her legs was broken. I hid her
in the barn so my father would not know
about her. She stayed there about two weeks
and when the leg had healed I let her out in
the yard with the other chickens. When my
father did find her he said she would
not have to be killed if I would take care of
her and feed her because she could not
scratch for worms like the other chickens.
Her leg healed all right, but it was crooked
and she limped every step she took.

"Well," Aunt Nellie said to my mother,
"that is a shame. If he doesn't like to hunt
he won't grow up to be a real Southern
gentleman."

"But, Nellie," my mother protested for
me, "Johnny does not like to kill things."

"Nonsense," Aunt Nellie said derisively.
"Any man who is a real Southern gentleman
likes to hunt. The Lord only knows what he
will turn out to be."

My father would have taken up for me
too if he had been in the room just then. My
father did not like to kill things either.

"I'm disappointed in having a nephew
who is not a real Southern gentleman. He
will never be one if he never goes hunting."
Aunt Nellie always talked a long time about
the same thing once she got started.

I was not greatly interested in being a
real Southern gentleman when I grew up,
but I did not want her to talk about me that
way. Every summer she wrote my mother a
letter inviting me up to her home in
Maryland, and I wanted to go again this
year.

My father heard what she said and went
out in the backyard and threw pebbles
against the barn side.

I went into the dining room where the
shotgun was kept and took it off the rack.
The gun was fired off to scare crows when

they came down in the spring to pull up the corn sprouts in the new ground. My father never aimed to kill the crows: he merely fired off the shotgun to make the crows so gun-shy they would not come back to the cornfield.

Taking the shotgun and half a dozen shells I went out the front door without anybody seeing me leave. I went down the road towards the schoolhouse at the crossroads. I had seen dozens of rabbits down at the first creek every time I went to school and came home. They were large rabbits with gray backs and white undercoats. All of them had long thin ears and a ball of white fur on their tails. I liked them a lot.

At the first creek I stopped on the bridge and rested against the railing. In a few minutes I saw two rabbits hop across the road ahead. Picking up the gun I started after them. A hundred yards from the bridge the road had been cut down into the hill and the banks on each side were fifteen and twenty feet high. At this time of year when there was nearly always a heavy frost each morning the bank facing the south was the warmer because the sun shone against it most of the day. I had seen several rabbits sitting in holes in the bank and I was sure that was where these rabbits were going now.

Sure enough when I got there a large gray-furred rabbit was sitting on the sunny bank backed into a hole. When I saw the rabbit I raised the shotgun to my shoulder and took good aim. The rabbit blinked her eyes and chewed a piece of grass she had found under a log somewhere. I was then only ten or twelve feet away but I thought I had better get closer so I should be certain to kill her. I would take the rabbit home and show my aunt. I wanted her to invite me to spend the summer at her house again.

I edged closer and closer to the rabbit until I stood in the drain ditch only three

feet from her. She blinked her eyes and chewed on the grass. I hated to kill her because she looked as if she wanted to live and sit on the sunny bank chewing grass always. But my Aunt Nellie thought a boy should be a sportsman and kill everything in sight.

There was nothing else I could do. I would have to shoot the poor rabbit and take her back for my aunt to see.

I took steady aim along the center of the double-barreled shotgun, shut both eyes, and pulled the triggers one after the other. When I opened my eyes the rabbit was still sitting there looking at me. I was so glad after the gun went off that the rabbit was not dead that I dropped the gun and crawled up the bank and caught the rabbit by her long ears. I lifted her in my arms and held her tightly so she could not run away. She was so frightened by the gunshots she was trembling all over like a whipped dog. When I put her in my arms she snuggled her nose against my sweater and stopped quivering while I stroked her fur.

Holding the rabbit tight in my right arm I picked up the shotgun and ran home as fast as I could.

My father was still sitting in the back yard when I got there.

"What's that you've got under your arm?" he asked.

"A rabbit," I told him.

"How did you catch it?"

"I shot at her and missed her. Then I caught her by the ears and brought her home."

"Look here, Johnny," he said to me. "You didn't shoot at that rabbit while it was sitting down, did you?"

"I guess I did," I admitted; adding hastily, "but I didn't hit her, anyway."

"Well, it's a good thing you didn't hit it. A good sportsman never shoots at a rabbit while it is sitting down. A good sportsman never shoots at a bird until it flies. A real sportsman always gives the game he is after

a chance for its life."

"But Aunt Nellie said I had to kill something and she didn't say not to kill things standing still."

"You stop paying attention to your Aunt Nellie. She doesn't know what she's talking about anyway."

I let my father hold the rabbit while I fixed a box to keep her in. When I was ready I put her in it and shut her up tight.

"What are you going to do with the rabbit?" he asked me.

"Keep her."

"I wouldn't put it in a box," he said with a queer look on his face. "If it wants to stay it won't run off. And if it doesn't want to stay it will worry itself to death in that box all the time. Turn it loose and let's see what it will do."

I was afraid to turn my rabbit loose because I did not want her to run away. But my father knew a lot more about rabbits than I did. Just then Aunt Nellie and my mother came out on the back porch.

"What have you got there in the box?" Aunt Nellie asked me.

"A rabbit," I said.

"Where did you get it?"

"I shot at her with the gun but I didn't hit her and she didn't run away so I brought her home."

My aunt turned to my mother in disgust.

"There you are, Bess! What did I tell you?"

I did not hear what my mother said. But my father got up and went down to the barn. Aunt Nellie went into the house and slammed shut the door behind her. My mother stood looking at me for several minutes as if I had done the right thing after all.

Taking the rabbit out of the box I went down to the barn where my father was. He was sitting against the barn side shelling an ear of corn for half a dozen chickens around him. I sat down beside him and turned the rabbit loose. The rabbit hopped

around and around and then sat down and looked at us.

"Why don't you name it Molly Cotton-Tail?" my father suggested, throwing a handful of shelled corn to the chickens.

"What does that mean?" I asked.

"There are two kinds of rabbits around here: jack rabbits and molly cotton-tails. That one has a cotton-tail—see the ball of white fur on its tail that looks like a boll of cotton?"

The rabbit hopped around and around again and sat down on her cotton-tail. The chickens were not afraid of her. They went right up to where she sat and scratched for corn just as if she had been a chicken too.

"Why don't you go into the garden and get a head of lettuce for it? Get a good tender one out of the hot-bed. All rabbits like lettuce," he said.

I got the lettuce and gave it to my rabbit. She hopped up to where we sat against the barn side, asked for more. I gave her all I had and she ate out of my hand.

"If you had killed that rabbit with the gun you would be sorry now," my father said. Anybody could see that he was beginning to like my rabbit a lot.

She hopped around and around in front of us, playing with the chickens. The chickens liked her too.

"I'd lots rather have her living than dead," I said, suddenly realizing how much I liked her myself.

Molly hopped up between us and nibbled at my father's hand. He reached to stroke her fur with his hand but she hopped away.

"Whoa there, sooky," he soothed, reaching for our rabbit.

THE BAREFOOT BOY

Blessings on thee, little man,
Barefoot boy, with cheek of tan!
With thy turned-up pantaloons,
And thy merry whistled tunes;
With thy red lip, redder still
Kissed by strawberries on the hill;
With the sunshine on thy face,
Through thy torn brim's jaunty grace;
From my heart I give thee joy,—
I was once a barefoot boy!
Prince thou art,—the grown-up man
Only is republican.
Let the million-dollared ride!
Barefoot, trudging at his side,
Thou hast more than he can buy
In the reach of ear and eye,—
Outward sunshine, inward joy:
Blessings on thee, barefoot boy! . . .

John Greenleaf Whittier

ON HIS OWN TWO FEET

Grace Perkins Oursler

The boy had fallen, running home after school, and skinned his left knee. It was no more than a scratch—there wasn't even a rent in his trousers—but by night the knee started to ache. Nothing much, he thought, being 13 and the sturdy son of a frontiersman. Ignoring the pain, he knelt in his nightgown and said his prayers, then climbed into bed in the room where he and his brothers slept.

His leg was painful the next morning, but he still did not tell anyone. The farm kept the whole family relentlessly busy; always he had to be up at six to do his chores before school. And he must be thorough about them or he would be sent back to do them over again, no matter what else he had to miss, including meals. In their household, discipline was fair but stern.

Two mornings later the leg ached too badly for him to drag himself to the barn.

That was a Sunday and he could remain behind, while the rest of the family drove into town. School homework finished, he sat in the parlor rocker, examining and comparing the three family Bibles; one in German that held the records of all their births and deaths; another in Greek that was his father's proud possession and finally the King James version shared by mother and all the sons.

One night this week it would be the boy's turn to lead the family devotions. He could select his own passages from the Old and New Testaments and read them aloud and try to get a discussion going; sometimes they became exciting. But now the pain blurred his attention; he put aside the Scriptures and dozed until his brothers returned from Sunday school.

By the time dinner was ready the boy had climbed into bed. The shoe had to be cut off his swollen and discolored leg. Why on earth hadn't he told somebody? Go quick and fetch the doctor!

Mother bathed knee and foot and thigh, applied poultices and wiped the boy's sweating forehead with moist, cool cloth. She was an intense and vital woman. Confronted with this angry infection, her manner remained serene. Mom had nursed her brood through accidents and ailments from toothaches to scarlet fever; one son she had lost, but that only made her calmer and more determined when she had to fight for the others.

Old Dr. Conklin examined the leg and pursed his lips. "It's not likely we can save it!"

The invalid sat up stiffly. "What's that mean?" he asked huskily.

"It means," explained the doctor gently, "if things get worse we'll have to amputate."

"Not me!" stormed the boy. "I won't have it! I'd rather die!"

"The longer we wait, the more we will have to take off," urged the doctor.

"You won't take any off!" The boy's voice

broke with an adolescent crack, as his mother turned away, shaken. But there was no adolescence in the eyes that defied the doctor's reproachful gaze.

Dr. Conklin stalked out, nodding to the mother to follow him. As he stood in the hallway explaining to both parents about what could and probably would happen, they could hear the boy calling for his brother: "Ed! *Ed*! Come up here, will you?"

The brother stamped in and then they heard the sick lad's voice, high pitched with pain: "If I go out of my head, Ed, don't let them cut off my leg. Promise me, Ed—*promise*!"

In a moment Ed came out and stood outside the bedroom door, his arms folded. Quite clearly he was standing on guard.

Ed looked straight at old Dr. Conklin. "Nobody's going to saw off that leg!" he announced.

"But Ed—you'll be sorry," gasped the doctor.

"Maybe so, Doc. But I gave him my word."

And nothing changed that.

If Ed had not stood his ground, father and mother might have yielded. They were not yet convinced that amputation was necessary; they were doubtful. The adamant attitude first of the sick boy and then of his brother was incredible, for defiance of parental authority was unknown in this household. Yet there was Ed, standing before the sickroom door.

"Guess we'll wait and see how he looks by tonight, eh, Doc?" said the father.

For two days and nights Ed stood guard, sleeping at the threshold, not leaving even to eat. The fever mounted, and the suffering boy babbled in torment, but the older brother showed no weakening of resolve, even though the discoloration of the swollen leg was creeping toward the pelvis, just as the doctor had predicted. Ed remained firm because he had given his promise, and also because he shared the

frontiersmen's horror of being less than physically perfect.

The parents knew that their son would never forgive an amputation, and Ed's attitude continued to be decisive, time after time, when the doctor returned. Once, in helpless rage, Dr. Conklin shouted, "It's murder!" and slammed the front door. Nothing but a miracle could save the boy now!

Mother, father and watchful brother Ed shared the same thought, as their anxious eyes turned from the doorway. Had they forgotten their faith in the turmoil of their fears? Now, in this desperate hour, the three went to their knees at the bedside.

They prayed, taking turns in leading one another. Father, mother—and at last Edgar—would rise and go about the farm work and rejoin the continual prayer. During the second night the other four brothers would kneel from time to time and join in the prayers.

The next morning, when the faithful old doctor stopped by again, his experienced eye saw a sign. The swelling was going down! Dr. Conklin closed his eyes and made a rusty prayer of his own—a prayer of thanksgiving. Even after the boy dropped into a normal sleep, one member of the family after another kept the prayer vigil.

It was nightfall again and the lamps were lighted when the boy opened his eyes. The swelling was away down now, and the discoloration had almost faded. In three weeks—pale and weak, but with eyes clear and voice strong—the boy could stand up.

And Ike Eisenhower was ready to face life.

LITTLE BOY BLUE

The little toy dog is covered with dust,
  But sturdy and stanch he stands;
And the little toy soldier is red with rust,
  And his musket molds in his hands.
Time was when the little toy dog was new

And the soldier was passing fair;
And that was the time when our
   Little Boy Blue
   Kissed them and put them there.

"Now, don't you go till I come," he said,
   "And don't you make any noise!"
So, toddling off to his trundle-bed,
   He dreamed of the pretty toys;
And as he was dreaming, an angel song
   Awakened our Little Boy Blue—
Oh! the years are many, the years are long,
   But the little toy friends are true!

Aye, faithful to Little Boy Blue they stand,
   Each in the same old place—
Awaiting the touch of a little hand,
   And the smile of a little face;
And they wonder, as waiting these long years
     through
   In the dust of that little chair,
What has become of our Little Boy Blue,
   Since he kissed them and put them there.

Eugene Field

READ ALL ABOUT IT!

W. Clement Stone

I was six years old and scared. Selling newspapers on Chicago's tough South Side wasn't easy, especially with the older kids taking over the busy corners, yelling louder, and threatening me with clenched fists. The memory of those dim days is still with me, for it's the first time I can recall turning a disadvantage into an advantage. It's a simple story, unimportant now . . . and yet it was a beginning.

Hoelle's Restaurant was near the corner where I tried to work, and it gave me an idea. It was a busy and prosperous place that presented a frightening aspect to a child of six. I was nervous, but I walked in hurriedly and made a lucky sale at the first table. Then diners at the second and third tables bought papers. When I started for the fourth, however, Mr. Hoelle pushed me

out the front door.

But I had sold three papers. So when Mr. Hoelle wasn't looking, I walked back in and called at the fourth table. Apparently, the jovial customer liked my gumption; he paid for the paper and gave me an extra dime before Mr. Hoelle pushed me out once again. But I had already sold four papers and got a "bonus" dime besides. I walked into the restaurant and started selling again. There was a lot of laughter. The customers were enjoying the show. One whispered loudly, "Let him be," as Mr. Hoelle came toward me. About five minutes later, I had sold all my papers.

The next evening I went back. Mr. Hoelle again ushered me out the front door. But when I walked right back in, he threw his hands in the air and exclaimed, "What's the use!" Later, we became great friends, and I never had trouble selling papers there again.

THE ARTIST IN EVERY CHILD

Marjorie Holmes

A child's feeling for art is a strange and wonderful thing.

He clutches a crayon or pencil and tries to make it speak for him, often before he can otherwise express himself at all. His first efforts are wild and wonderful attacks upon the nearest surface, whether it be paper, picture book, or the family walls.

With vigor and joy he makes these glorious swatches of color, and no matter if they adhere to the firm outlines of the puppy, the flower, or the little girl in the fat soft book that has been provided for him.

With equal vigor and delight he loves to draw. His first efforts at depicting a man are marvels of simplicity—a round shape, usually, with a few sticks of sprouting limbs. Gradually, as his powers of observation and duplication come into focus, he adds the facial features and the refinements of clothes.

CHILDHOOD

Animals likewise grow under his fingers, fierce or gentle, according to his mood; and the sun in the sky burns a hot yellow, jutting rays like porcupine quills.

A child is truly an artist, no matter how lopsided or out of proportion his efforts, for in this early stage of his being he shares the emotions that the genuine artist knows: the sheer joy of creating, which hurls him bodily into his work. The child feels the hot sunlight he has beating down upon the cottage roof, runs in terror along with his Goldilocks, knows the forlorn disappointment of his three well-meaning bears.

This is the essence of a youngster's art. His capacity to live fully in the act of depicting. He bolts into a vivid world of color and action, of jagged seas and tossing ships, where he can stand on the bridge in command, or swim with the fishes beneath the brilliant blue waves.

And this selfsame quality of participation he brings to the pictures he sees. The comic strips are a world in microcosm, each frame a little stage. Without bothersome mental gymnastics, he is swept into the activities of their boldly drawn characters, who seem so real, not because of what they say but because of the way they are shown.

And their backgrounds! I still remember vividly the furnishings in Jiggs' and Maggie's house (those Oriental vases!) and Maggie's hair styles, and shrew though she was—her dashing wardrobes.

Children's illustrators know well this innate need of childhood to be captured by that rectangle into which the artist must compress all the magic at his fingertips. To be successful it must engage the child's emotions, his senses, so that he will pore over the scene and scarcely be able to leave it. Mrs. Dagmar Wilson, who has done so many children's books, says, "The nicest compliment I can hear is for a child to say, 'I'd like to be in that picture.' For you know when he says that, in his imagination he's already there."

LENT FOR AWHILE

"I'll lend you for a little time a child of Mine,"
    He said,
"For you to love the while he lives, and
    mourn for, when he's dead.
It may be six or seven years, or twenty-two or
    three.
But will you till I call him back, take care of
    him for Me?

He'll bring his charms to gladden you, and
    should his stay be brief,
You'll have his lovely memories as solace for
    your grief.
I cannot promise he will stay since all from
    earth return,
But there are lessons taught down there I
    wish this child to learn.

I've looked the wide world over in my search
    for teachers true,
And from the throngs that crowd life's lanes
    I have selected you.
Nor will you give him all your love, nor think
    the labor vain,
Nor hate me when I come to call to take him
    back again?"

I fancied that I heard them say, "Dear Lord,
    Thy will be done,
For all the joy Thy child shall bring, the risk
    of grief we'll run.
We'll shelter him with tenderness, we'll love
    him while we may,
And for the happiness we've known, forever
    grateful stay.

And should the Angels call for him much
    sooner than we've planned,
We'll brave the bitter grief that comes, and
    try to understand."

Edgar Guest

DAVID AND GOLIATH

The Living Bible, I *Samuel 17, 18*

The Philistines mustered their army for battle and camped between Socoh in Judah and Azekah in Ephes-dam-mim. Saul countered with a buildup of forces at Elah Valley. So the Philistines and Israelis faced each other on opposite hills, with the valley between them.

Then Goliath, a Philistine champion from Gath, came out of the Philistine ranks to face the forces of Israel. He was a giant of a man, measuring over nine feet tall! He wore a bronze helmet, a two-hundred-pound coat of mail, bronze leggings, and carried a bronze javelin several inches thick, tipped with a twenty-five-pound iron spearhead, and his armor bearer walked ahead of him with a huge shield.

He stood and shouted across to the Israelis, "Do you need a whole army to settle this? I will represent the Philistines, and you choose someone to represent you, and we will settle this in single combat! If your man is able to kill me, then we will be your slaves. But if I kill him, then you must be our slaves! I defy the armies of Israel! Send me a man who will fight with me!"

When Saul and the Israeli army heard this, they were dismayed and frightened. David (the son of aging Jesse, a member of the tribe of Judah who lived in Bethlehem-Judah) had seven older brothers. The three oldest—Eliab, Abinadab, and Shammah—had already volunteered for Saul's army to fight the Philistines. David was the youngest son, and was on Saul's staff on a part-time basis. He went back and forth to Bethlehem to help his father with the sheep. For forty days, twice a day, morning and evening, the Philistine giant strutted before the armies of Israel.

One day Jesse said to David, "Take this bushel of roasted grain and these ten loaves of bread to your brothers. Give this cheese to their captain and see how the boys are getting along; and bring us back a letter from them!"

(Saul and the Israeli army were camped at the valley of Elah.)

So David left the sheep with another shepherd and took off early the next morning with the gifts. He arrived at the outskirts of the camp just as the Israeli army was leaving for the battlefield with shouts and battle cries. Soon the Israeli and Philistine forces stood facing each other, army against army. David left his luggage with a baggage officer and hurried out to the ranks to find his brothers. As he was talking with them, he saw Goliath the giant step out from the Philistine troops and shout his challenge to the army of Israel. As soon as they saw him the Israeli army began to run away in fright.

"Have you seen the giant?" the soldiers were asking. "He has insulted the entire army of Israel. And have you heard about the huge reward the king has offered to anyone who kills him? And the king will give him one of his daughters for a wife, and his whole family will be exempted from paying taxes."

David talked to some others standing there to verify the report. "What will a man get for killing this Philistine and ending his insults to Israel?" he asked them. "Who is this heathen Philistine, anyway, that he is allowed to defy the armies of the living God?" And he received the same reply as before.

But when David's oldest brother, Eliab, heard David talking like that, he was angry. "What are you doing around here, anyway?" he demanded. "What about the sheep you're supposed to be taking care of? I know what a cocky brat you are; you just want to see the battle!"

"What have I done now?" David replied. "I was only asking a question!"

And he walked over to some others and asked them the same thing and received the

same answer. When it was finally realized what David meant, someone told King Saul, and the king sent for him.

"Don't worry about a thing," David told him. "I'll take care of this Philistine!"

"Don't be ridiculous!" Saul replied. "How can a kid like you fight with a man like him? You are only a boy and he has been in the army since he was a boy!"

But David persisted. "When I am taking care of my father's sheep," he said, "and a lion or a bear comes and grabs a lamb from the flock, I go after it with a club and take the lamb from its mouth. If it turns on me I catch it by the jaw and club it to death. I have done this to both lions and bears, and I'll do it to this heathen Philistine too, for he has defied the armies of the living God! The Lord who saved me from the claws and teeth of the lion and the bear will save me from this Philistine!"

Saul finally consented, "All right, go ahead," he said, "and may the Lord be with you!"

Then Saul gave David his own armor—a bronze helmet and a coat of mail. David put it on, strapped the sword over it, and took a step or two to see what it was like, for he had never worn such things before. "I can hardly move!" he exclaimed, and took them off again. Then he picked up five smooth stones from a stream and put them in his shepherd's bag and, armed only with his shepherd's staff and sling, started across to Goliath. Goliath walked out towards David with his shield bearer ahead of him, sneering in contempt at this nice little red-cheeked boy!

"Am I a dog," he roared at David, "that you come at me with a stick?" And he cursed David by the names of his gods. "Come over here and I'll give your flesh to the birds and wild animals," Goliath yelled.

David shouted in reply, "You come to me with a sword and a spear, but I come to you in the name of the Lord of the armies of heaven and of Israel—the very God whom

you have defied. Today the Lord will conquer you and I will kill you and cut off your head; and then I will give the dead bodies of your men to the birds and wild animals, and the whole world will know that there is a God in Israel! And Israel will learn that the Lord does not depend on weapons to fulfill his plans—he works without regard to human means! He will give you to us!"

As Goliath approached, David ran out to meet him and, reaching into his shepherd's bag, took out a stone, hurled it from his sling, and hit the Philistine in the forehead. The stone sank in, and the man fell on his face to the ground. So David conquered the Philistine giant with a sling and a stone. Since he had no sword, he ran over and pulled Goliath's from its sheath and killed him with it, and then cut off his head. When the Philistines saw that their champion was dead, they turned and ran.

Then the Israelis gave a great shout of triumph and rushed after the Philistines, chasing them as far as Gath and the gates of Ekron. The bodies of the dead and wounded Philistines were strewn all along the road to Shaaraim. Then the Israeli army returned and plundered the deserted Philistine camp.

(Later, David took Goliath's head to Jerusalem, but stored his armor in his tent.)

As Saul was watching David go out to fight Goliath, he asked Abner, the general of his army, "Abner, what sort of family does this young fellow come from?"

"I really don't know," Abner said.

"Well, find out!" the king told him.

After David had killed Goliath, Abner brought him to Saul with the Philistine's head still in his hand.

"Tell me about your father, my boy," Saul said.

And David replied, "His name is Jesse and we live in Bethlehem."

. . . King Saul kept David at Jerusalem and wouldn't let him return home any more. He

was Saul's special assistant, and he always
carried out his assignments successfully. So
Saul made him commander of his troops,
an appointment which was applauded by
the army and general public alike.

IT IS THE SEASON

It is the season now to go
About the country high and low,
Among the lilacs hand in hand,
And two by two in fairyland.

The brooding boy, the sighing maid,
Wholly fain and half afraid,
Now meet along the hazel'd brook
To pause and linger, pause and look.

A year ago, and blithely paired,
Their rough-and-tumble play they shared;
They kissed and quarrelled, laughed and
    cried,
A year ago at Eastertide.

With bursting heart, with fiery face,
She strove against him in the race;
He unabashed her garter saw,
That now would touch her skirts with awe.

Now by the stile ablaze she stops,
And his demurer eyes he drops;
Now they exchange averted sighs
Or stand and marry silent eyes.

And he to her a hero is
And sweeter she than primroses;
Their common silence dearer far
Than nightingale and mavis are.

Now when they sever wedded hands,
Joy trembles in their bosom-strands,
And lovely laughter leaps and falls
Upon their lips in madrigals.

Robert Louis Stevenson

"Keep this for me."
What child has not said this,
And placed a treasure in his Mother's hand
With strict injunction she should keep it safe
Till he return?
He knows with her it will be safe;
No troubled thought or anxious fear besets
    his mind,
And off he runs lighthearted to his play.

If children can so trust, why cannot we,
And place our treasures, too, in God's safe
    hand;
Our hopes, ambitions, needs, and those we
    love,
Just see them, in His all-embracing care,
And say with joyous heart, "They are with
    Thee."

Author Unknown

BEAUTY

A FRAGILE MOMENT . . .

I remember one October night visiting a friend who was lying very sick. There was a full moon that night; and as I walked down the village street on my sad mission I felt the silvery beauty of it quiet my heart. The world lay lustrous. There was no scrawny bush nor ugly clod that was not transfigured in that glory. A little breeze over the brimming salt tide brought aromatic marshy odors. It seemed to me that some power was trying to make beauty take away my sadness. I found my friend not less aware than I was of the beauty of the night. He could look from his window and see the argent glamour of it all: how it flooded the gleaming tide with celestial lights ; how it ran long white lances through the swarthy cedars; how it tinged with soft radiance the locusts and the mimosas. He felt the breeze too, and delighted in the odours that it brought of the happy world beyond his window. To my surprise, although he was very ill, he greeted me with a strangely elevated calmness and joy.

"I have been," he said, "in many waters, and they are still deep all about me. But God has been with me too. He has not failed me in my distress. Who but He could send this moonlight and this mockingbird singing. He brought them to me, and I think they bring Him near."

As I sat beside him, a mockingbird began to sing in the moonlight, chanting divinely. I know the song reached our spirits. On the table by the bed were all the necessities for a sick man; but he had small comfort from them. But the moonlight, and the hale fragrances, and the wild song of the bird— these brought peace to his heart.

Long afterward he said to me, "Do you remember that night? I thought it would be my last. But from the time the birdsong came through that window I felt that I would get well. I don't talk much about these things, but I felt that all that beauty and peace were really the love of God. I guess He does not love us with words: He loves us by giving us everything we need— in every way."

It must be as he said.

Archibald Rutledge

DAFFODILS

I wandered lonely as a cloud
   That floats on high o'er vales and hills,
When all at once I saw a crowd,
   A host, of golden daffodils;
Beside the lake, beneath the trees,
Fluttering and dancing in the breeze.

William Wordsworth

There are broad and peaceful meadows, which, I think are among the most satisfying objects in natural scenery. The heart reposes on them with a feeling that few things else can give, because almost all other objects are abrupt and clearly defined; but a meadow stretches out like a small infinity, yet with a secure homeliness which we do not find either in an expanse of water or of air.

Nathaniel Hawthorne

THERE IS NO FRIGATE LIKE A BOOK

There is no frigate like a book
To take us lands away,
Nor any coursers like a page
Of prancing poetry.

Emily Dickinson

THE MIRACLE OF SPRING

Gladys Tabor

April in New England is like first love. There is the tender excitement of gathering the first snowdrops, the only symbol of life in the deserted garden. They are the lyric expression of music to come—as the symphony of lilacs will surely come—because I am picking the cool delicate bells of this first flower. When I brought the first tiny bouquet in and put it in an antique pill bottle, the greenish glass was the color of the center of the snowdrops. I often wonder what pills went in the bottles for they are only half an inch to an inch high and pencil-slim. My own pill bottles look gigantic in comparison! And when I swallow my vitamins, I feel as if I were choking down acorns.

Aconite and quinine, I remember, were my father's Rx for most ailments, but these tiny bottles were much earlier, they belong to the days of bloodletting. Now they

minister to the winter-weary spirit by holding the snowdrops which are too small even for a demitasse cup. Possibly, I thought, as I set the miniature bouquet on the old trestle table, possibly God knows that if spring came all at once, we should die of it. So the fairy-size bells ring a chime to make it possible to bear the beauty that will come in May.

But like first love, April has bitter days. This morning, we woke to a sky as dark as the inside of a snowboot. Leftover wind from March crashed branches to the ground that had withstood all of the winter blizzards. The pond iced over in the night again, and as I made pancakes for breakfast, I had a silly fancy that winter had flung her last scarf across it because she did not need it any longer. The confused robins tipped around in a wormless world, and the winter birds made almost as much noise as a social hour after a Woman's Club meeting. The red-winged blackbirds swooped down from the sugar maples, and it seemed to me they sounded cross.

I could imagine the wives saying crossly to their mates that it was all their fault they had come north too soon. So I went out after breakfast to set up the birds' buffet. For a time we shall have both the winter birds that companioned us during the long cold, and the migratory ones coming from strange southern lands. The air is filled with the excitement of wings. However, much as I welcome the wanderers, I love most the chickadees, nuthatches and woodpeckers, for they have shared the bitter season with us, and never a blizzard too fierce for them to chatter away at the window feeder. I suspect we always love best those who share the hard things with us. Spring and summer friends are delightful, but give me winter friends for my dearest.

As I went back to the house to turn up the thermostat, I reflected that Stillmeadow has seen a lot of sharing since it was built in 1690. In the beginning, it was a world in

itself, for the village was a long way off when you had to walk there, or hitch up the horse. (It takes about five minutes now.) Families, in the early days, were units. They had to be. Aside from flour, molasses, tea and salt, most of the food was grown on the farm. Hams were smoked in the small smokehouse, home-grown herbs went into spicy sausage and scrapple at butchering time. Lye and wood ashes cooked in the big iron kettle we now use for kindling. I always imagine it still smells of soft soap. The carder and spinning wheel were busy. Fuel for the great fireplace and the three lesser fireplaces came from the woodlot up the hill, and all the cooking was done over the fire. Savory stews bubbled in the iron pot hanging over the embers, potatoes baked in the ashes, "punkin" pies went in the Dutch oven and came forth spicy and rich, and made a fine end to a supper eaten by firelight and the glow from tallow dips.

The end of winter in those days was a miracle, even more than now. For in April the heated warmers for the beds upstairs could be discarded. The featherbeds were warm enough. And the three-hour sermon in the unheated church was more comfortable when you no longer wrapped hot bricks or stones or flatirons and held them in your lap.

In April, then, as now, the men of the house went up to the woodlot to cut for next season. A countryman's life always moves steadily, with a pattern fitting the changing seasons. This week our neighbor, Joe, said he better get up to the woodlot. He does not have to chop and haul by hand. He has a small trailer to load the wood on, and he has a modern saw. But the pattern itself is the same. When the snow melt leaves a way to the woods open, the wood is cut.

The logs come down the hill to be piled near the back door against the next winter. The true country dweller is a conserva-tionist, and always cuts to keep the woods in good shape. In New England, we cut with an eye to taking out dying trees, lightning-blasted ones, or fallen old apple trees. Clearing out the dead apple trees, for instance, makes room for the new shoots which spring up around the old trunk. So another generation, God willing, will have a young orchard of wild apple trees on which, if they are so minded, they can graft any number of fancy apples.

Wood is still our staple for heat. A good many of our neighbors burn wood in their furnaces. Those who have gone so modern as to install coal or oil-burning units, still have the problem of four or five fireplaces in the pre-Revolutionary houses. I have yet to know of a central heating system that will prevent winter from walking right down a chimney, and indeed, in our house, it snows on the hearth unless we have a fire.

When we turn the thermostat up, it is hot as a freshly boiled egg in the kitchen, but the family room is still as cold as a polar bear. So when April walks over the countryside, we all hope we still have enough wood in the woodpile for a fire in the fireplace on cool summer evenings.

As the long lovely light of April falls on the meadow lately deep in snow, I think about the way time passes. "Time is but the stream I go fishing in," said Thoreau. "I drink at it; but while I drink, I see the sandy bottom and detect how shallow it is. Its thin current slides away, but eternity remains." I am not sure I understand this, for I am no philosopher, but it stretches my mind. The days I live now in the beginning of spring are certainly transient; dusk falls before I have sufficiently enjoyed the dew on the grass in early morning. We busy ourselves with all the things that must, we think, be done at once. "But eternity remains," said Thoreau. Days on the calendar come and go, but God is timeless. Love and faith and hope know no season; they are themselves,

I think, eternity.

And, in a sense, the miracle of spring is eternal also.

"Let us spend one day as deliberately as Nature," said Thoreau. Nature never hurries, season moves gently into season, day into night. If we would all, now and then, spend one day as deliberately as nature, we would have less tensions, less anxieties. We would find, I am sure, reserves of peace in ourselves.

And be renewed, as spring renews the frozen earth.

WHAT IS IT THAT I LOVE?

I love to rise at break of morn,
   And wander o'er the fertile plains,
When warblers sweet, proclaim the dawn,
   And fill the air with joyful strains.

I love to view the limpid stream,
   As it meanders gently by,
When sunset with a lingering beam,
   And golden tinge, illumes the sky.

I love the balmy air of eve,
   With dewy tears and zephyr sighs;
It doth the ruffled wind relieve,
   And soothes the spirit ere it flies.

I love the glorious orb of day,
   That gives a sunshine to the heart,
With radiance, gilds life's dreary way,
   And sheds on all an equal part.

I love the bud and blooming rose
   Whose grace and fragrance give delight;
The violet that humbly grows,
   That wins the sense and charms the sight.

I love, o'er all fair Nature's Sire,
   Who made the earth, the sea, the sky,
The architect whom all admire,
   The God Supreme who dwells on high.

Author Unknown

I'll tell you how the sun rose,
A ribbon at a time.
The steeples swam in amethyst,
The news like squirrels ran.

The hills untied their bonnets,
The bobolinks begun.
Then I said softly to myself,
"That must have been the sun!"

Emily Dickinson

SWAN LAKE

Marjorie Holmes

Even the ducks can't sleep on nights when the moon is full. Sluggards by day, often drowsing far into the morning with their heads curled under their wings, on moony nights they rouse, making raw little sounds of discovery and agitation. With a stretch of necks and flap of wings, they waddle to the edge of the black satin water and sink into it, to come coasting, like luminous white ghost ships trailing their reflections.

"Look at the ducks," the children say. "They're heading for the moonpath!" And true, they sail directly toward that diamond-riddled bar. Across it they glide, back and forth, tracing their own silvery patterns and making gay, raucous sounds, as if in retort to the frogs in the rushes.

"I'll get some bread." A child streaks bare-legged into the cabin and returns with a bulging sack. "Let me, let me throw some!" Others join her, squatting moon-traced on the float to fling the crusts.

The ducks circle in unison, their movements in such liquid precision that someone remarks, "Swan Lake!" For that is now the picture; they are a quartet of feathered dancers, snow-white, effortless, making their greedy yet graceful arabesques to the music of frogs and crickets and humming night things. While silently flooding the stage from above them the huge round spotlight of the moon shines down.

BEAUTY

SONG OF THE CREATURES

Most high, almighty, good Lord,
    to You belongs praise, glory, honor, all
      blessings—
    to You alone, most high, belongs all
      reverence.
    No man can fully speak of all Your
      wonders.

Be praised, my Lord, with all Your
      creation—
    especially our brother the sun,
    who brings us day and light:
    He is beautiful and radiant with splendor.
    Most High, he is a symbol of You!

Be praised, my Lord, for our sister the
      moon and the stars:
    You have placed them in the heavens—
    clear, priceless, and beautiful.
Be praised, my Lord, for our brother the
      wind and for air, good weather, and
      seasons through which your whole
      creation lives.

Be praised, my Lord, for our sister water,
      so useful, humble, precious, and chaste.
Be praised, my Lord, for our brother fire,
      who brightens the darkness of night.
    He is beautiful, happy, robust and strong.
Be praised, my Lord, for our sister mother
      earth:
    She supports, nourishes, and gives forth
      vegetations—colorful flowers
      and grass.

St. Francis of Assisi

THE OLD OAKEN BUCKET

How dear to my heart are the scenes of my
      childhood,
    When fond recollection presents them to
      view!
The orchard, the meadow, the deep
      tangled wildwood,
    And every loved spot which my infancy
      knew,

The wide-spreading pond and the mill that
      stood by it,
    The bridge and the rock where the
      cataract fell;
The cot of my father, the dairy house nigh
      it,
    And e'en the rude bucket that hung in
      the well.

That moss-covered bucket I hailed as a
      treasure,
    For often at noon, when returned from
      the field,
I found it the source of an exquisite
      pleasure,
    The purest and sweetest that nature can
      yield.
How ardent I seized it, with hands that
      were glowing,
    And quick to the white-pebbled bottom it
      fell.
Then soon, with the emblem of truth
      overflowing,
    And dripping with coolness, it rose from
      the well.

How sweet from the green, mossy brim to
      receive it,
    As, poised on the curb, it inclined to my
      lips!
Not a full, blushing goblet could tempt me
      to leave it,
    Tho' filled with the nectar that Jupiter
      sips.
And now, far removed from the loved
      habitation,
    The tear of regret will intrusively swell,
As fancy reverts to my father's plantation,
    And sighs for the bucket that hung in the
      well.

Samuel Woodworth

HEAVEN IS HEAVEN

When a mounting skylark sings
    In the sunlit summer morn,
I know that heaven is up on high,

And on earth are fields of corn.
But when a nightingale sings
  In the moonlit summer even,
I know not if earth is merely earth,
  Only that heaven is heaven.

Christina Rossetti

SENSORY SEASON

Hal Borland

There is a sweetness of May verging on
June that no other time in the whole year
can equal. And by sweetness is meant more
than flower fragrance or honey taste; this is
the greater sweetness of understanding and
emotion, the glow of pleasure in being.

This is the sensory season. Trees are in
leaf, even the cautious oaks and the casual
hickories. It is a green world, full of elusive
fragrances. Walk through an orchard and
you can smell as well as feel the strength of
grass underfoot, new grass reaching tall
toward the sun. Boughs naked only a little
while ago, then bright and heady with
bloom, now rustle with leaf and tingle with
the strength of fruition. Listen, and you can
almost hear the pulse of sap and the
mysterious workings of chlorophyll.

The hills are rounded with their own green
growth, the soft hills of a lush and friendly
land. The valleys sing with brooks, laughing
waters of spring and seep that have not yet
felt the thirst of summer. Even the stone
walls are alive with vine, the creeping
tendrils of life that would root in granite
and suck faint sustenance from sandstone.

The air vibrates with birdsong, which is
the great rhythm made palpable to the
human ear. The oriole's rounded notes are
as delightful to the ear as the tanager's
bright scarlet is delightful to the eager eye.
All the senses tingle, alive with the season as
the world itself is alive. Nothing is impossible at such a time. High achievement is all
around us, beating on every sense for
recognition.

HOW DOTH THE LITTLE BUSY BEE

How doth the little busy bee
  Improve each shining hour
And gather honey all the day
  From every passing flower!

How skillfully she builds her cell;
  How neat she spreads the wax!
And labours hard to store it well
  With the sweet food she makes.

Isaac Watts

THE STAR-CHILD

Oscar Wilde

Once upon a time two poor Woodcutters
were making their way home through a
great pine forest. It was winter, and a night
of bitter cold. The snow lay thick upon the
ground, and upon the branches of the
trees: the frost kept snapping the little twigs
on either side of them, as they passed: and
when they came to the Mountain-Torrent
she was hanging motionless in air, for the
Ice-King had kissed her.

So cold was it that even the animals and
the birds did not know what to make of it.

"Ugh!" snarled the Wolf, as he limped
through the brushwood with his tail
between his legs, "this is perfectly
monstrous weather. Why doesn't the
Government look to it?"

"Weet! weet! weet!" twittered the green
Linnets, "the old Earth is dead, and they
have laid her out in her white shroud."

"The Earth is going to be married, and
this is her bridal dress," whispered the
Turtle-doves to each other. Their little pink
feet were quite frost-bitten, but they felt
that it was their duty to take a romantic view
of the situation.

"Nonsense!" growled the Wolf. "I tell you
that it is all the fault of the Government,
and if you don't believe me I shall eat you."
The Wolf had a thoroughly practical mind,

and was never at a loss for a good argument.

"Well, for my own part," said the Woodpecker, who was a born philosopher, "I don't care an atomic theory for explanations. If a thing is so, it is so, and at present it is terribly cold."

Terribly cold it certainly was. The little Squirrels, who lived inside the tall fir-tree, kept rubbing each other's noses to keep themselves warm, and the Rabbits curled themselves up in their holes, and did not venture even to look out of doors. The only people who seemed to enjoy it were the great horned Owls. Their feathers were quite stiff with rime, but they did not mind, and they rolled their large yellow eyes, and called out to each other across the forest, "Tu-whit! Tu-whoo! Tu-whit! Tu-whoo! what delightful weather we are having!"

On and on went the two Woodcutters, blowing lustily upon their fingers, and stamping with their huge iron-shod boots upon the caked snow. Once they sank into a deep drift, and came out as white as millers are, when the stones are grinding; and once they slipped on the hard smooth ice where the marsh-water was frozen, and their faggots fell out of their bundles, and they had to pick them up and bind them together again; and once they thought that they had lost their way, and a great terror seized on them, for they knew that the Snow is cruel to those who sleep in her arms. But they put their trust in the good Saint Martin, who watches over all travellers, and retraced their steps, and went warily, and at last they reached the outskirts of the forest, and saw, far down in the valley beneath them, the lights of the village in which they dwelt.

So overjoyed were they at their deliverance that they laughed aloud, and the Earth seemed to them like a flower of silver, and the Moon like a flower of gold.

Yet, after that they had laughed they became sad, for they remembered their poverty, and one of them said to the other, "Why did we make merry, seeing that life is for the rich, and not for such as we are? Better that we had died of cold in the forest, or that some wild beast had fallen upon us and slain us."

"Truly," answered his companion, "much is given to some, and little is given to others. Injustice has parcelled out the world, nor is there equal division of aught save of sorrow."

But as they were bewailing their misery to each other this strange thing happened. There fell from heaven a very bright and beautiful star. It slipped down the side of the sky, passing by the other stars in its course, and, as they watched it wondering, it seemed to them to sink behind a clump of willow trees that stood hard by a little sheepfold no more than a stone's throw away.

"Why! there is a crock of gold for whoever finds it," they cried, and they set to and ran, so eager were they for the gold.

And one of them ran faster than his mate, and outstripped him, and forced his way through the willows, and came out on the other side, and lo! there was indeed a thing of gold lying on the white snow. So he hastened towards it, and stooping down placed his hands upon it, and it was a cloak of golden tissue, curiously wrought with stars, and wrapped in many folds. And he cried out to his comrade that he had found the treasure that had fallen from the sky, and when his comrade had come up, they sat them down in the snow, and loosened the folds of the cloak that they might divide the pieces of gold. But, alas! no gold was in it, nor silver, nor, indeed, treasure of any kind, but only a little child who was asleep.

And one of them said to the other: "This is a bitter ending to our hope, nor have we any good fortune, for what doth a child profit to a man? Let us leave it here, and go our ways, seeing that we are poor men, and have children of our own whose bread we

may not give to another."

But his companion answered him: "Nay, but it were an evil thing to leave the child to perish here in the snow, and though I am as poor as thou art, and have many mouths to feed, and but little in the pot, yet will I bring it home with me, and my wife shall have care of it."

So very tenderly he took up the child, and wrapped the cloak around it to shield it from the harsh cold, and made his way down the hill to the village, his comrade marvelling much at his foolishness and softness of heart.

And when they came to the village, his comrade said to him, "Thou hast the child, therefore give me the cloak, for it is meet that we should share."

But he answered him: "Nay, for the cloak is neither mine nor thine, but the child's only," and he bade him Godspeed, and went to his own house and knocked.

And when his wife opened the door and saw that her husband had returned safe to her, she put her arms round his neck and kissed him, and took from his back the bundle of faggots, and brushed the snow off his boots, and bade him come in.

But he said to her, "I have found something in the forest, and I have brought it to thee to have care of it," and he stirred not from the threshold.

"What is it?" she cried. "Show it to me, for the house is bare, and we have need of many things." And he drew the cloak back and showed her the sleeping child.

"Alack, good man!" she murmured, "have we not children of our own, that thou must needs bring a changeling to sit by the hearth? And who knows if it will not bring us bad fortune? And how shall we tend it?" And she was wroth against him.

"Nay, but it is a Star-Child," he answered; and he told her the strange manner of the finding of it.

But she would not be appeased, but mocked at him, and spoke angrily, and cried: "Our children lack bread, and shall we feed the child of another? Who is there who careth for us? And who giveth us food?"

"Nay, but God careth for the sparrows even, and feedeth them," he answered.

"Do not the sparrows die of hunger in the winter?" she asked. "And is it not winter now?" And the man answered nothing, but stirred not from the threshold.

And a bitter wind from the forest came in through the open door, and made her tremble, and she shivered, and said to him: "Wilt thou not close the door? There cometh a bitter wind into the house, and I am cold."

"Into a house where a heart is hard cometh there not always a bitter wind?" he asked. And the woman answered him nothing, but crept closer to the fire.

And after a time she turned round and looked at him, and her eyes were full of tears. And he came in swiftly, and placed the child in her arms, and she kissed it, and laid it in a little bed where the youngest of their own children was lying. And on the morrow the Woodcutter took the curious cloak of gold and placed it in a great chest, and a chain of amber that was round the child's neck his wife took and set it in the chest also.

So the Star-Child was brought up with the children of the Woodcutter, and sat at the same board with them, and was their playmate. And every year he became more beautiful to look at, so that all those who dwelt in the village were filled with wonder, for, while they were swarthy and black-haired, he was white and delicate as sawn ivory, and his curls were like the rings of the daffodil. His lips, also, were like the petals of a red flower, and his eyes were like violets by a river of pure water, and his body like the narcissus of a field where the

mower comes not.

Yet did his beauty work him evil. For he grew proud, and cruel, and selfish. The children of the Woodcutter, and the other children of the village, he despised, saying that they were of mean parentage, while he was noble, being sprung from a Star, and he made himself master over them, and called them his servants. No pity had he for the poor, or for those who were blind or maimed or in any way afflicted, but would cast stones at them and drive them forth onto the highway, and bid them beg their bread elsewhere, so that none save the outlaws came twice to that village to ask for alms. Indeed, he was as one enamoured of beauty, and would mock at the weakly and ill-favoured, and make jest of them; and himself he loved, and in summer, when the winds were still, he would lie by the well in the priest's orchard and look down at the marvel of his own face, and laugh for the pleasure he had in his fairness.

Often did the Woodcutter and his wife chide him, and say: "We did not deal with thee as thou dealest with those who are left desolate, and have none to succour them. Wherefore art thou so cruel to all who need pity?"

Often did the old priest send for him, and seek to teach him the love of living things, saying to him: "The fly is thy brother. Do it no harm. The wild birds that roam through the forest have their freedom. Snare them not for thy pleasure. God made the blind-worm and the mole, and each has its place. Who art thou to bring pain into God's world? Even the cattle of the field praise Him."

But the Star-Child heeded not their words, but would frown and flout, and go back to his companions, and lead them. And his companions followed him, for he was fair, and fleet of foot, and could dance, and pipe, and make music. And wherever the Star-Child led them they followed, and whatever the Star-Child bade them do, that

did they. And when he pierced with a sharp reed the dim eyes of the mole, they laughed; and when he cast stones at the leper they laughed also. And in all things he ruled them, and they became hard of heart even as he was.

Now there passed one day through the village a poor beggar-woman. Her garments were torn and ragged, and her feet were bleeding from the rough road on which she had travelled, and she was in very evil plight. And being weary she sat her down under a chestnut tree to rest.

But when the Star-Child saw her, he said to his companions, "See! There sitteth a foul beggar-woman under that fair and green-leaved tree. Come, let us drive her hence, for she is ugly and ill-favoured."

So he came near and threw stones at her, and mocked her, and she looked at him with terror in her eyes, nor did she move her gaze from him. And when the Woodcutter, who was cleaving logs in a haggard hard by, saw what the Star-Child was doing, he ran up and rebuked him, and said to him: "Surely thou art hard of heart and knowest not mercy, for what evil has this poor woman done to thee that thou shouldst treat her in this wise?"

And the Star-Child grew red with anger, and stamped his foot upon the ground, and said, "Who art thou to question me what I do? I am no son of thine to do thy bidding."

"Thou speakest truly," answered the Woodcutter, "yet did I show thee pity when I found thee in the forest."

And when the woman heard these words she gave a loud cry, and fell into a swoon. And the Woodcutter carried her to his own house, and his wife had care of her, and when she rose up from the swoon into which she had fallen, they set meat and drink before her, and bade her have comfort.

But she would neither eat nor drink, but said to the Woodcutter, "Didst thou not say that the child was found in the forest? And was it not ten years from this day?"

And the Woodcutter answered, "Yea, it was in the forest that I found him, and it is ten years from this day."

"And what signs didst thou find with him?" she cried. "Bare he not upon his neck a chain of amber? Was not round him a cloak of gold tissue broidered with stars?"

"Truly," answered the Woodcutter, "it was even as thou sayest." And he took the cloak and the amber chain from the chest where they lay, and showed them to her.

And when she saw them she wept for joy, and said, "He is my little son whom I lost in the forest. I pray thee send for him quickly, for in search of him have I wandered over the whole world."

So the Woodcutter and his wife went out and called to the Star-Child, and said to him, "Go into the house, and there shalt thou find thy mother, who is waiting for thee."

So he ran in, filled with wonder and great gladness. But when he saw her who was waiting there, he laughed scornfully and said, "Why, where is my mother? For I see none here but this vile beggar-woman."

And the woman answered him, "I am thy mother."

"Thou art mad to say so," cried the Star-Child angrily. "I am no son of thine, for thou art a beggar, and ugly, and in rags. Therefore get thee hence, and let me see thy foul face no more."

"Nay, but thou art indeed my little son, whom I bare in the forest," she cried, and she fell on her knees, and held out her arms to him. "The robbers stole thee from me, and left thee to die," she murmured, "but I recognized thee when I saw thee, and the signs also have I recognized, the cloak of golden tissue and the amber chain. Therefore I pray thee come with me, for over the whole world have I wandered in search of thee. Come with me, my son, for I have need of thy love."

But the Star-Child stirred not from his place, but shut the doors of his heart against her, nor was there any sound heard save the sound of the woman weeping for pain.

And at last he spoke to her, and his voice was hard and bitter. "If in very truth thou art my mother," he said, "it had been better hadst thou stayed away, and not come here to bring me to shame, seeing that I thought I was the child of some Star, and not a beggar's child, as thou tellest me that I am. Therefore get thee hence, and let me see thee no more."

"Alas! my son," she cried, "wilt thou not kiss me before I go? For I have suffered much to find thee."

"Nay," said the Star-Child, "but thou art too foul to look at, and rather would I kiss the adder or the toad than thee."

So the woman rose up, and went away into the forest weeping bitterly, and when the Star-Child saw that she had gone, he was glad, and ran back to his playmates that he might play with them.

But when they beheld him coming, they mocked him and said, "Why, thou art as foul as the toad, and as loathsome as the adder. Get thee hence, for we will not suffer thee to play with us," and they drave him out of the garden.

And the Star-Child frowned and said to himself, "What is this that they say to me? I will go to the well of water and look into it, and it shall tell me of my beauty."

So he went to the well of water and looked into it, and lo! his face was as the face of a toad, and his body was scaled like an adder. And he flung himself down on the grass and wept, and said to himself, "Surely this has come upon me by reason of my sin. For I have denied my mother, and driven her away, and been proud, and cruel to her. Wherefore I will go and seek her through the whole world, nor will I rest till I

have found her."

And there came to him the little daughter of the Woodcutter, and she put her hand upon his shoulder and said, "What doth it matter if thou hast lost thy comeliness? Stay with us, and I will not mock at thee."

And he said to her, "Nay, but I have been cruel to my mother, and as a punishment has this evil been sent to me. Wherefore I must go hence, and wander through the world till I find her and she give me her forgiveness."

So he ran away into the forest and called out to his mother to come to him, but there was no answer. All day long he called to her, and when the sun set he lay down to sleep on a bed of leaves, and the birds and the animals fled from him, for they remembered his cruelty, and he was alone save for the toad that watched him, and the slow adder that crawled past.

And in the morning he rose up, and plucked some bitter berries from the trees and ate them, and took his way through the great wood, weeping sorely. And of everything that he met he made inquiry if perchance they had seen his mother.

He said to the Mole, "Thou canst go beneath the earth. Tell me, is my mother there?"

And the Mole answered, "Thou hast blinded mine eyes. How should I know?"

He said to the Linnet, "Thou canst fly over the tops of the tall trees, and canst see the whole world. Tell me, canst thou see my mother?"

And the Linnet answered, "Thou hast clipt my wings for thy pleasure. How should I fly?"

And to the little Squirrel who lived in the fir tree, and was lonely, he said, "Where is my mother?"

And the Squirrel answered, "Thou hast slain mine. Doest thou seek to slay thine also?"

And the Star-Child wept and bowed his head, and prayed forgiveness of God's things, and went on through the forest, seeking for the beggar-woman. And on the third day he came to the other side of the forest and went down into the plain.

And when he passed through the villages the children mocked him, and threw stones at him, and the carlots would not suffer him even to sleep in the byres lest he might bring mildew on the stored corn, so foul was he to look at, and their hired men drave him away, and there was none who had pity on him. Nor could he hear anywhere of the beggar-woman who was his mother, though for the space of three years he wandered over the world, and often seemed to see her on the road in front of him, and would call to her, and run after her till the sharp flints made his feet to bleed. But overtake her he could not, and those who dwelt by the way did ever deny that they had seen her, or any like to her, and they made sport of his sorrow.

For the space of three years he wandered over the world, and in the world there was neither love nor loving-kindness nor charity for him, but it was even such a world as he had made for himself in the days of his great pride.

And one evening he came to the gate of a strong-walled city that stood by a river, and, weary and footsore though he was, he made to enter in. But the soldiers who stood on guard dropped their halberts across the entrance, and said roughly to him, "What is thy business in the city?"

"I am seeking for my mother," he answered, "and I pray ye to suffer me to pass, for it may be that she is in this city."

But they mocked at him, and one of them wagged a black beard, and set down his shield and cried, "Of a truth, thy mother

will not be merry when she sees thee, for thou art more ill-favoured than the toad of the marsh, or the adder that crawls in the fen. Get thee gone. Get thee gone. Thy mother dwells not in this city."

And another, who held a yellow banner in his hand, said to him, "Who is thy mother, and wherefore art thou seeking for her?"

And he answered, "My mother is a beggar even as I am, and I have treated her evilly, and I pray ye to suffer me to pass that she may give me her forgiveness, if it be that she tarrieth in this city." But they would not, and pricked him with their spears.

And, as he turned away weeping, one whose armour was inlaid with gilt flowers, and on whose helmet crouched a lion that had wings, came up and made inquiry of the soldiers who it was who had sought entrance. And they said to him, "It is a beggar and the child of a beggar, and we have driven him away."

"Nay," he cried, laughing, "but we will sell the foul thing for a slave, and his price shall be the price of a bowl of sweet wine."

And an old evil-visaged man who was passing by called out, and said, "I will buy him for that price," and, when he had paid the price, he took the Star-Child by the hand and led him into the city.

And after they had gone through many streets they came to a little door that was set in a wall that was covered with a pomegranate tree. And the old man touched the door with a ring of graved jasper and it opened, and they went down five steps of brass into a garden filled with black poppies and green jars of burnt clay. And the old man took then from his turban a scarf of figured silk, and bound with it the eyes of the Star-Child, and drave him in front of him. And when the scarf was taken off his eyes, the Star-Child found himself in a dungeon, and that was lit by a lantern of horn.

And the old man set before him some mouldy bread on a trencher and said, "Eat," and some brackish water in a cup and said, "Drink," and when he had eaten and drunk, the old man went out, locking the door behind him and fastening it with an iron chain.

And on the morrow the old man, who was indeed the subtlest of the magicians of Libya and had learned his art from one who dwelt in the tombs of the Nile, came in to him and frowned at him, and said, "In a wood that is nigh to the gate of this city of Giaours there are three pieces of gold. One is of white gold, and another is of yellow gold, and the gold of the third one is red. Today thou shalt bring me the piece of white gold, and if thou bringest it not back, I will beat thee with a hundred stripes. Get thee away quickly, and at sunset I will be waiting for thee at the door of the garden. See that thou bringest the white gold, or it shall go ill with thee, for thou art my slave, and I have bought thee for the price of a bowl of sweet wine." And he bound the eyes of the Star-Child with the scarf of figured silk, and led him through the house and through the garden of poppies, and up the five steps of brass. And having opened the little door with his ring he set him in the street.

And the Star-Child went out of the gate of the city, and came to the wood of which the Magician had spoken to him.

Now this wood was very fair to look at from without, and seemed full of singing birds and of sweet-scented flowers, and the Star-Child entered it gladly. Yet did its beauty profit him little, for wherever he went harsh briars and thorns shot up from the ground and encompassed him, and evil nettles stung him, and the thistle pierced him with her daggers, so that he was in sore distress. Nor could he anywhere find the piece of white gold of which the Magician had spoken, though he sought for it from morn to noon, and from noon to sunset.

And at sunset he set his face towards home, weeping bitterly, for he knew what fate was in store for him.

But when he had reached the outskirts of the wood, he heard from a thicket a cry as of someone in pain. And forgetting his own sorrow he ran back to the place, and saw there a little Hare caught in a trap that some hunter had set for it.

And the Star-Child had pity on it, and released it, and said to it, "I am myself but a slave, yet may I give thee thy freedom."

And the Hare answered him, and said: "Surely thou hast given me freedom, and what shall I give thee in return?"

And the Star-Child said to it, "I am seeking for a piece of white gold, nor can I anywhere find it, and if I bring it not to my master he will beat me."

"Come thou with me," said the Hare, "and I will lead thee to it, for I know where it is hidden, and for what purpose."

So the Star-Child went with the Hare, and lo! in the cleft of a great oak tree he saw the piece of white gold that he was seeking. And he was filled with joy, and seized it, and said to the Hare, "The service that I did to thee thou hast rendered back again many times over, and the kindness that I showed thee thou hast repaid a hundredfold."

"Nay," answered the Hare. "But as thou dealt with me, so I did deal with thee," and it ran away swiftly, and the Star-Child went towards the city.

Now at the gate of the city there was seated one who was a leper. Over his face hung a cowl of grey linen, and through the eyelets his eyes gleamed like red coals. And when he saw the Star-Child coming, he struck upon a wooden bowl, and clattered his bell, and called out to him, and said, "Give me a piece of money, or I must die of hunger. For they have thrust me out of the city, and there is no one who has pity on me."

"Alas!" cried the Star-Child, "I have but one piece of money in my wallet, and if I bring it not to my master he will beat me, for I am his slave."

But the leper entreated him, and prayed of him, till the Star-Child had pity, and gave him the piece of white gold.

And when he came to the Magician's house, the Magician opened to him, and brought him in, and said to him, "Hast thou the piece of white gold?" And the Star-Child answered, "I have it not." So the Magician fell upon him, and beat him, and set before him an empty trencher, and said, "Eat," and an empty cup, and said, "Drink," and flung him again into the dungeon.

And on the morrow the Magician came to him, and said, "If today thou bringest me not the piece of yellow gold, I will surely keep thee as my slave, and give thee three hundred stripes."

So the Star-Child went to the wood, and all day long he searched for the piece of yellow gold, but nowhere could he find it. And at sunset he sat him down and began to weep, and as he was weeping there came to him the little Hare that he had rescued from the trap.

And the Hare said to him, "Why art thou weeping? And what dost thou seek in the wood?"

And the Star-Child answered, "I am seeking for a piece of yellow gold that is hidden there, and if I find it not my master will beat me, and keep me as a slave."

"Follow me," cried the Hare, and it ran through the wood till it came to a pool of water. And at the bottom of the pool the piece of yellow gold was lying.

"How shall I thank thee?" said the Star-Child, "for lo! this is the second time that you have succoured me."

"Nay, but thou hadst pity on me first," said the Hare, and it ran away swiftly.

And the Star-Child took the piece of yellow gold, and put it in his wallet, and

hurried to the city. But the leper saw him coming, and ran to meet him, and knelt down and cried, "Give me a piece of money or I shall die of hunger."

And the Star-Child said to him, "I have in my wallet but one piece of yellow gold, and if I bring it not to my master he beat me and keep me as his slave."

But the leper entreated him sore, so that the Star-Child had pity on him, and gave him the piece of yellow gold.

And when he came to the Magician's house, the Magician opened to him, and brought him in, and said to him, "Hast thou the piece of yellow gold?" And the Star-Child said to him, "I have it not." So the Magician fell upon him, and beat him, and loaded him with chains, and cast him again into the dungeon.

And on the morrow the Magician came to him, and said, "If today thou bringest me the piece of red gold I will set thee free, but if thou bringest it not I will surely slay thee."

So the Star-Child went to the wood, and all day long he searched for the piece of red gold, but nowhere could he find it. And at evening he sat him down and wept, and as he was weeping there came to him the little Hare.

And the Hare said to him, "The piece of red gold that thou seekest is in the cavern that is behind thee. Therefore weep no more but be glad."

"How shall I reward thee?" cried the Star-Child. "For lo! this is the third time thou has succoured me."

"Nay, but thou hadst pity on me first," said the Hare, and it ran away swiftly.

And the Star-Child entered the cavern, and in its farthest corner he found the piece of red gold. So he put it in his wallet, and hurried to the city. And the leper seeing him coming, stood in the centre of the road, and cried out, and said to him, "Give me the piece of red money, or I must die," and the Star-Child had pity on him

again, and gave him the piece of red gold, saying, "Thy need is greater than mine." Yet was his heart heavy, for he knew what evil fate awaited him.

But lo! as he passed through the gate of the city, the guards bowed down and made obeisance to him, saying, "How beautiful is our lord!" and a crowd of citizens followed him, and cried out, "Surely there is none so beautiful in the whole world!" so that the Star-Child wept, and said to himself, "They are mocking me, and making light of my misery." And so large was the concourse of the people, that he lost the threads of his way, and found himself at last in a great square, in which there was a palace of a King.

And the gate of the palace opened, and the priests and the high officers of the city ran forth to meet him, and they abased themselves before him, and said, "Thou art our lord for whom we have been waiting, and the son of our King."

And the Star-Child answered them and said, "I am no king's son, but the child of a poor beggar-woman. And how say ye that I am beautiful, for I know that I am evil to look at?"

Then he, whose armour was inlaid with gilt flowers, and on whose helmet crouched a lion that had wings, held up a shield, and cried, "How saith my lord that he is not beautiful?"

And the Star-Child looked, and lo! his face was even as it had been, and his comeliness had come back to him, and he saw that in his eyes which he had not seen there before.

And the priests and the high officers knelt down and said to him, "It was prophesied of old that on this day should come he who was to rule over us. Therefore, let our lord take this crown and this sceptre, and be in his justice and mercy our King over us."

But he said to them, "I am not worthy, for

BEAUTY

I have denied the mother who bare me, nor may I rest till I have found her, and known her forgiveness. Therefore, let me go, for I must wander again over the world, and may not tarry here, though ye bring me the crown and the sceptre." And as he spake he turned his face from them towards the street that led to the gate of the city, and lo! amongst the crowd that pressed round the soldiers, he saw the beggar-woman who was his mother, and at her side stood the leper, who had sat by the road.

And a cry of joy broke from his lips, and he ran over, and kneeling down he kissed the wounds on his mother's feet, and wet them with his tears. He bowed his head in the dust, and sobbing, as one whose heart might break, he said to her: "Mother, I denied thee in the hour of my pride. Accept me in the hour of my humility. Mother, I gave thee hatred. Do thou give me love. Mother, I rejected thee. Receive thy child now." But the beggar-woman answered him not a word.

And he reached out his hands, and clasped the white feet of the leper, and said to him: "Thrice did I give thee of my mercy. Bid my mother speak to me once." But the leper answered him not a word.

And he sobbed again and said: "Mother, my suffering is greater than I can bear. Give me thy forgiveness, and let me go back to the forest." And the beggar-woman put her hand on his head, and said to him, "Rise," and the leper put his hand on his head, and said to him, "Rise," also.

And he rose up from his feet, and looked at them, and lo! they were a King and a Queen.

And the Queen said to him, "This is thy father whom thou hast succoured."

And the King said, "This is thy mother whose feet thou hast washed with thy tears."

And they fell on his neck and kissed him, and brought him into the palace and clothed him in fair raiment, and set the crown upon his head, and the sceptre in his hand, and over the city that stood by the river he ruled, and was its lord. Much justice and mercy did he show to all, and the evil Magician he banished, and to the Woodcutter and his wife he sent many rich gifts, and to their children he gave high honour. Nor would he suffer any to be cruel to bird or beast, but taught love and loving-kindness and charity, and to the poor he gave bread, and to the naked he gave raiment, and there was peace and plenty in the land.

PSALM 8

O Lord, our Lord,
   how majestic is your name in all the earth!

You have set your glory
   above the heavens.
From the lips of children and infants
   you have ordained praise
because of your enemies,
   to silence the foe and the avenger.

When I consider your heavens,
   the work of your fingers,
the moon and the stars,
   which you have set in place,
what is man that you are mindful of him,
   the son of man that you care for him?
You made him a little lower than the
     heavenly beings
   and crowned him with glory and honor.

You made him ruler over the works of
     your hands;
   you put everything under his feet:
all flocks and herds,
   and the beasts of the field,
the birds of the air,
   and the fish of the sea,
   all that swim the paths of the seas.

O Lord, our Lord,
   how majestic is your name in all the earth!

from N.I.V. Bible

TRADITIONS

A FRAGILE MOMENT . . .

Whenever I see our national flag, bright against the summer sky, two things come into my mind: a memory and a question.

The memory goes back to a little ceremony that took place every Fourth of July around the flagpole in my grandparents' front yard on Long Island, when I was a little girl of five or six or so.

Their house was right across the street from ours, so at the crack of dawn I'd dress hurriedly and race over to ring their doorbell. Fortunately, Grandpa was an early riser. Out he'd come carrying the neatly folded flag over his arm. At the pole, he'd untie ropes and fumble with different catches and pulley while I'd jump up and down, eager for what I considered the *big* moment.

Grandpa would give the rope a couple of test tugs. Then, with a nod in my direction, he'd begin to raise the flag.

"Oh, Columbia, the gem of the ocean," I'd sing out in my high, piping, child's voice, "the home of the brave and the free. . . ." Grandpa always joined in the chorus: "Three cheers for the red, white and blue," while a warm breeze gently blew the flag, now flying high at the top of the pole.

After this Grandpa and I would go into his kitchen where we'd eat cereal smothered with blueberries and cream while he told me stories about life in his native Germany and how he came to the United States when he was a young boy of 14. "I'm so grateful to God," Grandpa would say, "for the privilege of living in such a wonderful country. Always remember, Eleanor, how lucky you are. . . ."

So that's the memory. And the question? It's this: Does a person have to come from someplace else to appreciate—really appreciate—all that our country's flag stands for, all that it means?

I hope not. I pray not.

Eleanor V. Sass

God of our fathers, give unto us, Thy servants, a true appreciation of our heritage, of great men and great deeds in the past, but let us not be intimidated by feelings of our own inadequacy for this troubled hour.

Remind us that the God they worshiped, and by whose help they laid the foundations of our Nation, is still able to help us uphold what they bequeathed and to give it new meanings.

Remind us that we are not called to fill the places of those who have gone, but to fill our own places, to do the work Thou hast laid before us, to do the right as Thou hast given us to see the right, always to do the very best we can, and to leave the rest to Thee.

Peter Marshall

THE CONCORD HYMN

By the rude bridge that arched the flood,
Their flag to April's breeze unfurled,
Here once the embattled farmers stood,
And fired the shot heard round the world.

The foe long since in silence slept;
Alike the conqueror silent sleeps;
And Time the ruined bridge has swept
Down the dark stream which seaward
        creeps.

On this green bank, by this soft stream,
We set today a votive stone;
That memory may their dead redeem,
When, like our sires, our sons are gone.

Spirit, that made those spirits dare
To die, and leave their children free,
Bid Time and Nature gently spare
The shaft we raise to them and Thee.

Ralph Waldo Emerson

WHEN I TOUCHED THE LIBERTY BELL

Donna Geyer

Just before Christmas one year, an ear infection prevented my flying back home to Denver from New Jersey, where I had been staying. The two days on the train and the two-hour stopover in Philadelphia loomed as interminable. Philadelphia? The Liberty Bell. I'd always wanted to see it. Why not?

The train conductor looked doubtful, but told me how to go.

The bus driver said he went within a "coupla blocks" of the Liberty Bell, but that "the whole thing was probably closed." I dared not look at my watch. I was committed now.

"Here's your stop, lady. Straight ahead—but it's pretty dark."

It was dark. There seemed to be sudden isolation. But by now, I had to find the Liberty Bell.

As my eyes grew accustomed to the dark, I made out a familiar silhouette off to my right. I'd seen that steeple in my history books. The Bell must be there.

I walked fast but carefully. My hands found an old wall, and I could make out narrow windows. Moving around the building I turned the corner and saw a shaft of light falling on the ground from a glass pane in a door.

I pressed my face and hands against the glass, and there it was, heavy and curved and huge and familiar. Unaccountable tears started to flow down my cheeks. A guard sitting inside saw me and called out, "We're closed, but would you like to come in?"

"Please!"

I stood back staring, gripped by the sudden, inexpressibly strong realization of what this Bell and this building, Independence Hall, had meant to those times.

The guard, a man of infinite understanding, watched me. "Would you like to touch the Bell?"

At my nod he said, "Go ahead."

I put the tips of my fingers on vibrant metal. With the touch came an overwhelming feeling of the potential, the power and the dignity of man.

I stood only a moment. "Thank you so very much. I have to catch a train."

Wet-cheeked, I plunged through the dark. Which way? If I were headed right, I might catch my train. If I were headed wrong, it wouldn't matter. There is no measure for how much of too late. Moreover, one woman missing a train seemed unimportant alongside the vision of courage and dedication I had experienced.

I came to a bus stop and four middle-aged people waiting. "Does this bus go to the railroad station?"

A tired, kind-looking woman glanced at me suspiciously and then with concern. She spoke with a rich accent.

"Yah. But why you cry?"

"Because"—all my exhilaration flooded into my voice—"Because I've just seen the Liberty Bell. And," I added proudly, "I touched it."

"You were born in this country?" she asked.

"Yes."

"You hear?" the woman demanded of the others. "She was born here, but she understands about the Liberty Bell."

They nodded and murmured as the bus drew up and we got in. I opened my bag to get my fare, but my new friend stayed my hand.

"No," she said. She turned to the people on the bus. "This lady," she announced, "cried because she sees the Liberty Bell. We pay her fare. Here is my nickel." Money was held out to her until she had enough. Proudly she dropped it into the fare box and turned to smile at me. "Driver, Penn Central Railroad Station."

Everyone was looking at me. I was choked up all over again by this fantastic gift. "Thank you. Thank you all for everything!"

The train lurched forward as the conductor pulled me onto the steps. "Did you see it?"

"See it? I touched it."

As I rode the miles toward Denver, I knew I had touched something more than the great metal Bell. Touching the Bell and touched by the good people to whom it symbolized shelter, I knew that this was my country I was crossing. The American Dream, which I had come to regard with cynical suspicion, was a flame I would keep warm and unquenched.

Remember the sabbath day, to keep it holy.

Exodus 20:8

THE STAR-SPANGLED BANNER

O say, can you see, by the dawn's early light,
What so proudly we hailed at the twilight's last gleaming.
Whose broad stripes and bright stars, through the perilous fight,
O'er the ramparts we watched were so gallantly streaming!
And the rockets' red glare, the bombs bursting in air,
Gave proof through the night that our flag was still there:
O say, does that star-spangled banner yet wave
O'er the land of the free and the home of the brave?

O thus be it ever, when free men shall stand
Between their loved homes and the war's desolation!
Blest with victory and peace, may the heaven-rescued land
Praise the Power that hath made and preserved us a nation.
Then conquer we must, when our cause it is just,
And this be our motto: "In God is our trust,"
And the star-spangled banner in triumph shall wave
O'er the land of the free and the home of the brave!

Francis Scott Key

STRANGERS IN A STRANGE LAND

They came, these Pilgrims, to a strange, wild land,
With none to know which day would be their last.
In their native country they had never known
So bitter a winter, so piercing an icy blast.
They never had dreamed that food could be so scarce,
While famine and death stalked darkly by their side.

They paid for toil with cruelly aching backs,
While far too often many a loved one died.
Then strangely, one day, they who possessed
   no wealth
Sat down to a hoarded feast; they bowed in
   prayer
To the God of mercy, lifting grateful hearts
For the little they had, and for His gracious
   care.
They thanked Him for their lives that He
   had spared.
They had their freedom for the days ahead:
What more need man require, when all is
   said?
Unknowingly they passed some virtue on
To us in our strange wilderness today.
Remembering them, we join their simple
   fare,
And humbled, as we should be, we, too, pray.

Grace Noll Crowell

THE NEW COLOSSUS

Not like the brazen giant of Greek fame,
With conquering limbs astride from land to
   land;
Here at our sea-washed, sunset gates shall
   stand
A mighty woman with a torch, whose flame
Is the imprisoned lightning, and her name
Mother of Exiles. From her beacon-hand
Glows world-wide welcome; her mild eyes
   command
The air-bridged harbor that twin cities
   frame.
"Keep, ancient lands, your storied pomp!"
   cries she
With silent lips. "Give me your tired, your
   poor,
Your huddled masses yearning to breathe
   free,
The wretched refuse of your teeming shore.
Send these, the homeless, tempest-tossed to
   me,
I lift my lamp beside the golden door!"

Emma Lazarus

DOLLY MADISON

Margaret Chase Smith and H. Paul Jeffers

Life on the Payne plantation in Scotchtown, Virginia, was simple. John and Mary Payne lived quietly, although Mr. Payne was regarded as a wealthy man. The mansion at Scotchtown was large and richly furnished. There were many servants.

Despite her father's wealth, young Dolly Payne wore coarse, plain clothes. Secretly, she longed for silk dresses, jewelry and fine laces. She wanted gaiety, laughter, parties—things which she could only dream about at Scotchtown.

It was a little girl's dream, but it came true because Dolly married the dashing James Madison. Then, in 1801, Thomas Jefferson became the third President of the United States and asked James Madison to be his Secretary of State. Because Jefferson was a widower, he wanted Dolly Madison to be the "hostess" for his administration in the new capital city, Washington.

Dolly quickly learned that parties, entertainments, and social gatherings can be important to men in politics. The parties and dinners which she gave as the hostess for President Jefferson made it possible for Madison to meet and get to know the important men of the country, men who eventually supported him for President.

In March 1809, with the inauguration of James Madison as President of the United States, Dolly Madison became the First Lady. She took great interest in the President's house, redecorating it in bright colors—yellow, white, blue and gold. The mansion became a glittering centerpiece for the rough, muddy and still-incomplete capital city.

There was a good deal of criticism of James Madison as President as a war between England and France threatened to involve the United States. Each country tried to keep the United States from trading with its enemy, but the English were

more guilty of this than the French. They went so far as to stop American ships and force American sailors into the English navy. At last, on June 1, 1812, President Madison asked Congress to declare war on England.

Late in the summer of 1814 the British sent a fleet and an army into Chesapeake Bay. Their orders were "to destroy and lay waste such towns and districts upon the coast" as the British officers saw fit. One of those towns was to be Washington, D. C.

On Tuesday afternoon, August 23, 1814, President Madison was with the army in Maryland. Except for a servant, Dolly was alone in the President's house. The street, usually one of the quietest in Washington, was clogged with speeding wagons and running men. Their angry, frightened shouts filled the air.

"What is it?" Dolly asked.

French John, her butler, who had been standing on the porch observing the confusion in the street, turned and shook his head sadly. Tears ran down his face. "It's the army," he said. "These men have just come from Maryland. The British have beaten us. Now they say there's nothing to keep them from marching right on into Washington. What are we going to do, ma'am?"

Dolly's blue eyes filled with tears. This, she told herself, was no time for crying. She would have to keep calm.

"If you must leave Washington," she remembered her husband saying to her, "you must take the Cabinet papers and other documents with you."

"French John," she said to the servant, "fetch a wagon and then find as many trunks and boxes as you can. We've got a lot of packing to do."

Following her husband's instructions, and with the help of French John, she went through the house stuffing papers and documents into the trunks he had found. Among the documents she packed was the

Declaration of Independence in a silver-and-glass frame.

She then went to her room and opened the closets filled with her many beautiful clothes. Each garment reminded her of happier times. She couldn't bear the thought that any of them would fall into the hands of British soldiers marching through Washington. "I'll take them all," Dolly said to herself.

Then she saw the Gilbert Stuart portrait of President Washington. It was her favorite painting, so lifelike, so much like Washington. The large painting was in a heavy frame screwed to the wall. To Dolly, the painting of the Father of the Country appeared as important to the United States as any of the papers and documents crammed into the one wagon French John was able to find.

"We should leave right away, ma'am," French John said quietly as he came into the room to find Dolly standing in front of the portrait.

"Is there any room in the wagon?" she asked.

French John shook his head.

"Remove as many trunks as necessary. My trunks," was Dolly Madison's response.

French John struggled with the frame, but it would not budge.

"Break the frame," Dolly instructed him. "Remove the canvas."

Cracking, splintering noises filled the house as French John smashed the frame and removed the painting. Dolly watched him as he carried the big painting outside and put it into the wagon. Then, at last, Dolly Madison climbed into the wagon and headed across the Potomac River into Virginia.

The British army sacked and burned Washington. The soldiers set fire to private homes, the Capitol building, other government property, and the President's house. From Virginia, Dolly Madison watched the sky above the city turn fiery

red. With a shudder she realized that the mansion was being destroyed and with it so many of the things she treasured and held dear.

Four days later, Dolly and James Madison went back to Washington. The British troops were gone, leaving behind smoldering ruins. The President was saddened by what he saw and discouraged about rebuilding the capital. "Perhaps we should go back to Philadelphia," he sighed.

Taking her husband's hand, Dolly looked at the charred and blackened walls of the President's house. "Leave Washington? But this is the capital, James. We belong here. We can't leave it like this. It means too much to us and to the country."

Although the Madisons never lived in the mansion again, they had the ruined building restored.

The portrait of Washington which Dolly Madison saved is the only furnishing from that original Presidential mansion in the White House today. It hangs in the East Room, a reminder of the gallant woman who in a moment of personal danger thought first about her country's heritage.

INNOMINATUS

Breathes there a man with soul so dead,
Who never to himself hath said,
"This is my own, my native land!"
Whose heart hath ne'er within him burn'd
As home his footsteps he hath turn'd
From wandering on a foreign strand?
If such there breathe, go, mark him well;
For him no Minstrel raptures swell;
High though his titles, proud his name,
Boundless his wealth as wish can claim;
Despite those titles, power, and pelf,
The wretch, concentered all in self,
Living, shall forfeit fair renown,
And, doubly dying, shall go down
To the vile dust from whence he sprung,
Unwept, unhonour'd, and unsung.

Sir Walter Scott

EMIL'S THANKSGIVING

Louisa May Alcott

The "Brenda" was scudding along with all sails set to catch the rising wind, and everyone on board was rejoicing, for the long voyage was drawing toward an end.

"Four weeks more, Mrs. Hardy, and we'll give you a cup of tea such as you never had before," said second mate Hoffmann, as he paused beside two ladies sitting in a sheltered corner of the deck.

"I shall be glad to get it, and still gladder to put my feet on solid ground," answered the elder lady, smiling, for our friend Emil was a favorite, as well he might be, since he devoted himself to the captain's wife and daughter.

"Is this likely to be a gale, think ye?" added Mrs. Hardy, with an anxious glance at the west, where the sun was setting redly.

"Only a capful of wind, ma'am, just enough to send us along lively," answered Emil, with a comprehensive glance aloft and alow.

Mrs. Hardy suddenly exclaimed, "What's that?"

Emil's quick eye saw at once the little puff of smoke coming up a hatchway where no smoke should be, and his heart seemed to stand still for an instant as the dread word "Fire!" flashed through his mind. Then he was quite steady, and strolled away, saying quietly,

"Smoking not allowed there, I'll go and stop it." But the instant he was out of sight his face changed, and he leaped down that hatchway.

He was gone a few minutes, and when he came up, half stifled with smoke, he was as white as a very brown man could be, but calm and cool as he went to report to the captain.

"Fire in the hold, sir."

"Don't frighten the women," was Captain Hardy's first order; then both bestirred

themselves to discover how strong the treacherous enemy was.

In spite of the streams of water poured into the hold it was soon evident that the ship was doomed. The rising gale soon fanned the smoldering fire to flames that began to break out here and there, telling the dreadful truth too plainly for any one to hide. Mrs. Hardy and Mary bore the shock bravely when told to be ready to quit the ship at a minute's notice; the boats were hastily prepared, and the men worked with a will to batten down every loophole whence the fire might escape. Soon the poor "Brenda" was a floating furnace, and the order to "Take to the boats!" came for all. The women first, of course, and it was fortunate that, being a merchantman, there were no more passengers on board, so there was no panic, and one after the other the boats pushed off. That in which the women were lingered near, for the brave Captain would be the last to leave his ship.

Emil stayed by him till ordered away, and reluctantly obeyed, but it was well for him he went, for just as he had regained the boat, rocking far below, half hidden by a cloud of smoke, a mast, undermined by the fire now raging in the bowels of the ship, fell with a crash, knocking Captain Hardy overboard. The boat soon reached him as he floated out from the wreck, and Emil sprung into the sea to rescue him, for he was wounded and senseless. This accident made it necessary for the young man to take command, and he at once ordered the men to pull for their lives, as an explosion might occur at any moment.

The other boats were out of danger, and all lingered to watch the splendid yet awesome spectacle of the burning ship alone on the wide sea, reddening the night sky and casting a lurid glare upon the water, where floated the frail boats filled with pale faces, all turned for a last look at the fated "Brenda," slowly settling to her watery grave. No one saw the end, however, for the gale soon swept the watchers far away and separated them.

The boat whose fortunes we must follow was alone when dawn came up, showing these survivors all the dangers of their situation. Food and water had been put in, and such provision for comfort and safety as time allowed, but it was evident that with a badly wounded man, two women, and seven sailors, their supply would not last long, and help was sorely needed. Their only hope was in meeting a ship, although the gale, which had raged all night, had blown them out of their course. To this hope all clung, and whiled away the weary hours, watching the horizon and cheering one another with prophecies of speedy rescue.

Second mate Hoffmann was very brave and helpful, though this unexpected responsibility weighed heavily on his shoulders, for the Captain's state seemed desperate, the poor wife's grief wrung his heart, and the blind confidence of the young girl in his power to save them, made him feel that no sign of doubt or fear must lessen it.

The first day and night passed in comparative comfort, but when the third came, things looked dark and hope began to fail. The wounded man was delirious, the wife worn out with anxiety and suspense, the girl weak for want of food, having put away half her biscuit for her mother, and given her share of water to wet her father's feverish lips. The sailors ceased rowing and sat grimly waiting, some openly reproaching their leader for not following their advice, others demanding more food, all waxing dangerous as privation and pain brought out the animal instinct lurking in them. Emil did his best, but mortal man was

helpless there. All day he tried to cheer and comfort them, while hunger gnawed, thirst parched, and growing fear lay heavy at his heart. He told stories to the men, implored them to bear up for the helpless women's sake, and promised rewards if they would pull while they had strength to regain the lost route, as nearly as he could make it out, and increase their chance of rescue. He rigged an awning of sailcloth over the suffering man and tended him like a son, comforted the wife, and tried to make the pale girl forget herself, by singing every song he knew or recounting his adventures by land and sea, till she smiled and took heart, for all ended well.

The fourth day came, and the supply of food and water was nearly gone. Emil proposed to keep it for the sick man and the women, but two of the men rebelled, demanding their share. Emil gave up his as an example, and several of the good fellows followed it. This shamed the others, and for another day an ominous peace reigned in that little world of suffering.

Another trial came to them that left all more despairing than before. A sail appeared, and a frenzy of joy prevailed, to be turned to disappointment when it passed by, too far away to see the signals waved to them or hear the frantic cries for help. Emil's heart sunk then, for the Captain seemed dying, and the women could not hold out much longer. He kept up till night came; then, in the darkness, broken only by the feeble murmuring of the sick man, the whispered prayers of the poor wife, the ceaseless swash of waves, Emil hid his face, and had an hour of silent agony.

As he sat there with his head in his hands, bowed down by the first great trial of his young life, the starless sky overhead, the restless sea beneath, and all around him suffering, for which he had no help, a soft sound broke the silence, and he listened like one in a dream. It was Mary singing to

her mother, who lay sobbing in her arms, spent with this long anguish. A very faint and broken voice it was, for the poor girl's lips were parched with thirst, but the loving heart turned instinctively to the great Helper in this hour of despair, and He heard her feeble cry. It was a sweet old hymn often sung at Plumfield, and as he listened, all the happy past came back so clearly that Emil forgot the bitter present, and was at home again.

Then, as the soft voice crooned on to lull the weary woman to a fitful sleep, Emil for a little while forgot his burden (in a dream of Plumfield).

A sudden shout startled him from that brief rest, and a drop on his forehead told him that the blessed rain had come at last, bringing salvation with it, for thirst is harder to bear than hunger, heat, or cold. Welcomed by cries of joy, all lifted up their parched lips, held out their hands, and spread their garments to catch the great drops that soon came pouring down to cool the sick man's fever, quench the agony of thirst, and bring refreshment to every weary body in the boat. The clouds broke away at dawn, and Emil sprung up, wonderfully braced and cheered by those hours of silent gratitude for this answer to their cry for help. But this was not all; as his eye swept the horizon, clear against the rosy sky shone the sails of a ship.

One cry broke from all those eager throats and rung across the sea, as every man waved hat or handkerchief, and the women stretched imploring hands toward this great white angel of deliverance.

No disappointment now; answering signals assured them of help, and in the rapture of that moment the happy women fell on Emil's neck, giving him his reward in tears and blessings as their grateful hearts overflowed.

When all were safely aboard the good "Urania," Emil saw his friends in tender

hands, his men among their mates, and told the story of the wreck before he thought of himself. The savory odor of the soup, carried by to the cabin for the ladies, reminded him that he was starving, and a sudden stagger betrayed his weakness. He was instantly borne away, to be half killed by kindness, and, being fed, clothed, and comforted, was left to rest. Just as the surgeon left the stateroom, he asked in his broken voice, "What day is this? My head is so confused, I've lost my reckoning."

"Thanksgiving Day, man! And we'll give you a regular New England dinner, if you'll eat it," answered the surgeon heartily.

But Emil was too spent to do anything except lie still and give thanks, more fervently and gratefully than ever before, for the blessed gift of life, which was the sweeter for a sense of duty faithfully performed.

CHRISTMAS BELLS

I heard the bells on Christmas Day
Their old, familiar carols play,
  And wild and sweet
  The words repeat
Of peace on earth, good will to men!

Henry Wadsworth Longfellow

THE CHRISTMAS TREE IN BROOKLYN

Betty Smith

Christmas was a charmed time in Brooklyn. It was in the air, long before it came. The first hint of it was Mr. Morton going around

the schools teaching Christmas carols, but the first sure sign was the store windows.

You have to be a child to know how wonderful is a store window filled with dolls and sleds and other toys. And this wonder came free to Francie. It was nearly as good as actually having the toys to be permitted to look at them through the glass window.

Oh, what a thrill there was for Francie when she turned a street corner and saw another store all fixed up for Christmas! Ah, the clean shining window with cotton batting sprinkled with stardust for a carpet! There were flaxen-haired dolls and others which Francie liked better who had hair the color of good coffee with lots of cream in it. Their faces were perfectly tinted and they wore clothes the like of which Francie had never seen on earth. The dolls stood upright in flimsy cardboard boxes. They stood with the help of a bit of tape passed around the neck and ankles and through holes at the back of the box. Oh, the deep blue eyes framed by thick lashes that stared straight into a little girl's heart and the perfect miniature hands extended, appealingly asking, "Please, won't *you* be my mama?" And Francie had never had a doll except a two-inch one that cost a nickel.

And the sleds! (Or, as the Williamsburg children called them, the sleighs.) There was a child's dream of heaven come true! A new sled with a flower someone had dreamed up painted on it—a deep blue flower with bright green leaves—the ebony-black painted runners, the smooth steering bar made of hard wood and gleaming varnish over all! And the names painted on them! "Rosebud!" "Magnolia!" "Snow King!" "The Flyer!" Thought Francie, "If I could only have one of those, I'd never ask God for another thing as long as I live."

There were roller skates made of shining nickel with straps of good brown leather and silvered nervous wheels, tensed for rolling, needing but a breath to start them turning, as they lay crossed one over the other, sprinkled with mica snow on a bed of cloudlike cotton.

There were other marvelous things. Francie couldn't take them all in. Her head spun and she was dizzy with the impact of all the seeing and all the making up of stories about toys in the shop windows.

The spruce trees began coming into Francie Nolan's neighborhood the week before Christmas. Their branches were corded to make shipping easier. Vendors rented space on the curb before a store and stretched a rope from pole to pole and leaned the trees against it. All day they walked up and down this one-sided avenue of aromatic leaning trees, blowing on stiff ungloved fingers. And the air was cold and still, and full of the pine smell and the smell of tangerines which appeared in the stores only at Christmas time and the mean street was truly wonderful for a little while.

There was a cruel custom in the neighborhood. At midnight on the Eve of our dear Saviour's birth, the kids gathered where there were unsold trees. There was a saying that if you waited until then, you wouldn't have to buy a tree, that "they'd chuck 'em at you." This was literally true. The man threw each tree in turn, starting with the biggest. Kids volunteered to stand up against the throwing. If a boy didn't fall down under the impact, the tree was his. If he fell, he forfeited his chance at winning a tree. Only the roughest boys and some of the young men elected to be hit by the big trees. The others waited shrewdly until a tree came up that they could stand against. The littlest kids waited for the tiny, foot-high trees and shrieked in delight when they won one.

On the Christmas Eve when Francie was

ten and her brother Neeley, nine, Mama consented to let them go down and have their first try for a tree. Francie had picked out her tree earlier in the day. She had stood near it all afternoon and evening praying that no one would buy it. To her joy, it was still there at midnight. It was ten feet tall and its price was so high that no one could afford to buy it. Its branches were bound with new white rope and it came to a sure point at the top.

The man took this tree out first. Before Francie could speak up, a neighborhood bully, a boy of eighteen known as Punky Perkins, stepped forward and ordered the man to chuck the tree at him. The man hated the way Punky was so confident. He looked around and asked, "Anybody else wanna take a chance on it?"

Francie stepped forward. "Me, Mister."

A spurt of derisive laughter came from the tree man. The kids snickered. A few adults who had gathered to watch the fun guffawed. "Aw g'wan. You're too little," the tree man objected.

"Me and my brother—we're not too little together."

She pulled Neeley forward. The man looked at them—a thin girl of ten with starveling hollows in her cheeks but with the chin still baby-round. He looked at the little boy with his fair hair and round eyes—Neeley Nolan, just nine years old, all innocence and trust.

"Two ain't fair," yelped Punky.

"Shut your lousy trap," advised the man, who held all power in that hour. "These here kids is got nerve. Stand back, the rest of youse. These kids is goin' to have a show at this tree."

The others made a wavering lane, a human funnel with Francie and her brother making the small end of it. The big man at the other end flexed his great arms to throw the great tree. He noticed how tiny the children looked at the end of the short lane. For the split part of a moment, the

tree thrower went through a kind of Gethsemane.

Oh, his soul agonized, *why don't I just give 'em the tree and say Merry Christmas? I can't sell it no more this year and it won't keep till next year.* The kids watched him solemnly as he stood there in his moment of thought. *But then*, he rationalized, *if I did that, all the others would expect to get 'em handed to 'em. And next year, nobody a'tall would buy a tree off of me. I ain't a big enough man to give this tree away for nothin'. No, I gotta think of myself and my own kids.* He finally came to his conclusion. *Them two kids is gotta live in this world. They got to learn to give and to take punishment.* As he threw the tree with all his strength, his heart wailed out, *It's a rotten, lousy world!*

Francie saw the tree leave his hands. The whole world stood still as something dark and monstrous came through the air. There was nothing but pungent darkness and something that grew and grew as it rushed at her. She staggered as the tree hit them. Neeley went to his knees but she pulled him up fiercely before he could go down. There was a mighty swishing sound as the tree settled. Everything was dark, green and prickly. Then she felt a sharp pain at the side of her head where the trunk of the tree had hit her. She felt Neeley trembling.

When some of the older boys pulled the tree away, they found Francie and her brother standing upright, hand in hand. Blood was coming from scratches on Neeley's face. He looked more like a baby than ever with his bewildered blue eyes and the fairness of his skin made more noticeable because of the clear red blood. But they were smiling. Had they not won the biggest tree in the neighborhood? Some of the boys hollered, "Hooray!"

It wasn't easy dragging that tree home. They were handicapped by a boy who ran alongside yelping, "Free ride! All aboard!" who'd jump on and make them drag him along. But he got sick of the game

eventually and went away.

In a way, it was good that it took them so long to get the tree home. It made their triumph more drawn out. Francie glowed when a lady said, "I never saw such a big tree!" The cop on their corner stopped them, examined the tree, and solemnly offered to buy it for fifteen cents if they'd deliver it to his home. Francie nearly burst with pride although she knew he was joking.

They had to call to Papa to help them get the tree up the narrow stairs. Papa came running down. His amazement at the size of the tree was flattering. He pretended to believe that it wasn't theirs. Francie had a lot of fun convincing him although she knew all the while that the whole thing was make-believe. Papa pulled in front and Francie and Neeley pushed in back and they began forcing the big tree up the two narrow flights of stairs. Papa started singing, not caring that it was rather late at night. He sang "Holy Night." The narrow walls took up his clear sweet voice, held it for a breath and gave it back with doubled sweetness. Doors creaked open and families gathered on the landings, pleased and amazed at something unexpected being added to that moment of their lives.

Francie saw the Tynmore sisters, who gave piano lessons, standing together in their doorway, their gray hair in crimpers, and ruffled, starched nightgowns showing under the voluminous wrappers. They added their thin poignant voices to Papa's. Floss Gaddis, her mother and her brother, Henny, who was dying of consumption, stood in their doorway. Henny was crying and when Papa saw him he let the song trail off; he thought maybe it made Henny too sad.

Flossie was in a Klondike-dance-hall-girl

costume waiting for an escort to take her to a masquerade ball which started soon after midnight. More to make Henny smile than anything else, Papa said, "Floss, we got no angel for the top of this Christmas tree. How about your obliging?"

Floss was all ready to make a smart-alecky reply, but there was something about the big proud tree, the beaming children and the rare good will of the neighbors that changed her mind. All she said was, "Gee, ain't you the kidder, Mr. Nolan."

They set the tree up in the front room after Mama had spread a sheet to protect the carpet from falling pine needles. The tree stood in a big tin bucket with broken bricks to hold it upright. When the rope was cut away, the branches spread out to fill the room. They draped over the piano and some of the chairs stood among the branches. There was no money to buy decorations or lights. But the great tree standing there was enough. The room was cold. It was a poor year, that one—too poor for them to buy the extra coal for the front-room stove. The room smelled cold and clean and aromatic.

Every day, during the week the tree stood there, Francie put on her sweater and stocking cap and went in and sat under the tree. She sat there and enjoyed the smell and the dark greenness of it.

Oh, the mystery of a great tree, a prisoner in a tin bucket in a tenement front room!

I have always thought of Christmas time, when it has come round, as a good time: a kind, forgiving, charitable, pleasant time: the only time I know of in the long calendar of the year when men and women seem by one consent to open their shut-up hearts freely, and to think of people below them as if they really were fellow passengers, and not another race of creatures bound on other journeys. And therefore, though it has never put a scrap of gold or silver in my pocket, I believe that it has done me good, and will do me good, and I say, God bless it!

Charles Dickens

Dear Lord, I offer Thee this day
All I shall think, or do, or say.

Author Unknown

And He took bread, gave thanks and broke it, and gave it to them, saying, "This is my body given for you; do this in remembrance of me."

Luke 22:19, N.I.V. Bible

YOUTH

A FRAGILE MOMENT . . .

Recently after a heavy blizzard my car was stuck in a
snowpile, and my efforts to get it moving only dug its
wheels in deeper and deeper. Down the street came a
muscular teen-ager carrying a shovel. When he saw my
problem he promptly got to work and set the car free.

"Many thanks," I said gratefully as I reached to hand
him some folded bills.

"No way," he said with a smile. "I belong to the DUO
Club."

"Never heard of it," I replied.

"Sure you have," he grinned. "It's the do-unto-others-as-
you-would-have-them-do-unto-you club." And with a wave
of his hand and another big smile, he was on his way.

Arve Hatcher

I walk with God daily.

Helen Keller

HOW DO YOU TACKLE YOUR WORK?

How do you tackle your work each day?
  Are you scared of the job you find?
Do you grapple the task that comes your
    way
  With a confident, easy mind?
Do you stand right up to the work ahead
  Or fearfully pause to view it?
Do you start to toil with a sense of dread
  Or feel that you're going to do it?

You can do as much as you think you can,
  But you'll never accomplish more;
If you're afraid of yourself, young man,
  There's little for you in store.

For failure comes from the inside first,
  It's there if we only knew it,
And you can win, though you face the
    worst,
  If you feel that you're going to do it.

Success! It's found in the soul of you,
  And not in the realm of luck!
The world will furnish the work to do,
  But you must provide the pluck.
You can do whatever you think you can,
  It's all in the way you view it.
It's all in the start that you make, young
    man:
  You must feel that you're going to do it.

How do you tackle your work each day?
  With confidence clear, or dread?
What to yourself do you stop and say

When a new task lies ahead
What is the thought that is in your mind?
　Is fear ever running through it?
If so, tackle the next you find
　By thinking you're going to do it.

Edgar Guest

No coward soul is mine,
No trembler in the world's storm-troubled
　　sphere:
　I see Heaven's glories shine,
And faith shines equal, arming me from
　　fear.

Emily Brontë

TRUCE IN THE FOREST

Fritz Vincken

When we heard the knock on our door that Christmas Eve in 1944, neither Mother nor I had the slightest inkling of the quiet miracle that lay in store for us.

I was 12 then, and we were living in a small cottage in the Hurtgen Forest, near the German-Belgian border. Father had stayed at the cottage on hunting weekends before the war; when Allied bombers partly destroyed our home town of Aachen, he sent us to live there. He had been ordered into the civil defense fire guard in the border town of Monschau, four miles away.

"You'll be safe in the woods," he had told me. "Take care of Mother. Now you're the man of the family."

But, nine days before Christmas, Field Marshal von Rundstedt had launched the last, desperate German offensive of the war, and now, as I went to the door, the Battle of the Bulge was raging all around us. We heard the incessant booming of field guns; planes soared continuously overhead; at night, searchlights stabbed through the darkness. Thousands of Allied and German soldiers were fighting and dying nearby.

When that first knock came, Mother quickly blew out the candles; then, as I went to answer it, she stepped ahead of me and pushed open the door. Outside, like phantoms against the snow-clad trees, stood two steel-helmeted men. One of them spoke to Mother in a language we did not understand, pointing to a third man lying in the snow. She realized before I did that these were American soldiers. Enemies!

Mother stood silent, motionless, her hand on my shoulder. They were armed and could have forced their entrance, yet they stood there and asked with their eyes. And the wounded man seemed more dead than alive. "Kommt rein," Mother said finally. "Come in." The soldiers carried their comrade inside and stretched him out on my bed.

None of them understood German. Mother tried French, and one of the soldiers could converse in that language. As Mother went to look after the wounded man, she said to me, "The fingers of those two are numb. Take off their jackets and boots, and bring in a bucket of snow." Soon I was rubbing their blue feet with snow.

We learned that the stocky, dark-haired fellow was Jim; his friend, tall and slender, was Robin. Harry, the wounded one, was now sleeping on my bed, his face as white as the snow outside. They'd lost their battalion and had wandered in the forest for three days, looking for the Americans, hiding from the Germans. They hadn't shaved, but still, without their heavy coats, they looked merely like big boys. And that was the way Mother began to treat them.

Now Mother said to me, "Go get Hermann. And bring six potatoes."

This was a serious departure from our pre-Christmas plans. Hermann was the plump rooster (named after portly Hermann Göring, Hitler's No. 2, for whom Mother had little affection) that we had been fattening for weeks in the hope that Father would be home for Christmas. But, some hours before, when it was obvious that

Father would not make it, Mother had decided that Hermann should live a few more days, in case Father could get home for New Year's. Now she had changed her mind again. Hermann would serve an immediate, pressing purpose.

While Jim and I helped with the cooking, Robin took care of Harry. He had a bullet through his upper leg, and had almost bled to death. Mother tore a bedsheet into long strips for bandages.

Soon, the tempting smell of roast chicken permeated our room. I was setting the table when once again there came a knock at the door. Expecting to find more lost Americans, I opened the door without hesitation. There stood four soldiers, wearing uniforms quite familiar to me after five years of war. They were Wehrmacht—Germans!

I was paralyzed with fear. Although still a child, I knew the harsh law: sheltering enemy soldiers constituted high treason. We could all be shot! Mother was frightened, too. Her face was white, but she stepped outside and said, quietly, "Frohliche Weihnachten." The soldiers wished her a Merry Christmas, too.

"We have lost our regiment and would like to wait for daylight," explained the corporal. "Can we rest here?"

"Of course," Mother replied, with a calmness born of panic. "You can also have a fine, warm meal, and eat till the pot is empty."

The Germans smiled as they sniffed the aroma through the half-open door. "But," Mother added firmly, "we have three other guests, whom you may not consider friends." Now her voice was suddenly sterner than I'd ever heard it before. "This is Christmas Eve, and there will be no shooting here."

"Who's inside?" the corporal demanded. "Amerikaner?"

Mother looked at each frost-chilled face. "Listen," she said slowly. "You could be my sons, and so could those in there. A boy with a gunshot wound, fighting for his life. His two friends—lost like you and just as hungry and exhausted as you are. This one night," she turned to the corporal and raised her voice a little, "this Christmas night, let us forget about killing."

The corporal stared at her. There were two or three endless seconds of silence. Then Mother put an end to indecision. "Enough talking!" she ordered and clapped her hands sharply. "Please put your weapons here on the woodpile—and hurry up before the others eat the dinner!"

Now, as Germans and Americans tensely rubbed elbows in the small room, Mother was really on her mettle. Never losing her smile, she went right on preparing dinner. But Hermann wasn't going to grow any bigger, and now there were four more mouths to feed. "Quick," she whispered to me, "get more potatoes and some oats. These boys are hungry, and a starving man is an angry one."

While foraging in the storage room, I heard Harry moan. When I returned, one of the Germans had put on his glasses to inspect the American's wound. "Do you belong to the medical corps?" Mother asked him. "No," he answered. "But I studied medicine at Heidelberg until a few months ago." Thanks to the cold, he told the Americans in what sounded like fairly good English, Harry's wound hadn't become infected. "He is suffering from a severe loss of blood," he explained to Mother. "What he needs is rest and nourishment."

Relaxation was now beginning to replace suspicion. Even to me, all the soldiers looked very young as we sat there together. Heinz and Willi, both from Cologne, were 16. The German corporal, at 23, was the oldest of them all. From his food bag Heinz managed to find a loaf of rye bread. Mother cut that in small pieces to be served with the dinner.

Then Mother said grace. I noticed that there were tears in her eyes as she said the

old, familiar words, "Komm, Herr Jesus. Be our guest." And as I looked around the table, I saw tears, too, in the eyes of the battle-weary soldiers, boys again, some from America, some from Germany, all far from home.

Our private armistice continued next morning. Harry woke in the early hours, and swallowed some broth that Mother fed him. With the dawn, it was apparent that he was becoming stronger. Mother now made him an invigorating drink from our one egg. Everyone else had oatmeal. Afterward, two poles and Mother's best tablecloth were fashioned into a stretcher for Harry.

The corporal then advised the Americans how to find their way back to their lines. Looking over Jim's map, the corporal pointed out a stream. "Continue along this creek," he said, "and you will find the 1st Army rebuilding its forces on its upper course." The medical student relayed the information in English.

"Why don't we head for Monschau?" Jim had the student ask. "Nein!" the corporal exclaimed. "We've taken Monschau."

Now Mother gave them all back their weapons. "Be careful, boys," she said. "I want you to get home someday where you belong. God bless you all!" The German and American soldiers shook hands and we watched them disappear in opposite directions.

When I returned inside, Mother had brought out the old family Bible. I glanced over her shoulder. The book was open to the Christmas story, the Birth in the Manger and how the Wise Men came from afar bearing their gifts. Her finger was tracing the last line from Matthew 2:12 ". . . they departed into their own country another way."

If ye have faith as a grain of mustard seed, ye shall say unto this mountain, Remove hence to yonder place; and it shall remove: and nothing shall be impossible unto you.

Matthew 17:20

THE WINDOWS OF GOLD

There is a legend that has often been told
Of the boy who searched for the windows
    of gold,
The beautiful windows he saw far away
When he looked in the valley at sunrise
    each day,
And he yearned to go down to the valley
    below
But he lived on a mountain that was
    covered with snow
And he knew it would be a difficult trek,
But that was a journey he wanted to
    make—
So he planned by day and he dreamed by
    night
Of how he could reach The Great Shining
    Light . . . .
And one golden morning when dawn broke
    through
And the valley sparkled with diamonds of
    dew
He started to climb down the mountainside
With the Windows of Gold as his goal and
    his guide . . . .
He traveled all day and, weary and worn,
With bleeding feet and clothes that were
    torn
He entered the peaceful valley town
Just as the Golden Sun Went Down . . . .
But he seemed to have lost his "Guiding
    Light,"
The windows were dark that had once been
    bright,
And hungry and tired and lonely and cold
He cried, "Won't You Show Me The
    Windows Of Gold?"

And a kind hand touched him and said,
 "Behold!
High On The Mountain Are The Windows
 Of Gold"—
For the sun going down in a great golden
 ball
Had burnished the windows of his cabin so
 small,
And The Kingdom of God with its Great
 Shining Light,
Like the Golden Windows that shone so
 bright,
Is not a far distant place, somewhere,
It's as close to you as a silent prayer—
And your search for God will end and begin
When you look for Him and Find Him
 within.

Helen Steiner Rice

If you have built castles in the air your
work need not be lost; that is where they
should be built; now put foundations under
them.

Henry Thoreau

Labour to keep alive in your breast that
little spark of celestial fire—conscience.

George Washington

SNOWFALL IN CHILDHOOD

Ben Hecht

I got out of bed to see what had happened
in the night. I was thirteen years old. I had
fallen asleep watching the snow falling
through the half-frosted window.

But though the snow had promised to
keep falling for a long time, perhaps three
or four days, on opening my eyes I was full
of doubts. Snowstorms usually ended too
soon.

While getting out of bed I remembered
how, as I was nearly asleep, the night
outside the frosted window had seemed to
burst into a white jungle. I had dreamed of
streets and houses buried in snow.

I hurried barefooted to the window. It
was scribbled with a thick frost and I
couldn't see through it. The room was cold
and through the open window came the
fresh smell of snow like the moist nose of an
animal resting on the ledge and breathing
into the room.

I knew from the smell and the darkness
of the window that snow was still falling. I
melted a peephole on the glass with my
palms. I saw that this time the snow had not
fooled me. There it was, still coming down
white and silent and too thick for the wind
to move, and the streets and houses were
almost as I had dreamed. I watched,
shivering and happy. Then I dressed,
pulling on my clothes as if the house were
on fire. I was finished with breakfast and
out in the storm two hours before school
time.

The world had changed. All the houses,
fences and barren trees had new shapes.
Everything was round and white and
unfamiliar.

I set out through these new streets on a
voyage of discovery. The unknown
surrounded me. Through the thick falling
snow, the trees, houses and fences looked
like ghost shapes that had floated down out
of the sky during the night. The morning
was without light, but the snowfall hung
and swayed like a marvelous lantern over
the streets. The snowbanks, already over
my head in places, glowed mysteriously.

I was pleased with this new world. It
seemed to belong to me more than that
other world which lay hidden.

I headed for the school, jumping like a
clumsy rabbit in and out of snowbanks. It
seemed wrong to spoil the smooth outlines
of these snowdrifts and I hoped that
nobody else would pass this way after me.
In that case the thick falling snow would

soon restore the damage. Reassured by this hope I continued on my devastations like some wanton explorer. I began to feel that no one would dare the dangers of my wake. Then, as I became more aware of the noble proportions of this snowstorm I stopped worrying altogether about the marring of this new and glowing world. Other snows had melted and been shoveled away, but this snow would never disappear. The sun would never shine again and the little Wisconsin town through which I plunged and tumbled to school on this dark storm-filled morning was from now on an arctic land full of danger and adventure.

When eventually, encased in snow, I arrived at the school, I found scores of white-covered figures already there. The girls had taken shelter inside, but the boys stayed in the storm. They jumped in and out of the snowdrifts and tumbled through the deep unbroken white fields in front of the school.

Muffled cries filled the street. Someone had discovered how far away our voices sounded in the snowfall and this started the screaming. We screamed for ten minutes, delighted with the fact that our voices no longer carried and that the snowstorm had made us nearly dumb.

Tired with two hours of such plunging and rolling, I joined a number of boys who like myself had been busy since dawn and who now stood for the last few minutes before the school bell with half-frozen faces staring at the heavily falling snow as if it were some game they could not bear to leave.

When we were finally seated in our grade room we continued to watch the snowstorm through the windows. The morning had grown darker as we had all hoped it would and it was necessary to turn on the electric lights in the room. This was almost as thrilling as the pale storm still floating outside the windows.

In this yellow light the school seemed to disappear and in its place a picnic spread around us. The teachers themselves seemed to change. Their eyes kept turning toward the windows and they kept looking at us behind our desks as if we were strangers. We grew excited and even the sound of our lessons—the sentences out of geography and arithmetic books—made us tremble.

Passing through the halls during recess we whispered to one another about the snowstorm, guessing at how deep the snowdrifts must be by this time. We looked nervously at our teachers who stood in the classroom doorways stiff and far removed from our secret whispers about the snow.

I felt sorry for these teachers, particularly for the one who had taught me several years ago when I was in the Fifth Grade. I saw her as I walked by the opened door of her room. She was younger than the other teachers, with two dark braids coiled around her head, a white starched shirtwaist and soft dark eyes that had always looked kindly at me when I was younger. I saw her now sitting behind her large desk looking over the heads of her class out of the window and paying no attention to the whispers and giggles of her pupils.

As for my own teacher, a tall, thin woman with a man's face, by afternoon I had become so happy I could no longer hear what she was saying. I sat looking at the large clock over her head. My feeling on the way to school that it would never be light again and that the snowstorm would keep on forever had increased so that it was something I now knew rather than hoped. My eagerness to get out into the world of wind, gloom and perpetual snow, kept lifting me out of my seat.

At three o'clock we rushed into the storm. Our screams died as we reached the school entrance. What we saw silenced us.

Under the dark sky the street lay piled in an unbroken bank of snow. And above it the snowfall still hung in a thick and moving cloud. Nothing was visible but snow. Everything else had disappeared. Even the sky was gone.

I saw the teachers come out and look around them, frowning. The children of the lower grades stood chattering and frightened near the teachers. I waited until the teacher with the two black braids saw me and then, paying no attention to her warning, spoken in a gentle voice, I plunged into the storm. I felt brave but slightly regretful that Miss Wheeler could no longer see me as I pushed into the head-high piles of snow and vanished fearlessly into the storm. But I was certain that she was still thinking of me and worrying about my safety. This thought added excitement to the snowstorm.

After an hour I found myself alone. My legs were tired with jumping and my face burned. It had grown darker and the friendliness seemed to have gone out of the storm. The wind bit with a sharper edge and I turned toward home.

I arrived at the house that now looked like a snowdrift and ploughed my way up to its front door. My heart was beating violently. I stopped to take a last look at the storm. It was hard to leave it. But for the first time in my life an adult logic instructed me. There would be even more snow tomorrow. And in this wind and snow-filled gloom and even in the marvelously buried street, there was something now unplayful.

I entered the house calling for something to eat, but as soon as I had taken my coat off and shaken myself clean, I was at the window again. The way this storm was keeping on was hard to believe.

At the table I was too excited to eat. I trembled and was unable to hear what was being said around me. In this room I could feel the night outside and the storm still blowing on my face. It seemed as if I were still in the street. My eyes kept seeing snow and my nose breathing it. The room and the people in it became far away. I left the table, taking a slice of bread and butter with me, and ran upstairs to my own room.

There were a lot of things to do, such as making my leather boots more waterproof by rubbing lard on them, putting my stamp collection in order, sharpening a deer's-foot knife I had recently acquired, winding tape on my new hockey stick, or reading one of the half dozen new books I had bought with my last birthday money. But none of these activities or even redrawing the plans for the ice boat on which I was working was possible. I sat in a chair near the window unable to think. The pale storm in the night seemed to spin like a top and, keeping the window frost melted with my palms, I sat and watched it snowing for an hour. Then, becoming sleepy, I went to bed. I thought drowsily of how happy Miss Wheeler would be to see me alive on Monday after the way I had rushed into the storm.

There was no seeing through my window when I awoke. The furnace never got going until after seven and before that hour on a winter's morning the house creaked with cold and the windows were sheeted thick with ice. But I knew as I dressed that the snowfall was over. There was too much wind blowing outside and the breath that came in from the snow-banked window ledge was no longer as fresh as it had been.

It was still dark. The bleak and gusty dawn lay over the snow like a guttering candle. The sky had finished with its snowing but now the wind sent the snowbanks ballooning into the air and the rooftops burst into little snowstorms.

I went outside and explored for ten minutes. When I came back into the house I needed no warning against going out to play. My skin was almost frozen and the wind was too strong to stand up in. I settled

down as a prisoner in front of the fireplace after breakfast, lying on my stomach and turning the pages of a familiar oversized edition of Dante's "Inferno." It was full of Doré's nightmarish pictures.

The house bustled with cooking and cleaning. But these were the dim activities of grown-ups. I felt alone and took care of the fire to keep it from going out and leaving me to freeze to death. I carried logs all morning from the cellar and lay perspiring and half-scorched on the hearthstone. Every half-hour I went to the window to have a look at the enemy. The sight of the whirling snowbanks and the sound of the brutal wind as it hit against the houses sent me back to the fireplace to scorch myself anew.

In this way I spent the day until late afternoon. It grew dark early. The snow turned leaden. The wind stopped. The dead storm lay in the street and as far as I could see from the window there were no inhabitants in the world. The dark snow was empty. I shivered and went back to the fireplace.

A half-hour later our door bell rang. Company had arrived for supper. They were the Joneses, who lived in the town of Corliss some eight miles away. They had brought their daughter Anna.

The lights went on in the house. Baked and dizzy with the fire's heat, I joined the two families in the larger parlor. Accounts of store windows blown in, roofs blown off, signs blown, and wagons abandoned in the drifts, were exchanged and I listened happily. Later when the talk turned to duller topics I became aware of Anna.

She was sitting in a corner watching me. She was a blondish girl two years older than I was and she went to high school. I had known her for a long time but had never liked her because she was too calm, never laughing or running, but always looking at people with a sad smile or just a stare as if she had something important on her mind. But now that she was watching me that way I felt suddenly interested in her. I wondered what she could be thinking of me and what made her smile in that half-sad way at me.

I sat next to her at the table and after looking at her several times out of the side of my eyes and catching her eyes doing the same thing, my heart started beating faster. I lost interest in eating. I wanted to be alone with her so we could sit and look at each other without the others noticing.

After supper the two families let us go to the hall upstairs, where I kept most of my possessions, without asking us any questions. I found a deck of cards and a cribbage board for a table. Underneath the lapboard our knees touched.

She played cribbage better than I and smiled at me as I kept losing. But I was only half aware of the game. I kept looking at her, unable to talk, and the light pressure of her knees began to make me feel weak. Her face seemed to become brighter and more beautiful as we played. A mist appeared around her eyes and her smile became so close, as if it were moving swiftly toward me, that I began to tremble. I felt ashamed of being so tongue-tied and red-faced, but with a half-frightened blissful indifference to everything—even Anna—I kept on playing.

We hardly spoke. I grew too nervous to follow the game and I wanted to stop. But I thought if we stopped we could no longer sit this way with our knees touching. At moments when Anna withdrew her touch I trembled and waited as if I were hanging from somewhere. When finally her knees returned to their place against mine, I caught my breath and frowned at the cards as if I were completely taken up with them.

As the hour passed, my face began to feel swollen and lopsided and it seemed to me my features had grown ugly beyond words.

I tried to distract Anna's attention from this phenomenon by twisting my mouth, screwing up my eyes and making popping noises with my cheeks as we played. But a new fear arrived to uncenter my attention. I became afraid now that Anna would notice her knees were touching mine and move them away. I began at once pretending a deeper excitement in the game, complaining against my bad luck and denouncing her for cheating. I was determined to keep her interested in the game at any cost, believing that her interest in what we were doing made her unaware of her knees touching mine.

Finally Anna said she was tired of the game. She pushed the cribbage board away. I waited, holding my breath, for her to realize where her knees were and to move them away. I tried not to look at her but I was so frightened of this happening that I found myself staring at her. She seemed to be paying no attention to me. She was leaning back in her chair and her eyes were half closed. Her face was unsmiling and I felt she was thinking of something. This startled me. My throat filled with questions but I was so afraid of breaking this hidden embrace of our knees under the lapboard that I said nothing.

The mist seemed to have spread from her eyes to her hair and over the rest of her face. Wherever I looked this same glow rested around her. I noticed then that her hand was lying on the lapboard. I thought desperately of touching it but there was something disillusioning in this thought. I watched her fingers begin to tap gently on the board as if she were playing the piano. There was something strange about her hand as if it did not belong to the way her knees were touching mine or to the mist that rose from her eyes.

The minutes passed in silence and then Anna's mother called her from downstairs.

"I guess they're going home," I said and

Anna nodded. She pressed closer against me but in my confusion I couldn't figure out whether this was the accidental result of her starting to get out of her chair or on purpose.

"Why don't you ride out with us?" she said. She leaned over the lapboard toward me. "We've got the wagon sleigh and there's plenty of room."

Before I could answer she had stood up. My knees felt suddenly cold. I slid the lapboard to the floor, ashamed and sad. Anna, without looking back at me, had gone down the stairs. I kept myself from running after her. I was sure she was laughing at me and that she was saying to herself, "He's a big fool. He's a big fool."

The Joneses were ready to leave when I came into the parlor. Anna's mother smiled at me.

"Why don't you come and visit us over Sunday?" she said. "There's even more snow in Corliss than here."

"More snow than you can shake a stick at," said another member of the Jones family. They all laughed and while they were laughing my mother hustled me off for my wraps. I was to drive away with the Jones family in the sleigh drawn by the two strong horses that stood in front of our house.

I pulled on my leather boots, sweater and overcoat while goodbyes were being made. I kept trying to catch Anna's attention, but she was apparently unaware that I was in the room. This made me sad, and slowly my eagerness to go to Corliss left me. I wanted instead to go up to my room and slam the door forever on all the Joneses. Anna's gaiety, the way she said goodbye over and over again and laughed and kissed all the members of my family as if nothing had happened to her, as if she hadn't sat with her eyes closed, pressing against my knees in the hallway upstairs, made me almost ill. I felt abandoned and

forgotten.

Finally I stood muffled and capped and scowling as my family offered some final instructions for my behavior. I heard nothing of what was said but turned over and over in my mind what I was going to do on the ride and after we got to Corliss. Chiefly I was going to ignore Anna, neither speak to her nor show her by a single look that I knew she was alive.

At this point Anna, having said goodbye to everybody several times, seized my arm unexpectedly and whispered against my ear.

"Come, hurry," she said. "We want to get a good place."

Without a word I rushed out of the house, slipping down the snow-caked steps and tumbling headlong into a snowdrift. I scrambled after Anna into the wagon sleigh. It was a low-sided farm wagon placed on wide, heavy wooden runners and piled with warm hay and horse blankets. There was room for only one on the seat. The rest of the Joneses, seven including me, would have to lie in the hay covered by the robes.

Anna was already in the wagon half-buried in the hay, a blanket over her. She gave me excited orders to brush the snow from my clothes, to cover myself well and not to get out and run alongside the horses when we were going uphill.

"It doesn't help any," she said. "They can pull just the same if you stay in here. And besides I don't want you to."

The rest of the Joneses came out and crowded into the wagon around us. Anna's father took his place on the driver's seat, assuring my mother, who had come out with a shawl over her head, that there was no danger because the State plow had cleared the road even to way beyond Corliss. I heard my mother ask where I was. Mrs. Jones answered that I was buried somewhere in the hay and Anna whispered

close to me not to answer or say anything. I obeyed her.

The sleigh started off. I heard the horses thumping in the snow and the harness bells falling into a steady jangling. Lying on my back I looked into the night. Stars filled the sky and a white glare hung over the house tops. The street was silent. I could no longer see the snow-covered houses with their lighted windows. My nose filled with the fresh smell of snow and the barn smells of hay and horse blankets, I lay listening to the different sounds—the harness bells and the snow crunching under the runners.

The stillness of this winter's night was as intense as the storm that had raged for three days. I felt that all the wind and snow there was had blown themselves out forever and that the night as far as the highest star had been emptied by the storm. This emptiness as I lay looking into it was like being hypnotized. It was something to run out into, to fly up into, as the snowfall had been. I began to want to see further and the star-filled sky that had seemed so vast a few minutes ago now didn't seem vast enough.

I had almost forgotten about Anna when I felt a now familiar warmth press against me. She had moved closer as if joggled by the sleigh. I held my breath waiting for her to order me to move away and give her room but she was silent.

My hand at my side touched her fingers. Now I forgot the sky and the great sprinkle of stars that seemed like a thin, far-away snowfall that had stopped moving. The night, the glare of snow, the jingling harness bells died away; only my fingers were alive. When I had looked at her hand tapping gently on the lapboard, it had seemed strange and the thought of touching it somehow disillusioning. But now under the horse blankets, hidden in the hay, this hand seemed more breathing and mysterious and familiar than anything

about her. I lay unable to move closer to it, our fingertips barely touching. I grew dizzy wishing to reach her hand but I felt as powerless to move toward it as to fly.

The minutes passed. Two of the Joneses started singing. The thump of the horses, the jingling of the sleighbells, and the crunching of the snow under the runners seemed part of this soft singing. I too wished to sing, to stand up suddenly in this sweeping-along sleigh and bellow at the silent night.

Then the fingers for which I had been wishing until I was dizzy, seemed to start walking under the horse blankets, seemed to be running toward me in the warm hay. They came as far as my hand, closed around it, and I felt the throb of their tips against my palm. The night turned into a dream. I opened my eyes to the wide sprinkle of stars and a mist seemed to have come over them. The snow-covered hills over which we were gliding sparkled behind a mist and suddenly the night into which I was looking lost its hours. It stretched away without time as if it were not something that was passing like our sleigh over the snow, but a star-filled winter's night that would never change and never move.

Lying beside Anna, her hand in mine, with the sleigh now flying in a whirl of snow down the white hill, I thought this night would never end.

LOOK UP

Look up and not down.
Look forward and not back.
Look out and not in.
Lend a hand.

Edward Everett Hale

ADVERBS

May I seek to live this day
   quietly, easily,
leaning on Your mighty strength
   trustfully, restfully,
meeting others in the path
   peacefully, joyously,
waiting for Your will's unfolding
   patiently, serenely,
facing what tomorrow brings
   confidently, courageously.

Author Unknown

WEDDING BY THE SEA

Arthur Gordon

From the start, they didn't want a formal wedding. No bridesmaids, no wedding march, nothing like that. "The old language and the old ritual are beautiful," our daughter said, "but they belong to millions of people. Ken and I want something of our own."

In an old town like ours, tradition binds with silver chains. "Well," we said a bit doubtfully, "it's your wedding. How do you want it, and when, and where?"

"At sundown," said Dana dreamily, shaking back her long blond hair. "On the beach. As near the ocean as we can get. With a minister who understands how we feel and who can say some words that belong in the twentieth century."

"But what will you *wear*?" her mother asked, naturally.

"A long white dress," she said. "With a bouquet made of sea oats. But no shoes. I want to feel the sand under my feet. I don't know why—but I do."

She's choosing the beach, I said to myself, *because you taught her to love it. Some deep instinct in her knows that life makes tremendous silent statements where sand and salt water meet. She's following that instinct, and she's right.*

So I was pleased, but still a faint, strange sense of apprehension seemed to shadow

the pleasure. Nothing to do with Ken—a fine boy, strong and tall, with a skilled surfer's easy grace and a teaching career stretching out ahead of him. Nothing to do with anything graspable, really. *You're afraid*, I told myself finally, *that's it. Afraid that something very important in your life may be ending. Afraid that a closeness may be vanishing. You may be able to conceal the feeling, or even deny it, but you won't be able to push it away. It goes too deep for reason—or for words.*

"Arrange for a big, high tide, will you?" said Dana, giving us both a casual hug. "And no thunderstorms, please."

"I'm not entirely in charge of such things," I told her. "But we'll do the best we can."

The time came. We stood—friends, neighbors, relatives—in a little amphitheatre made by the dunes. Behind us the dying sun hurled spears of amber light. Ahead, the ocean came surging joyously, all ivory and jade and gold. The young minister stood facing us, the crimson-lined hood of his robe fluttering in the wind, tongues of foam licking at his heels. He had to lift his voice above the clamor of the waves.

"Friends, we are here this afternoon to share with Ken and Dana a most important moment in their lives. In places like this they have learned to know and love each other. Now they have decided to live their lives together as husband and wife. . . ."

In places like this . . . Under the overlay of time, I could feel the pictures form and dissolve in my mind. Years ago on this same beach, not many yards away, a placid pool left by the ebbing tide. One moment a three-year-old playing at the edge. The next moment—incredibly—vanished. And the heart-stopping realization, the frantic plunge, the lunge that raised the small dripping figure back into the sunlight, the overwhelming relief that somehow she had

remembered what she had been taught about holding her breath. Then the wide gray eyes opening and the small, reproachful voice: "Why didn't you come *sooner*? It's all dark and bubbly down there!"

Or the day years later, when she was perhaps eleven or twelve, and we found the old pelican, sick and shivering. Nothing could be done; we had to watch him die. And the impact as death for the first time became a reality, and the piercing pain of compassion striking the unarmored spirit. "Oh," she said finally through her tears, groping for something to ease her anguish, "I'm glad we didn't know him very well."

And then, still later, the golden afternoons when she would go out saying gravely that she had to walk her dog, but knowing that we knew she really hoped to find Ken surfing. He was hardly aware of her then, but she would sit on a dune with arms clasped around her knees and her heart full of love and longing and the big German shepherd motionless as a statue by her side.

In places like this . . . Why does time slide by so fast, I asked myself. *Why does nothing stay?*

Serenely the young minister's voice went on:

"We have been invited to hear Ken and Dana as they promise to face the future together, accepting whatever joy or sadness may lie ahead. These surroundings were not chosen by chance. Those who love the sea can hear in it the heartbeat of Creation as the tides ebb and flow, the sun rises and sets, and the stars come nightly to the sky. For the beauty around us, for the strength it offers, for the peace it brings, we are grateful."

Yes, I thought, *it does give strength. To find endurance all we have to do is seek out places where great and elemental things prevail. For some of us the sea. For some the mountains, as the psalmist knew. I will lift up mine eyes. . . .*

Now the words were being spoken directly to the young couple:

"Dana and Ken, nothing is easier than saying words.

Nothing is harder than living them, day after day.

What you promise today must be renewed and redecided tomorrow and each day that stretches out before you.

At the end of this ceremony, legally you will be man and wife, but still you must decide each day that you want to be married."

Can they understand that? I asked myself, watching the clear young profiles. *Can they possibly grasp it now? Or will the realization take years, as it has for most of us, and then come so quietly that they're not even sure that it's there?*

The young minister was saying tenderly:

"All of us know that you are deeply in love. But beyond the warmth and glow, the excitement and romance, what is love, really?

Real love is caring as much about the welfare and happiness of your marriage partner as about your own.

Real love is not possessive or jealous; it is liberating; it sets you free to become your best self.

Real love is not total absorption in each other; it is looking outward in the same direction—together.

Love makes burdens lighter, because you divide them. It make joys more intense, because you share them. It makes you stronger, so that you can reach out and become involved with life in ways you dared not risk alone."

True, I was thinking. *All true. But you can't learn it from hearing it. You have to learn it by living it, and even then no one but a saint can apply more than fragments of it to his own marriage or his own life. All we can do, even the best of us, is try. And even the trying is hard.*

Now the time had come for the questions, and indeed the language did belong to the twentieth century:

"Ken, will you take Dana to be your wife? Will you love and respect her? Will you be honest with her always? Will you stand by her through whatever may come? Will you make whatever adjustments are necessary so that you can genuinely share your life with her?"

"I will," said the tall boy, and to the same questions the slender girl gave the same answer.

Now the minister's steady gaze fell upon us.

"Who brings this woman to stand beside this man?"

"We do," my wife and I said together. We could not give our child away, for she was not our possession. She was uniquely and eternally herself. And yet, but for our own love, she would not be here under this tranquil sky, close to this restless sea.

The same question to Ken's parents. The same answer. And then a challenge to the four of us:

"Are you willing, now and always, to support and strengthen this marriage by upholding both Ken and Dana with your love and concern?"

"We are," we said, and now all of us were a part of the commitment. No favoritism. No side-taking. Just a quiet, constant defense against the fierce centrifugal forces that threaten every marriage. *This at least*, I thought, *is wholly within our power; this much we can do.*

Now for a moment the wind seemed to hush itself and around us the swaying sea oats grew almost still. I saw Dana's fingers tremble as she put her hand in Ken's, waiting for the ancient symbol of fidelity and love.

"I give you this ring," the tall boy said. "Wear it with love and joy. I choose you to be my wife this day and every day."

"I accept this ring," our child said in a small voice—but a woman's voice. "I will

wear it with love and joy. I choose you to be my husband this day and every day."

Silence, then, for a moment or two. No one stirred. The faces of the onlookers were touched with something indefinable, a kind of timelessness, a sense of life fulfilling itself and moving on. *Perhaps this is the way that everything of consequence begins*, I thought. *No certainty. No guarantees. Just a choice, an intention, a promise, a hope....*

The minister reached forward and took the couple's clasped hands in his own.

"Ken and Dana, we have heard you promise to share your lives in marriage. We recognize and respect the covenant you have made. It's not a minister standing before you that makes your marriage real, but the honesty and sincerity of what you have said and done here before your friends and parents and in the sight of God. On behalf of all those present, I take your hands and acknowledge that you are husband and wife."

He smiled and released their hands.

"Now the ceremony is over and the experience of living day by day as married people is about to begin. Go forth to meet it gladly. Love life, so that life will love you.

The blessing of God be with you.

So be it."

So be it, I thought, watching Dana kiss her husband and turn to embrace her mother. *So be it!* cried all the hugs and the handshakes, the excited laughter and the unashamed tears. *So be it*, murmured the wind and the waves, turning away once more from human things.

And when I looked for the apprehension that had been in me, it was gone.

LISTEN CAREFULLY

Sue Kidd

Not long ago I heard a story about a young man and an old preacher. The young man had lost his job and didn't know which way to turn. So he went to see the old preacher. Pacing about the preacher's study, the young man ranted about his problem. Finally he clenched his fist and shouted, "I've begged God to say something to help me. Tell me, Preacher, why doesn't God answer?"

The old preacher, who sat across the room, spoke something in reply— something so hushed it was indistinguishable. The young man stepped across the room. "What did you say?" he asked.

The preacher repeated himself, but again in a tone as soft as a whisper. So the young man moved closer until he was leaning on the preacher's chair. "Sorry," he said. "I still didn't hear you."

With their heads bent together, the old preacher spoke once more. "God sometimes whispers," he said, "so we will move closer to hear Him." This time the young man heard and he understood.

We all want God's voice to thunder through the air with the answer to our problem. But God's is the still, small voice ... the gentle whisper. Perhaps there's a reason. Nothing draws human focus quite like a whisper. God's whisper means I must stop my ranting and move close to Him, until my head is bent together with His. And then, as I listen, I will find my answer. Better still, I find myself closer to God.

GREATNESS

A FRAGILE MOMENT . . .

One of the best speeches I ever heard was made by a little man who came into our schoolroom one day and was invited to say a few words to us. I don't remember who he was, and probably I am not quoting him verbatim, but what he said was very close to this: Love life. Be grateful for it always. And show your gratitude by not shying away from its challenges. Try always to live a little bit beyond your capacities. You'll find that you never succeed.

Arthur Gordon

THE LEGEND OF THE WINGLESS BIRDS

"Oh for the wings of a bird," we cry,
 To carry us off to an untroubled sky
Where we can dwell untouched by care
 And always be free as a bird in the air—
But there is a legend that's very old,
 Not often heard and seldom told,
That once all birds were wingless, too,
 Unable to soar through the skies of blue—
For, while their plumage was beautifully
  bright
 And their chirping songs were liltingly
  light.
They, too, were powerless to fly
 Until one day when the Lord came by
And laid at the feet of the singing birds
 Gossamer wings as He spoke these words:
"Come take these burdens, so heavy now,
 But if you bear them you'll learn somehow
That as you wear them they'll grow light

And soon you can lift yourself into
 flight"—
So folding the wings beneath their hearts,
 And after endless failures and starts,
They lifted themselves and found with de-
 light
 The wings that were heavy had grown so
  light—
So let us, too, listen to God's wise words,
 For we are much like the "wingless birds,"
And if we would shoulder our daily trials
 And learn to wear them with sunny smiles
We'd find they were wings that God had sent
 To lift us above our heart's discontent—
For The Wings that Lift us out of despair
 Are made by God from the weight of care,
So whenever you cry for "the wings of a bird"
 Remember this little legend you've heard
And let God give you a heart that sings
 As He turns your burdens to "silver
  wings."

Helen Steiner Rice

KEEPING CHRISTMAS

Henry van Dyke

It is a good thing to observe Christmas day. The mere marking of times and seasons, when men agree to stop work and make merry together, is a wise and wholesome custom. It helps one to feel the supremacy of the common life over the individual life. It reminds a man to set his own little watch, now and then, by the great clock of humanity which runs on sun time.

But there is a better thing than the observance of Christmas day, and that is keeping Christmas.

Are you willing to forget what you have done for other people, and to remember what other people have done for you; to ignore what the world owes you, and to think what you owe the world; to put your rights in the background, and your duties in the middle distance, and your chances to do a little more than your duty in the foreground; to see that your fellowmen are just as real as you are, and try to look behind their faces to their hearts hungry for joy, to own that probably the only good reason for your existence is not what you are going to get out of life, but what you are going to give to life; to close your book of complaints against the management of the universe, and look around you for a place where you can sow a few seeds of happiness—are you willing to do these things even for a day? Then you can keep Christmas.

Are you willing to stoop down and consider the needs and the desires of little children; to remember the weakness and loneliness of people who are growing old; to stop asking how much your friends love you, and ask yourself whether you love them enough; to bear in mind the things that other people have to bear in their hearts; to try to understand what those who live in the same house with you really want, without waiting for them to tell you; to trim your lamp so that it will give more light and less smoke, and to carry it in front so that your shadow will fall behind you; to make a grave for your ugly thoughts and a garden for your kindly feelings, with the gate open—are you willing to do these things even for a day? Then you can keep Christmas.

Are you willing to believe that love is the strongest thing in the world—stronger than hate, stronger than evil, stronger than death—and that the blessed life which began in Bethlehem nineteen hundred years ago is the image and brightness of the Eternal Love? Then you can keep Christmas.

And if you can keep it for a day, why not always? But you can never keep it alone.

That best portion of a good man's life—
His little, nameless, unremembered acts
Of kindness and of love.

William Wordsworth

I hope I shall always possess firmness and virtue enough to maintain what I consider the most enviable of all titles, the character of an "Honest Man."

George Washington

IT CAN BE DONE

Norman Vincent Peale

I met one of the world's great positive thinkers in the wilderness of Judea, where, in the long ago, John the Baptist preached. His name is Musa Alami and he has made the desert to blossom as the rose—a desert that in all the history of the world had never blossomed before. He succeeded because he believed that he could, and he kept at it until he did, which, of course, is the way you succeed at anything.

Musa, an Arab boy, was educated at Cambridge, went back to Palestine where

he became a well-to-do man—well-to-do, that is, by Middle Eastern standards. Then, in political turmoil, he lost everything, including his home.

He went beyond Jordan to the edge of Jericho. Stretching away on either side was the great, bleak, arid desert of the Jordan valley. In the distance to the left, shimmering in the hot haze, loomed the mountains of Judea, and to the right the mountains of Moab.

With the exception of a few oases, nothing had ever been cultivated in this hot and weary land, and everyone said that nothing could be, for how could you bring water to it? To dam the Jordan River for irrigation was too expensive and besides, there was no money to finance such a project.

"What about underground water?" asked Musa Alami. Long and loud they laughed. Whoever heard of such a thing? There was no water under that hot, dry desert. Ages ago it had been covered by Dead Sea water; now the sand was full of salt, which added further to the aridity.

He had heard of the amazing rehabilitation of the California desert through subsurface water. He decided that he could find water here also. All the old-time Bedouin sheiks said it couldn't be done; government officials agreed, and so, solemnly, did the famous scientists from abroad. There was absolutely no water there. That was that.

But Musa was unimpressed. He thought there was. A few poverty-stricken refugees from the nearby Jericho Refugee Camp helped him as he started to dig. With well-drilling equipment? Not on your life. With pick and shovel. Everybody laughed as this dauntless man and his ragged friends dug away day after day, week after week, month after month. Down they went, slowly, deep into the sand into which no man since creation had plumbed for water.

For six months they dug; then one day the sand became wet and finally water, life-giving water, gushed forth. The Arabs who had gathered round did not laugh or cheer; they wept. Water had been found in the ancient desert!

A very old man, sheik of a nearby village, heard the amazing news. He came to see for himself. "Musa," he asked, "have you really found water? Let me see it and feel it and taste it."

The old man put his hand in the stream, splashed it over his face, put it on his tongue. "It is sweet and cool," he said. "It is good water." Then, placing his aged hands on the shoulder of Musa Alami, he said, "Thank God. Now, Musa, you can die." It was the simple tribute of a desert man to a positive thinker who did what everyone said could not be done.

Now, several years later, Musa Alami has fifteen wells supplying a ranch nearly three miles long and two miles wide. He raises vegetables, bananas, figs, citrus fruit, and boys. In his school he is growing citizens of the future, farmers and technicians, experts in the trades. Imitating Musa, others have also dug until forty thousand acres are under cultivation and the green is spreading over the sands.

I asked this amazing man what kept him going, kept him believing when everyone said it couldn't be done. "There was no alternative. It had to be done," he said, then added, "God helped me."

THE GREATNESS OF GOD

Charles L. Allen

Here is one of the grandest verses in the Bible: "When I consider Thy heavens, the work of Thy fingers, the moon and the stars, which Thou has ordained. . . ." (Psalm 8:3)

Have you ever wondered why God made the world so beautiful, so impressive, so big? Nobody knows how big the heavens are with their millions, maybe billions, of stars. God didn't have to make it that big in order

GREATNESS

for the earth to exist. Why did God make it so that every morning the glory of a sunrise would come over the earth and every evening the quiet beauty of a sunset? He could have arranged it so the day would come and go in some less impressive manner.

Have you ever looked at a great mountain range and wondered why God made those high peaks? God could have left the mountains out of His creation. Mountains aren't really good for anything. They can't be cultivated; and beyond a certain point, they don't even grow trees. We do not need mountains in order to live on this earth.

I have flown across the trackless deserts of the West. As I looked at the endless miles of hot sand, I wondered why God made them that way. The deserts aren't good for anything. No food can grow there; the few creatures who live there are worthless to mankind.

Most impressed am I when I look at the ocean. Nobody really knows how big the ocean is. In places it is literally miles deep. It seems an awful waste. God could have fixed His creation so that rain could come without creating that vast reservoir of water. Why did He make the ocean?

God had a reason for making oceans, mountains, skies and deserts. He never wastes anything. The Psalmist said, "When I consider thy heavens. . . . " The tragedy is that many people live amid God's creation and never consider it. A thoughtless person once said to Helen Keller, "Isn't it awful to be blind?" She replied, "Not half so bad as to have two good eyes and never see anything."

And there are people who are content with a mighty small world. They never "consider the heavens." They never really see anything big.

When you look into the face of the sky and consider something of its infinite size,

you realize that no little God created it. He had to have big ideas and unlimited abilities. Truly we come to realize, "Our God is a great God." Realizing His greatness, we are not as afraid of what might happen in His world. Our troubles seem hard to bear, but nothing can defeat the will and purposes of the Eternal Father.

I have watched colossal storms roar across the mountains. Heavy clouds come thundering in and everything gets dark. You begin to wonder if the world isn't going to be destroyed. Then, the clouds break up and you see the green mountainside bathed in sunlight. And you know that if you wait out the storm, there will be sunlight again. When we have trouble and everything seems lost, with a picture of the greatness of God in mind, we gain courage and calmness.

On the other hand, when the sun is shining and the breezes are gentle, we know it will not always remain so. Sooner or later it will cloud up and rain again. So we make preparation during the good weather for the bad that is sure to follow. Likewise, when we are blessed with a life that is smooth and good, we remember that we must be ready for the trouble that is sure to come.

Realizing the greatness of God, our minds are stretched to take the long view of life, not living for just the moment but considering the whole.

We are in too big a hurry, and we run by far more than we catch up with. The Bible tells us to "be still, and know that I am God." (Psalm 46:10) Beauty doesn't shout. Loveliness is quiet. Our finest moods are not clamorous. The familiar appeals of the Divine are always in calm tones, a still, small voice. Here is the New Testament picture of Jesus: "Behold, I stand at the door, and knock: if any man hear My voice, and open the door, I will come in to him, and will sup

with him, and he with me." (Revelation 3:20) The Divine is not obtrusive. He bursts in no one's life unbidden. He is reserved and courteous.

People who are faithful in that which is least wear very radiant crowns. They are the people who are great in little tasks. They are scrupulous in the rutty roads of drudgery. They win triumphs amid small irritations. They are as loyal when wearing aprons in the kitchen as if they wore purple and fine linen in the visible presence of the king.

They finish the most obscure bit of work as if it were to be displayed before an assembled heaven by Him who is the Lord of light and glory. Great souls are those who are faithful in that which is least.

J. H. Jowett

Let me not pray to be sheltered from dangers, but to be fearless in facing them.

Rabindranath Tagore

PAUL REVERE'S RIDE

Listen, my children, and you shall hear
Of the midnight ride of Paul Revere,
On the eighteenth of April, in Seventy-five;
Hardly a man is now alive
Who remembers that famous day and year.

He said to his friend, "If the British march
By land or sea from the town tonight,
Hang a lantern aloft in the belfry arch
Of the North Church tower as a signal
    light—
One, if by land, and two, if by sea;
And I on the opposite shore will be,
Ready to ride and spread the alarm
Through every Middlesex village and farm
For the country folk to be up and to arm."

Then he said, "Good night!" and with muf-
    fled oar
Silently rowed to the Charlestown shore,
Just as the moon rose over the bay,
Where swinging wide at her moorings lay
The Somerset, British man-of-war;
A phantom ship, with each mast and spar
Across the moon like a prison bar,
And a huge black hulk, that was magnified
By its own reflection in the tide.

Meanwhile, his friend, through alley and
    street,
Wanders and watches, with eager ears,
Till in the silence around him he hears
The muster of men at the barrack door,
And the measured tread of the grenadiers,
Marching down to their boats on the shore.

Then he climbed to the tower of the Old
    North Church,
By the wooden stairs, with stealthy tread,
To the belfry-chamber overhead,
And startled the pigeons from their perch
On the somber rafters, that round him
    made
Masses and moving shapes of shade—
By the trembling ladder, steep and tall,
To the highest window in the wall,
Where he paused to listen and look down
A moment on the roofs of the town,
And the moonlight flowing over all.

Meanwhile, impatient to mount and ride,
Booted and spurred, with a heavy stride
On the opposite shore walked Paul Revere.
Now he patted his horse's side,
Now gazed at the landscape far and near,
Then, impetuous, stamped the earth,
And turned and tightened his saddle girth;
But mostly he watched with eager search
The belfry tower of the Old North Church,
As it rose above the graves on the hill,
Lonely and spectral and somber and still.
And lo! as he looks, on the belfry's height
A glimmer, and then a gleam of light!
He springs to the saddle, the bridle he turns,

But lingers and gazes, till full on his sight
A second lamp in the belfry burns!

A hurry of hoofs in a village street,
A shape in the moonlight, a bulk in the dark,
And beneath, from the pebbles, in passing,
  a spark
Struck out by a steed flying fearless and
  fleet:
That was all! And yet, through the gloom
  and the light,
That fate of a nation was riding that night;
And the spark struck out by that steed, in his
  flight,
Kindled the land into flame with its heat.

You know the rest. In the books you have
  read
How the British Regulars fired and fled—
How the farmers gave them ball for ball,
From behind each fence and farmyard wall,
Chasing the red-coats down the lane,
Then crossing the fields to emerge again
Under the trees at the turn of the road,
And only pausing to fire and load.

So through the night rode Paul Revere;
And so through the night went his cry of
  alarm
To every Middlesex village and farm—
A cry of defiance and not of fear,
A voice in the darkness, a knock at the door,
And a word that shall echo for evermore!
For, borne on the night-wind of the Past,
Through all our history, to the last,
In the hour of darkness and peril and need,
The people will awaken and listen to hear
The hurrying hoof-beats of the steed,
And the midnight message of Paul Revere.

Henry Wadsworth Longfellow

THE BLUE AND THE GRAY

By the flow of the inland river,
  Whence the fleets of iron have fled,
Where the blades of the grave-grass quiver,
  Asleep are the ranks of the dead:—
Under the sod and the dew,
  Waiting the Judgment Day:—
Under the one, the Blue;
  Under the other, the Gray.

These in the robings of glory,
  Those in the gloom of defeat,
All with the Battle-blood gory,
  In the dusk of eternity meet:—
Under the sod and the dew,
  Waiting the Judgment Day:—
Under the laurel, the Blue;
  Under the willow, the Gray.

From the silence of sorrowful hours
  The desolate mourners go,
Lovingly laden with flowers,
  Alike for the friend and the foe:—
Under the sod and the dew,
  Waiting the Judgment Day:—
Under the roses, the Blue;
  Under the lilies, the Gray.

No more shall the war cry sever,
  Or the winding rivers be red:—
They banish our anger forever
  When they laurel the graves of our dead!
Under the sod and the dew,
  Waiting the Judgment Day:—
Love and tears for the Blue;
  Tears and love for the Gray.

Francis Miles Finch

Be in the company of good books, beautiful pictures, and charming, delightful and inspiring music; and let all that one hears, sees, reads and thinks lift and inspire the higher. The man who does that is kept above the lower nature. Many and many a thing which is not directly religious, therefore, comes in to make up a part of the nourishment of the spiritual life.

Henry Drummond

Govern all by Thy wisdom, O Lord, so that my soul may be serving Thee as Thou dost will, and not as I may choose. Do not punish me, I beseech Thee, by granting that which I wish or ask, if it offend Thy love, which would always live in me. Let me die to myself, that I may serve Thee, who in Thyself art the true life. Amen.

St. Teresa of Avila

I HEAR AMERICA SINGING

I hear America singing, the varied carols I
    hear:
Those of mechanics—each one singing his,
    as it should be, blithe and strong;
The carpenter singing his, as he measures
    his plank or beam,
The mason singing his, as he makes ready
    for work, or leaves off work;
The boatman singing what belongs to him in
    his boat—the deckhand singing on the
    steamboat deck;
The shoemaker singing as he sits on his
    bench—the hatter singing as he stands;
The wood cutter's song—the ploughboy's
    on his way in the morning, or at noon
    intermission, or at sundown;
The delicious singing of the mother—or of
    the young wife at work—or of the girl
    sewing or washing—
Each singing what belongs to him or her and
    to none else;

The day what belongs to the day—at night,
    the party of young fellows, robust,
    friendly,
Singing, with open mouths, their strong
    melodious songs.

Walt Whitman

Before the mountains were brought forth, or ever Thou hadst formed the earth and the world, even from everlasting to everlasting, Thou art God.

Psalm 90:2

THE BIRDS' CHRISTMAS CAROL

Kate Douglas Wiggin

It was very early Christmas morning, and in the stillness of the dawn, with the soft snow falling on the housetops, a little child was born in the Bird household.

They had intended to name the baby Lucy, if it were a girl; but they had not expected her on Christmas morning, and a real Christmas baby was not to be lightly named—the whole family agreed in that.

They were consulting about it in the nursery. Mr. Bird said that he had assisted in naming three boys, and that he should leave this matter entirely to Mrs. Bird; Donald wanted the child called "Dorothy," after a pretty, curly-haired girl who sat next to him in school; Paul chose "Luella," for Luella was the nurse who had been with him during his whole babyhood, up to the time of his first trousers, and the name suggested all sorts of comfortable things. Uncle Jack said that the first girl should always be named for her mother, no matter how hideous the name happened to be.

Grandma said that she would prefer not to take any part in the discussion, and everybody suddenly remembered that Mrs. Bird had thought of naming the baby Lucy,

for Grandma herself; and while it would be indelicate for her to favor that name, it would be against human nature for her to suggest any other, under the circumstances.

Hugh, the "hitherto baby," if that is a possible term, sat in one corner and said nothing, but felt, in some mysterious way, that his nose was out of joint; for there was a newer baby now, a possibility he had never taken into consideration; and the "first girl," too—a still higher development of treason, which made him actually green with jealousy.

But it was too profound a subject to be settled then and there, on the spot; besides, Mamma had not been asked, and every-body felt it rather absurd, after all, to forestall a decree that was certain to be absolutely wise, just, and perfect.

So Donald took his new velocipede and went out to ride up and down the stone pavement and notch the shins of innocent people as they passed by, while Paul spun his musical top on the front steps.

But Hugh refused to leave the scene of action. He seated himself on the top stair in the hall, banged his head against the railing a few times, just by way of uncorking the vials of his wrath, and then subsided into gloomy silence, waiting to declare war if more "first girl babies" were thrust upon a family already surfeited with that unnecessary article.

Meanwhile dear Mrs. Bird lay in her room, weak, but safe and happy, with her sweet girl baby by her side and the heaven of motherhood opening again before her. Nurse was making gruel in the kitchen, and the room was dim and quiet. There was a cheerful open fire in the grate, but though the shutters were closed, the side windows that looked out on the Church of Our Saviour, next door, were a little open.

Suddenly a sound of music poured out into the bright air and drifted into the chamber. It was the boy choir singing Christmas anthems. Higher and higher rose the clear, fresh voices, full of hope and cheer, as children's voices always are. Fuller and fuller grew the burst of melody as one glad strain fell upon another in joyful harmony:—

"Carol, brother, carol,
  Carol joyfully,
Carol the good tidings,
  Carol merrily!
And pray a gladsome Christmas
  For all your fellow-men:
Carol, brother, carol,
  Christmas Day again."

Mrs. Bird thought, as the music floated in upon her gentle sleep, that she had slipped into heaven with her new baby, and that the angels were bidding them welcome. But the tiny bundle by her side stirred a little, and though it was scarcely more than the ruffling of a feather, she awoke; for the mother-ear is so close to the heart that it can hear the faintest whisper of a child.

She opened her eyes and drew the baby closer. It looked like a rose dipped in milk, she thought, this pink and white blossom of girlhood, or like a pink cherub, with its halo of pale yellow hair, finer than floss silk.

"Carol, brother, carol,
  Carol joyfully,
Carol the good tidings,
  Carol merrily!"

The voices were brimming over with joy.

"Why, my baby," whispered Mrs. Bird in soft surprise, "I had forgotten what day it was. You are a little Christmas child, and we will name you 'Carol'—mother's Christmas Carol!"

"What!" said Mr. Bird, coming in softly and closing the door behind him.

"Why, Donald, don't you think 'Carol' is a sweet name for a Christmas baby? It came to me just a moment ago in the singing, as I was lying here half asleep and half awake."

"I think it is a charming name, dear heart, and sounds just like you, and I hope

that, being a girl, this baby has some chance of being as lovely as her mother;"—at which speech from baby's papa, Mrs. Bird, though she was as weak and tired as she could be, blushed with happiness.

And so Carol came by her name.

Perhaps because she was born in holiday time, Carol was a very happy baby. Of course, she was too tiny to understand the joy of Christmas-tide, but people say there is everything in a good beginning, and she may have breathed in unconsciously the fragrance of evergreens and holiday dinners; while the peals of sleigh-bells and the laughter of happy children may have fallen upon her baby ears and wakened in them a glad surprise at the merry world she had come to live in.

Her cheeks and lips were as red as holly-berries; her hair was for all the world the color of a Christmas candle-flame; her eyes were bright as stars; her laugh like a chime of Christmas-bells, and her tiny hands forever outstretched in giving.

Such a generous little creature you never saw! A spoonful of bread and milk had always to be taken by Mamma or nurse before Carol could enjoy her supper; what-ever bit of cake or sweetmeat found its way into her pretty fingers was straightway broken in half to be shared with Donald, Paul or Hugh; and when they made believe to nibble the morsel with affected enjoy-ment, she would clap her hands and crow with delight.

"Why does she do it?" asked Donald thoughtfully. "None of us boys ever did."

"I hardly know," said Mamma, catching her darling to her heart, "except that she is a little Christmas child, and so she has a tiny share of the blessedest birthday the world ever knew!"

It was December, ten years later.

Carol had seen nine Christmas trees lighted on her birthdays, one after another; nine times she had assisted in the holiday festivities of the household, though in her babyhood her share of the gayeties was somewhat limited.

For five years, certainly, she had hidden presents for Mamma and Papa in their own bureau drawers, and harbored a number of secrets sufficiently large to burst a baby brain, had it not been for the relief gained by whispering them all to Mamma, at night, when she was in her crib, a proceeding which did not in the least lessen the value of a secret in her innocent mind.

For five years she had heard " 'Twas the night before Christmas," and hung up a scarlet stocking many sizes too large for her, and pinned a sprig of holly on her little white nightgown, to show Santa Claus that she was a "truly" Christmas child, and dreamed of fur-coated saints and toy-packs and reindeer, and wished everybody a "Merry Christmas" before it was light in the morning, and lent every one of her new toys to the neighbors' children before noon, and eaten turkey and plum-pudding, and gone to bed at night in a trance of happiness at the day's pleasures.

Donald was away at college now. Paul and Hugh were great manly fellows, taller than their mother. Papa Bird had gray hairs in his whiskers; and Grandma, God bless, had been four Christmases in heaven.

But Christmas in the Birds' Nest was scarcely as merry now as it used to be in the bygone years, for the little child, that once brought such an added blessing to the day, lay month after month a patient, helpless invalid in the room where she was born. She had never been very strong in body, and it was with a pang of terror her mother and father noticed, soon after she was five years old, that she began to limp ever so slightly, to complain too often of weariness, and to nestle close to her mother, saying she "would rather not go out to play, please." The illness was slight at first, and hope was

always stirring in Mrs. Bird's heart. "Carol would feel stronger in the summer-time;" or, "She would be better when she had spent a year in the country;" or, "She would outgrow it;" or, "They would try a new physician;" but by and by it came to be all too sure that no physician save One could make Carol strong again, and that no "summer-time" nor "country air," unless it were the everlasting summer-time in a heavenly country, could bring back the little girl to health.

The cheeks and lips that were once as red as holly-berries faded to faint pink; the star-like eyes grew softer, for they often gleamed through tears; and the gay child-laugh, that had been like a chime of Christmas bells, gave place to a smile so lovely, so touching, so tender and patient, that it filled every corner of the house with a gentle radiance that might have come from the face of the Christchild himself.

Love could do nothing; and when we have said that we have said all, for it is stronger than anything else in the whole wide world. Mr. and Mrs. Bird were talking it over one evening, when all the children were asleep. A famous physician had visited them that day, and told them that some time, it might be in one year, it might be in more, Carol would slip quietly off into heaven, whence she came.

"It is no use to close our eyes to it any longer," said Mr. Bird, as he paced up and down the library floor; "Carol will never be well again. It almost seems as if I could not bear it when I think of that loveliest child doomed to lie there day after day, and, what is still more, to suffer pain that we are helpless to keep away from her. Merry Christmas, indeed; it gets to be the saddest day in the year to me!" And poor Mr. Bird sank into a chair by the table, and buried his face in his hands to keep his wife from seeing the tears that would come in spite of all his efforts.

"But, Donald, dear," said sweet Mrs. Bird, with trembling voice, "Christmas Day may not be so merry with us as it used, but it is very happy, and that is better, and very blessed, and that is better yet. I suffer chiefly for Carol's sake, but I have almost given up being sorrowful for my own. I am too happy in the child, and I see too clearly what she has done for us and the other children. Donald and Paul and Hugh were three strong, willful, boisterous boys, but now you seldom see such tenderness, devotion, thought for others, and self-denial in lads of their years. A quarrel or a hot word is almost unknown in this house, and why? Carol would hear it, and it would distress her; she is so full of love and goodness. The boys study with all their might and main. Why? Partly, at least, because they like to teach Carol, and amuse her by telling her what they read. When the seamstress comes, she likes to sew in Miss Carol's room, because there she forgets her own troubles, which, Heaven knows, are sore enough! And as for me, Donald, I am a better woman every day for Carol's sake: I have to be her eyes, ears, feet, hands—her strength, her hope; and she, my own little child, is my example!"

"I was wrong, dear heart," said Mr. Bird more cheerfully; "we will try not to repine, but to rejoice instead that we have an 'angel of the house.' "

"And as for her future," Mrs. Bird went on, "I think we need not be over-anxious. I feel as if she did not belong altogether to us, but that when she has done what God sent her for, He will take her back to Himself—and it may not be very long!" Here it was poor Mrs. Bird's turn to break down, and Mr. Bird's turn to comfort her.

Carol herself knew nothing of motherly tears and fatherly anxieties; she lived on peacefully in the room where she was born.

But you never would have known that

room; for Mr. Bird had a great deal of money, and though he felt sometimes as if he wanted to throw it all in the sea, since it could not buy a strong body for his little girl, yet he was glad to make the place she lived in just as beautiful as it could be.

The room had been extended by the building of a large addition that hung out over the garden below, and was so filled with windows that it might have been a conservatory. The ones on the side were thus still nearer the Church of Our Saviour than they used to be; those in front looked out on the beautiful harbor, and those in the back commanded a view of nothing in particular but a narrow alley; nevertheless, they were pleasantest of all to Carol, for the Ruggles family lived in the alley, and the nine little, middle-sized, and big Ruggles children were a source of inexhaustible interest.

The shutters could all be opened and Carol could take a real sun-bath in this lovely glass house, or they could all be closed when the dear head ached or the dear eyes were tired. The carpet was of soft gray, with clusters of green bay and holly leaves. The furniture was of white wood, on which an artist had painted snow scenes and Christmas trees and groups of merry children ringing bells and singing carols.

Donald had made a pretty, polished shelf, and screwed it on the outside of the footboard, and the boys always kept this full of blooming plants, which they changed from time to time; the headboard, too, had a bracket on either side, where there were pots of maiden-hair ferns.

Love-birds and canaries hung in their golden houses in the windows, and they, poor caged things, could hop as far from their wooden perches as Carol could venture from her little white bed.

On one side of the room was a bookcase filled with hundreds—yes, I mean it—with hundreds and hundreds of books; books with gay-colored pictures, books without; books with black and white outline sketches, books with none at all; books with verses, books with stories; books that made children laugh, and some, only a few, that made them cry; books with words of one syllable for tiny boys and girls, and books with words of fearful length to puzzle wise ones.

This was Carol's "Circulating Library." Every Saturday she chose ten books, jotting their names down in a diary; into these she slipped cards that said:—

"Please keep this book two weeks and read it. With love,
Carol Bird."

Then Mrs. Bird stepped into her carriage and took the ten books to the children's Hospital, and brought home ten others that she had left there the fortnight before.

This was a source of great happiness; for some of the Hospital children that were old enough to print or write, and were strong enough to do it, wrote Carol sweet little letters about the books, and she answered them, and they grew to be friends.

There was a high wainscoting of wood about the room, and on top of this, in a narrow gilt framework, ran a row of illuminated pictures, illustrating fairy tales, all in dull blue and gold and scarlet and silver.

Then there was a great closet full of beautiful things to wear, but they were all dressing-gowns and slippers and shawls; and there were drawers full of toys and games, but there were such as you could play on your lap. There were no ninepins, nor balls, nor bows and arrows, nor bean bags, nor tennis rackets; but, after all, other children needed these more than Carol Bird, for she was always happy and contented, whatever she had or whatever she lacked; and after the room had been made so lovely for her, on her eighth

GREATNESS

Christmas, she always called herself, in fun, a "Bird of Paradise."

On these particular December days she was happier than usual, for Uncle Jack was coming from England to spend the holidays. Dear, funny, jolly, loving, wise Uncle Jack, who came every two or three years, and brought so much joy with him that the world looked as black as a thunder-cloud for a week after he went away again.

Donald came, too; Donald, with a line of down upon his upper lip, and Greek and Latin on his tongue, and stores of knowl-edge in his handsome head, and stories—bless me, you couldn't turn over a chip without reminding Donald of something that happened "at College." One or the other was always at Carol's bedside, for they fancied her paler then she used to be, and they could not bear her out of sight. It was Uncle Jack, though, who sat beside her in the winter twilights. The room was quiet, and almost dark, save for the snowlight outside, and the flickering flame of the fire, that danced over the "Sleeping Beauty's" face and touched the Fair One's golden locks with ruddier glory. Carol's hand (all too thin and white these latter days) lay close clasped in Uncle Jack's, and they talked together quietly of many, many things.

"I want to tell you all about my plans for Christmas this year, Uncle Jack," said Carol, on the first evening of his visit, "because it will be the loveliest one I ever had. The boys laugh at me for caring so much about it; but it isn't altogether because it is Christmas, nor because it is my birthday; but long, long ago, when I first began to be ill, I used to think, the first thing when I waked on Christmas morning, 'Today is Christ's birthday—and *mine*!' I did not put the words close together, you know, because that made it seem too bold; but I first said, 'Christ's birthday,' out loud, and then, in a minute softly to myself—'and mine!'

'Christ's birthday and mine!' And so I do not quite feel about Christmas as other girls do. Mamma says she supposes that ever so many other children have been born on that day. I often wonder where they are, Uncle Jack, and whether it is a dear thought to them, too, or whether I am so much in bed, and so often alone, that it means more to me. Oh, I do hope that none of them are poor, or cold, or hungry; and I wish—I wish they were all as happy as I, because they are really my little brothers and sisters. Now, Uncle Jack dear, I am going to try and make somebody happy every single Christmas that I live, and this year it is to be the 'Ruggleses in the rear.' "

"That large and interesting brood of children in the little house at the end of the back garden?"

"Yes; isn't it nice to see so many together?—and, Uncle Jack, why do the big families always live in the small houses, and the small families in the big houses? We ought to call them the Ruggles children, of course; but Donald began talking of them as the 'Ruggleses in the rear,' and Papa and Mamma took it up, and now we cannot seem to help it. The house was built for Mr. Carter's coachman, but Mr. Carter lives in Europe, and the gentleman who rents his place for him doesn't care what happens to it, and so this poor family came to live there. When they first moved in, I used to sit in my window and watch them play in their backyard; they are so strong, and jolly, and good-natured;—and then, one day, I had a terrible headache, and Donald asked them if they would please not scream quite so loud, and they explained that they were having a game of circus, but that they would change."

"Ha, ha, ha!" laughed Uncle Jack. "What an obliging family, to be sure!"

"Yes, we all thought it very funny, and I smiled at them from the window when I was well enough to be up again. Now, Sarah

Maud comes to her door when the children come home from school, and if Mamma nods her head, 'Yes,' that means 'Carol is very well,' and then you ought to hear the little Ruggleses yell—I believe they try to see how much noise they can make; but if Mamma shakes her head 'No,' they always play at quiet games. Then, one day, 'Cary,' my pet canary, flew out of her cage, and Peter Ruggles caught her and brought her back, and I had him up here in my room to thank him."

"Is Peter the oldest?"

"No, Sarah Maud is the oldest—she helps do the washing; and Peter is the next. He is a dressmaker's boy."

"And which is the pretty little red-haired girl?"

"That's Kitty."

"And the fat youngster?"

"Baby Larry."

"And that—most freckled one?"

"Now, don't laugh—that's Peoria."

"Carol, you are joking."

"No, really, Uncle dear. She was born in Peoria; that's all."

"And the next boy Oshkosh?"

"No," laughed Carol, "the others are Susan, and Clement, and Eily, and Cornelius; they all look exactly alike, except that some of them have more freckles than the others."

"How did you ever learn all their names?"

"Why, I have what I call a 'window-school.' It is too cold now; but in warm weather I am wheeled out on my balcony, and the Ruggleses climb up and walk along our garden fence, and sit down on the roof of our carriage-house. That brings them quite near, and I tell them stories. On Thanksgiving Day they came up for a few minutes—it was quite warm at eleven o'clock—and we told each other what we had to be thankful for; but they gave such queer answers that Papa had to run away for fear of laughing; and I couldn't

understand them very well. Susan was thankful for '*trunks*,' of all things in the world; Cornelius, for 'horse-cars;' Kitty, for 'pork steak;' while Clem, who is very quiet, brightened up when I came to him, and said he was thankful for '*his lame* puppy.' Wasn't that pretty?"

"It might teach some of us a lesson, mightn't it, little girl?"

"That's what Mamma said. Now I'm going to give this whole Christmas to the Ruggleses; and, Uncle Jack, I earned part of the money myself."

"You, my bird; how?"

"Well, you see, it could not be my own Christmas if Papa gave me all the money, and I thought to really keep Christ's birthday I ought to do something of my very own; and so I talked with Mamma. Of course she thought of something lovely; she always does: Mamma's head is just brimming over with lovely thoughts—all I have to do is ask, and out pops the very one I want. This thought was to let her write down, just as I told her, a description of how a child lived in her own room for three years, and what she did to amuse herself; and we sent it to a magazine and got twenty-five dollars for it. Just think!"

"Well, well," cried Uncle Jack, "my little girl a real author! And what are you going to do with this wonderful 'own' money of yours?"

"I shall give the nine Ruggleses a grand Christmas dinner here in this very room— that will be Papa's contribution—and afterwards a beautiful Christmas tree, fairly blooming with presents—that will be my part; for I have another way of adding to my twenty-five dollars, so that I can buy nearly anything I choose. I should like it very much if you would sit at the head of the table, Uncle Jack, for nobody could ever be frightened of you, you dearest, dearest, dearest thing that ever was! Mamma is going to help us, but Papa and the boys are

going to eat together downstairs for fear of making the little Ruggleses shy; and after we've had a merry time with the tree we can open my window and all listen together to the music at the evening church-service, if it comes before the children go. I have written a letter to the organist, and asked him if I might have the two songs I like best. Will you see if it is all right?"

> Birds' Nest, December 21, 188-.
> Dear Mr. Wilkie,—I am the little girl who lives next door to the church, and, as I seldom go out, the music on practice days and Sundays is one of my greatest pleases.
>
> I want to know if you can have "Carol, brothers, carol," on Christmas night, and if the boy who sings "My ain countree" so beautifully may please sing that too. I think it is the loveliest thing in the world, but it always makes me cry; doesn't it you?
>
> If it isn't too much trouble, I hope they can sing them both quite early, as after ten o'clock I may be asleep.
> Yours respectfully,
> Carol Bird.
>
> P.S.—The reason I like "Carol, brothers, carol," is because the choir-boys sang it eleven years ago, the morning I was born, and put it into Mamma's head to call me Carol. She didn't remember then that my other name would be Bird, because she was half asleep, and could only think of one thing at a time. Donald says if I had been born on the Fourth of July they would have named me "Independence," or if on the twenty-second of February, "Georgina," or even "Cherry," like Cherry in "Martin Chuzzlewit"; but I like my own name and birthday best.
> Yours truly,
> Carol Bird.

Uncle Jack thought the letter quite right, and did not even smile at her telling the organist so many family items.

The days flew by as they always fly in holiday time, and it was Christmas Eve before anybody knew it. The family festival was quiet and very pleasant, but almost overshadowed by the grander preparations for the next day. Carol and Elfrida, her pretty German nurse, had ransacked books, and introduced so many plans, and plays, and customs, and merry-makings from Germany, and Holland, and England, and a dozen other countries, that you would scarcely have known how or where you were keeping Christmas.

And when, after dinner, the whole family had gone to church to see the Christmas decorations, Carol limped out on her slender crutches, and with Elfrida's help, placed all the family boots in a row in the upper hall. That was to keep the dear ones from quarreling all through the year. There were Papa's stout top boots; Mamma's pretty buttoned shoes next; then Uncle Jack's, Donald's, Paul's, and Hugh's; and at the end of the line her own little white worsted slippers. Last, and sweetest of all, like the children in Austria, she put a lighted candle in her window to guide the dear Christchild, lest he should stumble in the dark night as he passed up the deserted street. This done, she dropped into bed, a rather tired, but very happy Christmas fairy . . . .

Carol's bed had been moved into the farthest corner of the room, and she was lying on the outside, dressed in a wonderful dressing gown that looked like a fleecy cloud. Her golden hair fell in fluffy curls over her white forehead and neck, her cheeks flushed delicately, her eyes beamed with joy, and the children told their mother, afterwards, that she looked as beautiful as the angels in the picture books.

There was a great bustle behind a huge screen in another part of the room, and at half past five this was taken away, and the Christmas dinner-table stood revealed. What a wonderful sight it was to the poor little Ruggles children, who ate their sometimes scanty meals on the kitchen table! It blazed with tall colored candles, it gleamed with glass and silver, it blushed with flowers, it groaned with good things to eat; so it was not strange that the Ruggleses, forgetting altogether that their mother was a McGrill, shrieked in admiration of the fairy spectacle. But Larry's behavior was the most disgraceful, for he stood not upon the order of his going, but went at once for a high chair that pointed unmistakably to him, climbed up like a squirrel, gave a comprehensive look at the turkey, clapped his hands in ecstasy, rested his fat arms on the table, and cried with joy, "I beat the hull lot o' yer!" Carol laughed until she cried, giving orders, meanwhile—"Uncle Jack, please sit at the head, Sarah Maud at the foot, and that will leave four on each side; Mamma is going to help Elfrida, so that the children need not look after each other, but just have a good time."

A sprig of holly lay by each plate, and nothing would do but each little Ruggles must leave his seat and have it pinned on by Carol, and as each course was served, one of them pleaded to take something to her. There was hurrying to and fro, I can assure you, for it is quite a difficult matter to serve a Christmas dinner on the third floor of a great city house; but if it had been neces-sary to carry every dish up a rope ladder the servants would gladly have done so. There was turkey and chicken, with delicious gravy and stuffing, and there were half a dozen vegetables, with cranberry jelly, and celery, and pickles; and as for the way these delicacies were served, the Ruggleses never forgot it as long as they lived.

Peter nudged Kitty, who sat next to him, and said, "Look, will yer, ev'ry feller's got his own partic'lar butter; I s'pose that's to show you can eat that 'n' no more. No, it ain't either, for that pig of a Peory's just gettin' another helpin'!"

"Yes," whispered Kitty, "an' the napkins is marked with big red letters! I wonder if that's so nobody'll nip 'em; an' oh, Peter, look at the pictures stickin' right on ter dishes! Did yee ever?"

"The plums is all took out o' my cramb'ry sarse an' it's friz to a stiff jell'!" whispered Peoria, in wild excitement.

"Hi—yah! I got a wish-bone!" sang Larry, regardless of Sarah Maud's frown; after which she asked to have his seat changed, giving as excuse that he "gen'ally set beside her, an' would feel strange"; the true reason being that she desired to kick him gently, under the table, whenever he passed what might be termed "the McGrill line."

"I declare to goodness," murmured Susan, on the other side, "there's so much to look at I can't scarcely eat nothin'!"

"Bet yer life I can!" said Peter, who had kept one servant busily employed ever since he sat down; for, luckily, no one was asked by Uncle Jack whether he would have a second helping, but the dishes were quietly passed under their noses, and not a single Ruggles refused anything that was offered him, even unto the seventh time.

Then, when Carol and Uncle Jack perceived that more turkey was a physical impossibility, the meats were taken off and the dessert was brought in— a dessert that would have frightened a strong man after such a dinner as had preceded it. Not so the Ruggleses—for a strong man is nothing to a small boy—and they kindled to the dessert as if the turkey had been a dream and the six vegetables an optical delusion. There were plum-pudding, mince-pie, and ice-cream; and there were nuts, and raisins, and oranges. Kitty chose ice-cream,

explaining that she knew it "by sight, though she hadn't never tasted none"; but all the rest took the entire variety, without any regard to consequences.

"My dear child," whispered Uncle Jack, as he took Carol an orange, "there is no doubt about the necessity of this feast, but I do advise you after this to have them twice a year, or quarterly perhaps, for the way these children eat is positively dangerous; I assure you I tremble for that terrible Peoria. I'm going to run races with her after dinner."

"Never mind," laughed Carol; "let them have enough for once; it does my heart good to see them, and they shall come oftener next year."

The feast being over, the Ruggleses lay back in their chairs languidly, like little gorged boa-constrictors, and the table was cleared in a trice. Then a door was opened into the next room, and there, in a corner facing Carol's bed, which had been wheeled as close as possible, stood the brilliantly lighted Christmas tree, glittering with gilded walnuts and tiny silver balloons, and wreathed with snowy chains of pop-corn. The presents had been bought mostly with Carol's story-money, and were selected after long consultations with Mrs. Bird. Each girl had a blue-knitted hood, and each boy a red-crocheted comforter, all made by Mamma, Carol, and Elfrida. ("Because if you buy everything, it doesn't show so much love," said Carol.) Then every girl had a pretty plaid dress of a different color, and every boy a warm coat of the right size. Here the useful presents stopped, and they were quite enough; but Carol had pleaded to give them something "for fun." "I know they need the clothes," she had said, when they were talking over the matter just after Thanksgiving, "but they don't care much for them, after all. Now, Papa, won't you *please* let me go without part of my presents this year, and give me the money they would

cost, to buy something to amuse the Ruggleses?"

"You can have both," said Mr. Bird, promptly; "is there any need of my little girl's going without her own Christmas, I should like to know? Spend all the money you like."

"But that isn't the thing," objected Carol, nestling close to her father; "it wouldn't be mine. What is the use? Haven't I almost everything already, and am I not the happiest girl in the world this year, with Uncle Jack and Donald at home? You know very well it is more blessed to give than to receive; so why won't you let me do it? You never look half as happy when you are getting your presents as when you are giving us ours. Now, Papa, submit, or I shall have to be very firm and disagreeable with you!"

"Very well, your Highness, I surrender."

So Carol had her way, as she generally did; but it was usually a good way, which was fortunate, under the circumstances; and Sarah Maud had a set of Miss Alcott's books, and Peter a modest silver watch, Cornelius a tool-chest, Clement a doghouse for his lame puppy, Larry a magnificent Noah's ark, and each of the younger girls a beautiful doll.

You can well believe that everybody was very merry and very thankful. All the family, from Mr. Bird down to the cook, said that they had never seen so much happiness in the space of three hours; but it had to end, as all things do. The candles flickered and went out, the tree was left alone with its gilded ornaments, and Mrs. Bird sent the children downstairs at half past eight, thinking that Carol looked tired.

"Now, my darling, you have done quite enough for one day," said Mrs. Bird, getting Carol into her little nightgown. "I'm afraid you will feel worse tomorrow, and that would be a sad ending to such a charming evening."

"Oh, wasn't it a lovely, lovely time," sighed Carol. "From first to last, everything was just right. I shall never forget Larry's face when he looked at the turkey; nor Peter's when he saw his watch; nor that sweet, sweet Kitty's smile when she kissed her dolly; nor the tears in Sarah Maud's eyes when she thanked me for her books ; nor"—

"But we mustn't talk any longer about it tonight," said Mrs. Bird, anxiously; "you are too tired, dear."

"I am not so very tired, Mamma. I have felt well all day; not a bit of pain anywhere. Perhaps this has done me good."

"Perhaps; I hope so. There was no noise or confusion; it was just a merry time. Now, may I close the door and leave you alone, dear? Papa and I will steal in softly by and by to see if you are all right; but I think you need to be very quiet."

"Oh, I'm willing to stay by myself; but I am not sleepy yet, and I am going to hear the music, you know."

"Yes, I have opened the window a little, and put the screen in front of it, so that you won't feel the air."

"Can I have the shutters open? And won't you turn my bed, please? This morning I woke ever so early, and one bright, beautiful star shone in that eastern window. I never noticed it before, and I thought of the Star in the East, that guided the wise men to the place where the baby Jesus was. Good-night, Mamma. Such a happy, happy day!"

"Good-night my precious Christmas Carol—mother's blessed Christmas child."

"Bend your head a minute, mother dear," whispered Carol, calling her mother back. "Mamma, dear, I do think that we have kept Christ's birthday this time just as He would like it. Don't you?"

"I am sure of it," said Mrs. Bird, softly.

The Ruggleses had finished a last romp in the library with Paul and Hugh, and

Uncle Jack had taken them home and stayed a while to chat with Mrs. Ruggles, who opened the door for them, her face all aglow with excitement and delight. When Kitty and Clem showed her the oranges and nuts that they had kept for her, she astonished them by saying that at six o'clock Mrs. Bird had sent her in the finest dinner she had ever seen in her life; and not only that, but a piece of dress-goods that must have cost a dollar a yard if it cost a cent.

As Uncle Jack went down the rickety steps he looked back into the window for a last glimpse of the family, as the children gathered about their mother, showing their beautiful presents again and again—and then upward to a window in the great house yonder. "A little child shall lead them," he thought. "Well, if—if anything ever happens to Carol, I will take the Ruggleses under my wing."

"Softly, Uncle Jack," whispered the boys, as he walked into the library a while later. "We are listening to the music in the church. The choir has sung 'Carol, brothers, carol,' and now we think the organist is beginning to play 'My ain countree' for Carol."

"I hope she hears it," said Mrs. Bird; "but they are very late tonight, and I dare not speak to her lest she should be asleep. It is almost ten o'clock."

The boy soprano, clad in white surplice, stood in the organ loft. The light shone full upon his crown of fair hair, and his pale face, with its serious blue eyes, looked paler than usual. Perhaps it was something in the tender thrill of the voice, or in the sweet words, but there were tears in many eyes, both in the church and in the great house next door.

There were tears in many eyes, but not in Carol's. The loving heart had quietly ceased to beat, and the "wee birdie" in the great house had flown to its "home next." Carol

had fallen asleep! But as to the song, I think perhaps, I cannot say, she heard it after all!

So sad an ending to a happy day! Perhaps—to those who were left; and yet Carol's mother, even in the freshness of her grief, was glad that her darling had slipped away on the loveliest day of her life, out of its glad content, into everlasting peace.

She was glad that she had gone as she had come, on the wings of song, when all the world was brimming over with joy; glad of every grateful smile, of every joyous burst of laughter, of every loving thought and word and deed the dear last day had brought.

Sadness reigned, it is true, in the little house behind the garden; and one day poor Sarah Maud, with a courage born of despair, threw on her hood and shawl, walked straight to a certain house a mile away, up the marble steps into good Dr. Bartol's office, falling at his feet as she cried, "Oh, sir, it was me an' our children that went to Miss Carol's last dinner-party, an' if we made her worse we can't never be happy again!" Then the kind old gentleman took her rough hand in his and told her to dry her tears, for neither she nor any of her flock had hastened Carol's flight; indeed, he said that had it not been for the strong hopes and wishes that filled her tired heart, she could not have stayed long enough to keep that last merry Christmas with her dear ones.

And so the old years, fraught with memories, die, one after another, and the new years, bright with hopes, are born to take their places; but Carol lives again in every chime of Christmas bells that peal glad tidings, and in every Christmas anthem sung by childish voices.

Blessed are the peacemakers: for they shall be called the children of God.

Matthew 5: 9

A PSALM OF LIFE

Tell me not, in mournful numbers,
  "Life is but an empty dream!"
For the soul is dead that slumbers,
  And things are not what they seem.

Life is real! Life is earnest;
  And the grave is not its goal;
"Dust thou art, to dust returnest,"
  Was not spoken of the soul.

Not enjoyment, and not sorrow,
  Is our destined end or way;
But to act, that each to-morrow
  Find us farther than to-day.

Art is long, and Time is fleeting,
  And our hearts, though stout and brave,
Still, like muffled drums, are beating
  Funeral marches to the grave.

In the world's broad field of battle,
  In the bivouac of Life,
Be not like dumb, driven cattle!
  Be a hero in the strife!

Trust no Future, howe'er pleasant!
  Let the dead Past bury its dead!
Act —act in the living Present!
  Heart within, and God o'erhead!

Lives of great men all remind us
  We can make our lives sublime,
And, departing, leave behind us
  Footprints on the sands of Time;

Footprints that perhaps another,
  Sailing o'er life's solemn main,
A forlorn and shipwrecked brother,
  Seeing, shall take heart again.

Let us, then, be up and doing,
  With a heart for any fate;
Still achieving, still pursuing,
  Learn to labour and to wait.

Henry Wadsworth Longfellow

LOVE

A FRAGILE MOMENT . . .

It may sound foolishly romantic, this custom we observe, but I believe that it enriches our life together. We play a trick on time.

We were married in May, Thomas and I, and every year as our anniversary comes near, we begin to relive in mind and heart those last charmed days of courtship. I look at my husband as I saw him then. I blot out his thinning hair, his eyes not quite so bright, his arthritic gait. I see instead a fine athlete straight from the football team of a large university. I see his strong face, his beautiful long eyelashes, his head topped with thick, wavy, dark brown hair. I see a young man moving to me with a lithe yet resolute step, and I go to meet him with the same joy, the same fluttering heart, the same courtesy as I did 41 years ago.

In turn, I trust that when he looks at me he sees beyond the pounds that I have gathered along the way. Perhaps his love for me will blot out some of my wrinkles. Maybe instead of my gray hair, he can see the rich, black locks that once were there.

And if the magic of memory should fail, if I should see his thinning hair, and he my wrinkles, it doesn't matter, for while we have lost some sprightliness and youthful energy, we have gained patience, understanding, tolerance, a willingness to yield and the ability to overlook trivialities.

I count this fair exchange.

Faye Field

SONNET CXVI

Let me not to the marriage of true minds
Admit impediments. Love is not love
Which alters when it alteration finds,
Or bends with the remover to remove:
O, no! it is an ever-fixed mark
That looks on tempests and is never
   shaken;

LOVE

It is the star to every wandering bark,
Whose worth's unknown, although his
   height be taken.
Love's not Time's fool, though rosy lips and
   cheeks
Within his bending sickle's compass come;
Love alters not with his brief hours and
   weeks,
But bears it out even to the edge of doom.
   If this be error and upon me proved,
   I never writ, nor no man ever loved.

William Shakespeare

THE GIFT OF THE MAGI

O. Henry

One dollar and eighty-seven cents. That
was all. And sixty cents of it was in pennies.
Pennies saved one and two at a time by
bulldozing the grocer and the vegetable
man and the butcher until one's cheeks
burned with the silent imputations of
parsimony that such close dealing implied.
Three times Della counted it. One dollar
and eighty-seven cents. And the next day
would be Christmas.

There was clearly nothing to do but flop
down on the shabby little couch and howl.
So Della did it. Which instigates the moral
reflection that life is made up of sobs,
sniffles, and smiles, with sniffles
predominating.

While the mistress of the home is
gradually subsiding from the first stage to
the second, take a look at the home. A
furnished flat at $8 per week. It did not
exactly beggar description but it certainly
had that word on the lookout for the
mendicancy squad.

In the vestibule below was a letterbox
into which no letter would go, and an
electric button from which no mortal finger
could coax a ring. Also appertaining
thereunto was a card bearing the name
"Mr. James Dillingham Young."

The "Dillingham" had been flung to the
breeze during a former period of
prosperity when its possessor was being
paid $30 per week. Now, when the income
was shrunk to $20, the letters of
"Dillingham" looked blurred, as though
they were thinking seriously of contracting
to a modest and unassuming D. But
whenever Mr. James Dillingham Young
came home and reached his flat above, he
was called "Jim" and greatly hugged by
Mrs. James Dillingham Young, already
introduced to you as Della. Which is all
very good.

Della finished her cry and attended to
her cheeks with the powder rag. She stood
by the window and looked out dully at a
gray cat walking a gray fence in a gray
backyard. Tomorrow would be Christmas
Day and she had only $1.87 with which to
buy Jim a present. She had been saving
every penny she could for months, with this
result. Twenty dollars a week doesn't go far.
Expenses had been greater than she had
calculated. They always are. Only $1.87 to
buy a present for Jim. Her Jim. Many a
happy hour she had spent planning for
something nice for him. Something fine
and rare and sterling—something just a
little bit near to being worthy of the honor
of being owned by Jim.

There was a pier glass between the
windows of the room. Perhaps you have seen
a pier glass in an $8 flat. A very thin and
very agile person may, by observing his
reflection in a rapid sequence of
longitudinal strips, obtain a fairly accurate
conception of his looks. Della, being
slender, had mastered the art.

Suddenly she whirled from the window
and stood before the glass. Her eyes were
shining brilliantly, but her face had lost its
color within twenty seconds. Rapidly she
pulled down her hair and let it fall to its
full length.

Now, there were two possessions of the

James Dillingham Youngs in which they both took a mighty pride. One was Jim's gold watch that had been his father's and his grandfather's. The other was Della's hair. Had the Queen of Sheba lived in the flat across the airshaft, Della would have let her hair hang out the window some day just to depreciate Her Majesty's jewels and gifts. Had King Solomon been the janitor, with all his treasures piled up in the basement, Jim would have pulled out his watch every time he passed, just to see him pluck at his beard from envy.

So now Della's beautiful hair fell about her, rippling and shining like a cascade of brown waters. It reached below her knee and made itself almost a garment for her. And then she did it up again nervously and quickly. Once she faltered for a minute and stood still while a tear or two splashed on the worn red carpet.

On went her old brown jacket; on went her old brown hat. With a whirl of skirts and with the brilliant sparkle still in her eyes, she fluttered out the door and down the stairs to the street.

Where she stopped the sign read: "Mme. Sofronie. Hair Goods of All Kinds." One flight up Della ran, and collected herself, panting. Madame, large, too white, chilly, hardly looked the "Sofronie."

"Will you buy my hair?" asked Della.

"I buy hair," said Madame. "Take yer hat off and let's have a sight at the looks of it."

Down rippled the brown cascade.

"Twenty dollars," said Madame, lifting the mass with a practiced hand.

"Give it to me quick," said Della.

Oh, and the next two hours tripped by on rosy wings. Forget the hashed metaphor. She was ransacking the stores for Jim's present.

She found it at last. It surely had been made for Jim and no one else. There was no other like it in any of the stores, and she had turned all of them inside out. It was a platinum fob chain simple and chaste in design, properly proclaiming its value by substance alone and not by meretricious ornamentation—as all good things should do. It was even worthy of The Watch. As soon as she saw it she knew that it must be Jim's. It was like him. Quietness and value—the description applied to both. Twenty-one dollars they took from her for it, and she hurried home with the 87 cents. With that chain on his watch Jim might be properly anxious about the time in any company. Grand as the watch was, he sometimes looked at it on the sly on account of the old leather strap that he used in place of a chain.

When Della reached home her intoxication gave way a little to prudence and reason. She got out her curling irons and lighted the gas and went to work repairing the ravages made by generosity added to love. Which is always a tremendous task, dear friends—a mammoth task.

Within forty minutes her head was covered with tiny, close-lying curls that made her look wonderfully like a truant schoolboy. She looked at her reflection in the mirror long, carefully, and critically.

"If Jim doesn't kill me," she said to herself, "before he takes a second look at me, he'll say I look like a Coney Island chorus girl. But what could I do—oh! what could I do with a dollar and eighty-seven cents?"

At 7 o'clock the coffee was made and the frying pan was on the back of the stove hot and ready to cook the chops.

Jim was never late. Della doubled the fob chain in her hand and sat on the corner of the table near the door that he always entered. Then she heard his step on the stair away down on the first flight, and she turned white for just a moment. She had a habit of saying little silent prayers about the simplest everyday things, and now she

whispered: "Please God, make him think I am still pretty."

The door opened and Jim stepped in and closed it. He looked thin and very serious. Poor fellow, he was only twenty-two and to be burdened with a family! He needed a new overcoat and he was without gloves.

Jim stepped inside the door, as immovable as a setter at the scent of quail. His eyes were fixed upon Della, and there was an expression in them that she could not read, and it terrified her. It was not anger, nor surprise, nor disapproval, nor horror, nor any of the sentiments that she had been prepared for. He simply stared at her fixedly with that peculiar expression on his face.

Della wriggled off the table and went for him.

"Jim, darling," she cried, "don't look at me that way. I had my hair cut off and sold it because I couldn't have lived through Christmas without giving you a present. It'll grow out again—you won't mind, will you? I just had to do it. My hair grows awfully fast. Say 'Merry Christmas!', Jim, and let's be happy. You don't know what a nice—what a beautiful, nice gift I've got for you."

"You've cut off your hair?" asked Jim, laboriously, as if he had not arrived at that patent fact yet even after the hardest mental labor.

"Cut it off and sold it," said Della. "Don't you like me just as well, anyhow? I'm me without my hair, ain't I?"

Jim looked about the room curiously.

"You say your hair is gone?" he said, with an air almost of idiocy.

"You needn't look for it," said Della. "It's sold, I tell you—sold and gone, too. It's Christmas Eve, boy. Be good to me, for it went for you. Maybe the hairs of my head were numbered," she went on with a sudden, serious sweetness, "but nobody could ever count my love for you. Shall I put the chops on, Jim?"

Out of his trance Jim seemed quickly to wake. He enfolded his Della. For ten seconds let us regard with discreet scrutiny some inconsequential object in the other direction. Eight dollars a week or a million a year—what is the difference? A mathematician or a wit would give you the wrong answer. The magi brought valuable gifts, but that was not among them. This dark assertion will be illuminated later on.

Jim drew a package from his overcoat pocket and threw it upon the table.

"Don't make any mistake, Dell," he said, "about me. I don't think there's anything in the way of a haircut or a shave or shampoo that could make me like my girl any less. But if you'll unwrap that package you may see why you had me going a while at first."

White fingers and nimble tore at the string and paper. And then an ecstatic scream of joy; and then, alas! a quick feminine change to hysterical tears and wails, necessitating the immediate employment of all of the comforting powers of the lord of the flat.

For there lay The Combs—the set of combs, side and back, that Della had worshiped for long in a Broadway window. Beautiful combs, pure tortoise shell, with jeweled rims—just the shade to wear in the vanished hair. They were expensive combs, she knew, and her heart had simply craved and yearned over them without the least hope of possession. And now, they were hers, but the tresses that should have adorned the coveted adornments were gone.

But she hugged them to her bosom, and at length she was able to look up with dim eyes and a smile and say: "My hair grows so fast, Jim!"

And then Della leaped up like a little singed cat and cried, "Oh, oh!"

Jim had not yet seen his beautiful present. She held it out to him eagerly upon her open palm. The dull precious metal

seemed to flash with a reflection of her bright and ardent spirit.

"Isn't it a dandy, Jim? I hunted all over town to find it. You'll have to look at the time a hundred times a day now. Give me your watch. I want to see how it looks on it."

Instead of obeying, Jim tumbled down on the couch and put his hands under the back of his head and smiled.

"Dell," said he, "let's put our Christmas presents away and keep 'em a while. They're too nice to use just at present. I sold the watch to get the money to buy your combs. And now suppose you put the chops on."

The magi, as you know, were wise men—wonderfully wise men—who brought gifts to the Babe in the manger. They invented the art of giving Christmas presents. Being wise, their gifts were no doubt wise ones possibly bearing the privilege of exchange in case of duplication. And here I have lamely related to you the uneventful chronicle of two foolish children in a flat who most unwisely sacrificed for each other the greatest treasures of their house. But in a last word to the wise of these days let it be said that of all who give gifts these two were the wisest. Of all who give and receive gifts, such as they are wisest. Everywhere they are wisest. They are the magi.

As the bow unto the cord is
So unto the man is woman.
Though she bends him, she obeys him,
Though she draws him, yet she follows,
Useless each without the other.

Henry Wadsworth Longfellow

From TWO FROM GALILEE

Marjorie Holmes

The betrothal had been fixed for the Wednesday three weeks hence, when the moon would be full for good luck.

Each night Joseph watched for its rising, and often he was still awake as it set. By the light of the moon and a single saucer of oil he worked on his gifts for Mary: A sewing box. A pair of slippers from some doeskin bought in the bazaars at Sepphoris. And his table. The moonlight poured across the doorstep, for he had flung the door wide; it made him feel closer to Mary. Everywhere things were blooming and bearing. The fragrance of almond and pomegranate blossoms drifted in, mingling with the odor of shavings and the cedar oil that he was rubbing into the table. Deeply, lovingly, with all his force to make it shine for her.

The moon plated it with silver. The moon was like a maiden itself, at first frail, fine-boned, but growing, nightly fleshing toward the fullness of love. Or it was like one of the ships that coasted across the blue lake of Galilee, too fragile, it seemed, for its cargo. But when the wind caught the sails how they billowed and strutted forward with their precious freight. The moon was like that, it drew his love along as it rose and nightly swelled. God's own moon watched over his labors and gave them light.

He no longer sang. A great silence had come upon him. The music within him was too mighty for words, even those of David or Solomon. He could make music only with his hands, working for the beloved.

"You should get your rest," his mother worried, holding him with her bright, penetrating gaze. "You'll be worn out before the betrothal, let alone the wedding."

And the children taunted him. "Joseph's sleep-walking—see, see, he doesn't hear a thing, Joseph's in love!"

LOVE

He laughed good-naturedly; they were all remote from him, outside the borders of his private journey. He was on his way to Mary.

He had scarcely seen her since the Sabbath when she had sat surrounded by other maids, with her hair unbound.... That hair. The scent of its rich, dark, tumbling tide ... he had had to turn away lest he press his face into it, disturb it with his fingers, make a fool of himself. And since then he had not dared draw near her house. For one thing, it was considered more seemly; for another, her parents were so busy. Hannah had hauled everything out onto the grass and was whitening the walls afresh. But most of all, he was restrained by his own desire. The image of her sitting, eyes downcast, so small and lovely in the intimate tent and shelter of her hair, was to rouse up such passion in him that he was afraid.

God had kept faith with him. He could not even imagine the consequences should he break faith with God.... As for Hannah! Joseph felt a flash of amused alarm. Or Mary—Mary herself. At this he had to retreat from his own tormented thoughts. For he saw her eyes, large with love. He saw her parted lips.

His heart stopped as it smote him how easily he might have been someone else. But she, a slight girl, had shown far more courage than he, standing up to her parents, an almost unheard-of thing. Before the spectacle of his own blind, wasted year, Joseph was appalled. Now he resolved to make it up to her. He would protect her from the emotions that sprang like lightning between them. He would keep himself distant. He would not suffer himself to touch her, not even a finger, or a strand of that sweet temptation of hair. As for the fine gifts that he could not bestow upon her, he suffered. Yet in his wretchedness he was also proud.

Weighing himself against them, he realized that Abner had his scholarship, his devotion to the Law. Cleophas had his wealth, his travels, his other women. He, Joseph, had only his love for Mary. She was his Temple, his wealth and his wisdom. And to her he would bring all that he possessed, every stitch, every penny, every eagerly hewn bit of wood. Every fiber of his strong young body, every thought that did not first belong to him who had made her for him, their God.

He was awed by the honor of his undertaking, but he was not humbled. He knew that the gift of total commitment is never small.

Joseph worked feverishly even the day of his betrothal. It would help to pass the hours until sundown. Furthermore, there had been a slight upsurge of business, as if already his union with the house of Joachim might become an asset to his family. He did not want to be found wanting, and he wanted to prosper. Soon he would have a wife to support.

Suddenly he could not believe it. The daze of sheer blind yielding, moving foward, ever forward in harmony with his fate deserted him. Something might happen even yet. Hannah might still hurl herself between them. Or some awful caprice of God might strike. His mother had gone up to help with the baking; any moment she might rush in, her eyes cold with horror. Or Timna would never return at all. The day would simply go on forever, with Mary ahead of him like a mirage on the desert, or a port toward which he was forever doomed to sail.

"My darling, you're still working?" His mother's hand parted the curtains, her concerned face peered through. "It's growing late, I'll fetch the water for your bath and lay out your garments." Flushed and perspiring but smiling, she pulled off her kerchief. Hannah had bade her come

up with the aunts and other kin to join in the joyous preparations. Kneading the dough and baking it in the ovens dug in the yard, setting out the vegetables that were now bursting in such abundance, polishing the bright fruit, checking the wine. And all the while they worked, caught up in the glittering net of women's talk. They had praised each other's efforts and each other's children, favoring her especially, as mother of the groom.

Home now, she looked about with her familiar anxiety for her husband. But Jacob was fine, Joseph assured her; only sleeping. "Good," she sighed, "he'll need the rest. We'll be up late. You should have rested too." She pressed his arm.

Joseph bathed and dressed and annointed his hair with olive oil. His confidence was returning. As the water had washed away the grime and sweat, so it cleansed him of his nervous, foolish imaginings. He felt the splendor of his own body in its pure white linen; he felt the wonder of his youth pulsing, urgent and eager. One small thing troubled him exceedingly—his hands. Although he scrubbed them nearly raw and rubbed them with the precious oil, he could do nothing about their calluses or the scarred, broken nails. He wanted to be perfect for Mary. He did not want his hands to be harsh, clasping hers, or to snag the betrothal veil.

His father puffed in and out, bumping into him, borrowing things, asking Joseph's help with the tying of his girdle. Jacob could never manage and his wife was busy with the girls. "And do I have to wear shoes?" he pleaded, exhibiting his poor swollen feet with their bunions. Squat, ruddy, his wispy hair combed futilely over his baldness, he looked uncomfortably clean and dressed up and rather pathetic. Yet it was he who reminded Joseph of the things that in his agitation he might forget: the purse of long-hoarded silver dinars, the

ring, the presents.

Together they set off at last, Joseph lugging the heavy table. Jacob limped along in his unaccustomed sandals. A brisk breeze set the palm trees clashing and blew their robes about their legs. The dusty cobbled streets seemed strangely empty, as if life had been suspended for this gravely impending hour. Behind a tumbled-down rock fence a camel lurched growling to his feet, a donkey worried a bucket and brayed. They trudged along the steep, narrow corridors in a strange silence. They were miserably aware, the nearer they drew to their destination, of the inadequacy of their offerings.

Ahead of them in the fast-falling darkness they saw the newly whitened bridal house in its clump of prickly pears. Fluttering from it like a beckoning arm was the pennant that proclaimed its festivities to passers-by. As they approached they saw that Joachim had stepped outside to light the torch of pitch-soaked rushes at the step. It blazed up suddenly, revealing his face with its unguarded look of grief. However quickly he jerked his head, there was no denying that naked sorrowing. Because of me? Joseph wondered, or only because his dearest child has so little time left to be under his roof? Promptly Joachim recovered himself and turned to welcome them. Courteously ignoring the gifts they carried, he led them inside.

The room had been transformed. This was no house now, but Eden; the women had gathered up armsful of Eden and brought it inside. The white walls struggled to hold up its colors—the shining green of dampened leaves, and blossoms that rose in a bright riot, to wind even into the rushes of the ceiling. Purple iris, scarlet carnations, pink and blue cyclamen, the ruddy cups of tulips, heavy-headed poppies, already beginning to swoon in the heat of the lamps that stood like little floating stars.

The largest lamp, burning the finest oil,

was placed at the head of the table where the bride and groom were led. Joseph found himself there as in a dream. Mary seemed unreal beside him, though her sweet flesh at times brushed against his. The scent of her was more heady than the overpowering fragrance of the flowers. He was stiff with guarding his emotions, remote from her, afraid. Her eyes had a fixed shining, she was smiling, smiling, laughing and smiling before the lavish compliments that each guest paid as he laid his gifts at her feet. Bolts of cloth, baskets, jugs, skeins of flax, countless tools for keeping house. The guests deposited them and then returned to their seats which were bedecked with olive boughs.

Finally an expectant hush; the scribe came forward. The rabbi nodded to Joseph, whose heart was large in his throat. With unsteady hands he drew from his girdle the purse containing the marriage fee, and turned to Mary, whose face floated before him. Not smiling now, but grave and as white as one of the pure white roses in her crown.

"And have you brought a token to give the bride to signify that this covenant is made?"

Nodding, Joseph unwound his girdle. His eyes did not leave Mary's as the rabbi took it and placed it across her uplifted hands.

"And have you other gifts?" the rabbi asked.

"Yes." If only there were more. . . . But nobody seemed to think ill of them, the shawl he had for Hannah, the fine hand chisel for Joachim. And for Mary—ah, for Mary, the sewing box, the soft little doeskin slippers, and the table that would be the first piece of furniture for their house. Plainly she loved them all, especially the slippers. She cried out with delight and thrust out her feet to their measure. There was an awkward moment for it seemed as if she would have him kneel there in the presence of everyone to put them on her.

He flushed and people laughed at his discomfort and the rabbi made stern noises in his throat. For the scribe sat waiting to pen the terms of the contract.

And when it was finished, Joseph spoke aloud the prescribed words: that he would work for her and honor her in the manner of Jewish husbands, and that all of his property would be hers forever. Thus did he openly take the vow already made within his heart.

It was over now, all but the draping of her face with the betrothal veil. But the children must first be called forward. They had been bouncing with impatience for their treats; now the rabbi beckoned, and the mothers who had been restraining them let them go. They came in an eager swarm, shrieking, hands outstretched for the nuts and cakes. The eyes of Mary and Joseph met, and between them ran a shining thread of wonder, for despite its festive nature, this too was a grave thing, this matter of bestowing the sweets. For it symbolized the fact that she had kept herself for him.

In the commotion he almost forgot the veil. "The veil, the veil!" various ones were whispering. "Quiet the children." An aunt shepherded most of them outside, the others clung to their mothers, eyes focused with a placid interest on the bride.

As Joseph had feared, his fingers caught on the delicate gossamer stuff, and his hands shook placing it with anguished care so that it fell before her face. Yet pride upheld him. This was his victory; he knew that he stood before them tall and comely, humble yet mighty, a man claiming his true bride.

A vast tenderness swept him, and a great reverence. Now she belonged to him and her face was his to shield. In regret and joy he draped her, his personal Torah, which now must be returned to the ark to await their covenant.

THE GREATEST OF THESE IS LOVE
Saint Paul

Though I speak with the tongues of men and of angels, and have not love, I am become *as* sounding brass, or a tinkling cymbal.

And though I have *the gift of* prophecy, and understand all mysteries, and all knowledge; and though I have all faith, so that I could remove mountains, and have not love, I am nothing.

And though I bestow all my goods to feed *the poor*, and though I give my body to be burned, and have not love, it profiteth me nothing.

Love suffereth long, *and* is kind; love envieth not; love vaunteth not itself, is not puffed up,

Doth not behave itself unseemly, seeketh not her own, is not easily provoked, thinketh no evil;

Rejoiceth not in iniquity, but rejoiceth in the truth;

Beareth all things, believeth all things, hopeth all things, endureth all things.

Love never faileth: but whether *there be* prophecies, they shall fail; whether *there be* tongues, they shall cease; whether *there be* knowledge, it shall vanish away.

For we know in part, and we prophesy in part.

But when that which is perfect is come, then that which is in part shall be done away.

When I was a child, I spake as a child, I understood as a child, I thought as a child: but when I became a man, I put away childish things.

For now we see through a glass, darkly; but then face to face: now I know in part; but then shall I know even as also I am known.

And now abideth faith, hope, love, these three; but the greatest of these *is* love.

I Corinthians 13:1-13

Lord, help me live from day to day
In such a self-forgetful way,
That even when I kneel to pray,
My prayer may be for—*others*.

Charles Dickens

Talk not of wasted affection, affection
  never was wasted;
If it enrich not the heart of another, its
  waters, returning
Back to their springs, like the rain, shall fill
  them full of refreshment;
That which the fountain sends forth
  returns again to the fountain.

Henry Wadsworth Longfellow

IN GRATITUDE FOR FRIENDS

I thank You, God in Heaven, for friends.
When morning wakes, when daytime ends,
  I have the consciousness
Of loving hands that touch my own,
Of tender glance and gentle tone,
  Of thoughts that cheer and bless!
If sorrow comes to me I know
That friends will walk the way I go
  And, as the shadows fall,
I know that I will raise my eyes
And see—ah, hope that never dies!—
  The dearest Friend of All.

Margaret E. Sangster

SUNDAY BEST
Dorothy Canfield Fisher

Many years ago when my great-grand-mother was a frisky, withered old woman, she heard that on one of the mountain farms way up on a steep side road, the farmer's wife never came down to the village to buy things or go to church because she was afraid people would laugh at her. Her mother had been an Indian,

and her skin was very dark. They were plain folks with little money, and she didn't think her clothes were good enough to go to church. She'd stayed away from people so long that she was shy—the way a deer is shy—and went into the house quickly and hid if a stranger happened to stop at the farm.

My great-grandmother no sooner heard that, than she got into the small battered old family phaeton and had a boy drive her to the Hunter farm. Mrs. Hunter was hanging out her clothes on the line when Great-grandmother drove into the yard. Before she could dodge away and hide, Great-grandmother hopped out of the low, little carriage and said, "Here, let me help you!" In a minute, with her mouth full of clothespins, she was standing by Mrs. Hunter, pinning up sheets and towels, and men's shirts. "My, how clean you get them!" she said mumblingly around the clothespins. "They're as white as new milk! How do you make your soap? Do you put any salt in it?"

By the time they had the big basket of wet clothes hung up, the dark-skinned, black-haired mountain wife couldn't feel shy of the quick-stepping little old woman from the valley. They had a pleasant time talking in the kitchen as they washed the breakfast dishes, and sat down together to the basket of mending. The question of going to church came up, along with all sorts of other subjects. Before the old visitor had gone, Mrs. Hunter said she would go to church the next Sunday, if she could go with Great-grandmother and sit in the same pew with her.

Sure enough, the next Sunday, Great-grandmother, her young-lady daughter and her little-girl granddaughter stood on their front porch. They were all in their best Sunday dresses, wore bonnets, had their prayer books in their hands. They smiled at Mrs. Hunter as Mr. Hunter drove

her up in the lumbering farm wagon.

Mrs. Hunter had a bonnet on over her sleek black hair. It was a cool day, she had put on a warm cloak, her shoes were brightly black with polish. And (she was a real country-woman whose idea of dressing up was a freshly-ironed clean apron) she had put on a big blue-checked gingham apron, nicely starched, over her coat, and tied the strings in the back.

My aunt, who was Great-grandmother's granddaughter, and who was the little girl on the front porch that day, said she and her young-lady aunt were so astonished to see a woman starting to church with a big apron on, over her coat, that their eyes opened wide, and they were just ready to put their hands up to their mouths to hide a smile. But Great-grandmother swung the little girl sharply around and shoved her back into the house, calling over her shoulder to Mrs. Hunter, "Well, would you believe it, the girls and I have forgotten to put our aprons on. We won't keep you waiting a minute."

Once inside, she hustled them into gingham aprons, which they tied on over their coats. She herself put on the biggest one she had, tied the strings in a dashing bowknot behind, and they sailed across to the church with Mrs. Hunter, aproned from chin to hem, all four of them.

People already in their pews looked astonished, but Great-grandmother put on a hard expression she sometimes used, and faced them down, so that they got the idea and made their children stop giggling.

At the end of the service, everybody came to shake hands with Mrs. Hunter. They knew Great-grandmother would have a thing or two to say to them, if they didn't. They told her and the rector of the church told her they were glad to see her out at church and they hoped she'd come often. After that Mrs. Hunter came every Sunday, the rest of her life—without an apron; for

some time during the next week, Great-grandmother let fall negligently that it wasn't really necessary to wear them on Sundays.

Long years after Great-grandmother and Mrs. Hunter were both in the old Burying Ground with tombstones over their graves, something else "happened" that would make you think, almost, that one action makes a natural channel along which other actions like it can flow more easily.

It was this way. One of the families in our town was very poor. The father had died, the mother was sick, the five children scratched along as best they could, with what help the neighbors could give them. But they had to go without things that you'd think were necessary.

They wore things that other people had given up because they were too ragged. Their mother, sitting up in bed, patched them as best she could, and the children wore them. When the oldest boy—he was a little fellow about fourteen years old—got a chance to go to work for a farmer over the mountain from our valley, he had nothing at all to wear but a very old shirt, some faded, much-patched blue denim overalls, and his work shoes.

The farmer and his wife had never seen anybody in such poor working clothes. It did not occur to them that the new-hired boy had no others at all. Saturday when the farmer's wife went to the village to sell some eggs, she bought young David a pair of blue jeans, so stiff they could almost stand alone—you know how brand-new overalls look.

The next day at breakfast they said they were going to church, and would David like to go along? Yes, indeed he would! So they went off to their rooms to get into their Sunday clothes. The farmer was dressed first, and sat down by the radio to get the time signals to set his watch. David walked in. His hair was combed slick with lots of

water, his work shoes were blacked, his face was clean as a china plate. And he had on those stiff, new blue jeans, looking as though they were made out of blue stovepipe.

The farmer opened his mouth to say, "We're almost ready to start. You'll be late if you don't get dressed for church," when he saw David's face. It was shining. He looked down at the blue jeans with a smile; he ran his hand lovingly over their stiff newness, and said ardently to the farmer, "Land! I'm so much obliged to you folks for getting me these new clothes in time to go to church in them."

The farmer had to blow his nose real hard before he could say, "Wait a minute." He went to take off his own black suit and put on a pair of blue jeans. Then he and David walked into church together, sat in the same pew, and sang out of the same hymnbook.

When true friends meet in adverse hour,
'Tis like a sunbeam through a shower.
A watery way an instant seen,
The darkly closing clouds between.

Sir Walter Scott

A true friend unbosoms freely, advises justly, assists readily, adventures boldly, takes all patiently, defends courageously, and continues a friend unchangeably.

William Penn

THE SELFISH GIANT
Oscar Wilde

Every afternoon, as they were coming from school, the children used to go and play in the Giant's garden.

It was a large lovely garden, with soft green grass. Here and there over the

grass stood beautiful flowers like stars, and there were twelve peach trees that in the springtime broke out into delicate blossoms of pink and pearl, and in the autumn bore rich fruit. The birds sat on the trees and sang so sweetly that the children used to stop their games in order to listen to them. "How happy we are here!" they cried to each other.

One day the Giant came back. He had been to visit his friend the Cornish ogre, and had stayed with him for seven years. After the seven years were over he had said all that he had to say, for his conversation was limited, and he determined to return to his own castle. When he arrived he saw the children playing in the garden.

"What are you doing here?" he cried in a very gruff voice, and the children ran away.

"My own garden is my own garden," said the Giant, "anyone can understand that, and I will allow nobody to play in it but myself." So he built a high wall all round it, and put up a notice board :

TRESPASSERS WILL BE PROSECUTED

He was a very selfish Giant.

The poor children had now nowhere to play. They tried to play on the road, but the road was very dusty and full of hard stones, and they did not like it. They used to wander round the high wall when their lessons were over, and talk about the beautiful garden inside. "How happy we were there," they said to each other.

Then the Spring came, and all over the country there were little blossoms and little birds. Only in the garden of the Selfish Giant it was still winter. The birds did not care to sing in it as there were no children, and the trees forgot to blossom. Once a beautiful flower put its head out from the grass, but when it saw the notice board it was so sorry for the children that it slipped back into the ground again, and went off to sleep. The only people who were pleased were the Snow and the Frost. "Spring has forgotten this garden," they cried, "so we will live here all the year round." The Snow covered up the grass with her great white cloak, and the Frost painted all the trees silver. Then they invited the North Wind to stay with them, and he came. He was wrapped in furs, and he roared all day about the garden, and blew the chimney pots down. "This is a delightful spot," he said. "We must ask the Hail on a visit." So the Hail came. Every day for three hours he rattled on the roof of the castle till he broke most of the slates, and then he ran round and round the garden as fast as he could go. He was dressed in grey, and his breath was like ice.

"I cannot understand why the Spring is so late in coming," said the Selfish Giant, as he sat at the window and looked out at his cold white garden. "I hope there will be a change in the weather."

But the Spring never came, nor the Summer. The Autumn gave golden fruit to every garden, but to the Giant's garden she gave none. "He is too selfish," she said. So it was always Winter there, and the North Wind, and the Hail, and the Frost, and the Snow danced about through the trees.

One morning the Giant was lying awake in bed when he heard some lovely music. It sounded so sweet to his ears that he thought it must be the King's musicians passing by. It was really only a little linnet singing outside his window, but it was so long since he had heard a bird sing in his garden that it seemed to him to be the most beautiful music in the world. Then the Hail stopped dancing over his head, and the North Wind ceased roaring, and a delicious perfume came to him through the open casement. "I believe the Spring has come at last," said the Giant, and he jumped out of bed and looked out.

What did he see?

He saw a most wonderful sight. Through a little hole in the wall the children had crept in, and they were sitting in the branches of the trees. In every tree that he could see there was a little child. And the trees were so glad to have the children back again that they had covered themselves with blossoms, and were waving their arms gently above the children's heads. The birds were flying about and twittering with delight, and the flowers were looking up through the green grass and laughing. It was a lovely scene; only in one corner it was still winter. It was the farthest corner of the garden, and in it was standing a little boy. He was so small that he could not reach up to the branches of the tree, and he was wandering all around it, crying bitterly. The poor tree was still quite covered with Frost and Snow, and the North Wind was blowing and roaring above it. "Climb up, little boy!" said the Tree, and it bent its branches down as low as it could; but the boy was too tiny.

And the Giant's heart melted as he looked out. "How selfish I have been!" he said. "Now I know why the Spring would not come here. I will put that poor little boy on the top of the tree, and then I will knock down the wall, and my garden shall be the children's playground for ever and ever." He was really very sorry for what he had done.

So he crept downstairs and opened the front door quite softly, and went out into the garden. But when the children saw him they were so frightened that they all ran away, and the garden became winter again. Only the little boy did not run, for his eyes were so full of tears that he did not see the Giant coming. And the Giant stole up behind him and took him gently in his hand, and put him up into the tree. And the tree broke at once into blossom, and the birds came and sang on it, and the little boy stretched out his two arms and flung them round the Giant's neck, and kissed him. And the other children, when they saw that the Giant was not wicked any longer, came running back, and with them came the Spring. "It is your garden now, little children," said the Giant, and he took a great axe and knocked down the wall. And when the people were going to market at twelve o'clock they found the Giant playing with the children in the most beautiful garden they had ever seen.

All day long they played, and in the evening they came to the Giant to bid him good-bye.

"But where is your little companion?" he said: "the boy I put into the tree." The Giant loved him the best because he had kissed him.

"We don't know," answered the children. "He has gone away."

"You must tell him to be sure and come here tomorrow," said the Giant. But the children said that they did not know where he lived, and had never seen him before; and the Giant felt very sad.

Every afternoon, when school was over, the children came and played with the Giant. But the little boy whom the Giant loved was never seen again. The Giant was very kind to all the children, yet he longed for his first little friend, and often spoke of him. "How I would like to see him!" he used to say.

Years went over, and the Giant grew very old and feeble. He could not play about any more, so he sat in a huge armchair, and watched the children at their games, and admired his garden. "I have many beautiful flowers," he said, "but the children are the most beautiful flowers of all."

One winter morning he looked out of his window as he was dressing. He did not hate the Winter now, for he knew that it was merely the Spring asleep, and that the flowers were resting.

Suddenly he rubbed his eyes in wonder,

and looked and looked. It certainly was a marvellous sight. In the farthest corner of the garden was a tree quite covered with lovely white blossoms. Its branches were all golden, and silver fruit hung down from them, and underneath it stood the little boy he had loved.

Downstairs ran the Giant in great joy, and out into the garden. He hastened across the grass, and came near to the child. And when he came quite close his face grew red with anger, and he said, "Who hath dared to wound thee?" For on the palms of the child's hands were the prints of two nails, and the prints of two nails were on the little feet.

"Who hath dared to wound thee?" cried the Giant. "Tell me, that I may take my big sword and slay him."

"Nay!" answered the child, "but these are the wounds of Love."

"Who art thou?" said the Giant, and a strange awe fell on him, and he knelt before the little child.

And the child smiled on the Giant, and said to him, "You let me play once in your garden, today you shall come with me to my garden, which is Paradise."

And when the children ran in that afternoon, they found the Giant lying dead under the tree, all covered with white blossoms.

OUTWITTED

He drew a circle that shut me out—
Heretic, rebel, a thing to flout.
But Love and I had the wit to win:
We drew a circle that took him in!

Edwin Markham

THE STEADFAST TIN SOLDIER

Hans Christian Andersen

There were once five and twenty tin soldiers, all brothers, for they were the offspring of the same old tin spoon. Each man shouldered his gun, kept his eyes well to the front, and wore the smartest red and blue uniform imaginable. The first thing they heard in their new world, when the lid was taken off the box, was a little boy clapping his hands and crying, "Soldiers, soldiers!" It was his birthday and they had just been given to him, so he lost no time in setting them up on the table. All the soldiers were exactly alike, with one exception, and he differed from the rest in having only one leg, for he was made last, and there was not quite enough tin left to finish him. However, he stood just as well on his one leg, as the others on two; in fact, he is the very one who is to become famous. On the table where they were being set up were many other toys; but the chief thing which caught the eye was a delightful paper castle. You could see through tiny windows, right into the rooms. Outside there were some little trees surrounding a small mirror, representing a lake, whose surface reflected the waxen swans which were swimming about on it. It was altogether charming, but the prettiest thing of all was a little maiden standing at the open door of the castle. She, too, was cut out of paper, but she wore a dress of the lightest gauze, with a dainty little blue ribbon over her shoulders, by way of a scarf, set off by a brilliant spangle as big as her whole face. The little maid was stretching out both arms, for she was a dancer, and in the dance one of her legs was raised so high into the air that the tin soldier could see absolutely nothing of it, and supposed that she, like himself, had one leg.

"That would be the very wife for me!" he

thought, "but she is much too grand; she lives in a palace, while I only have a box, and then there are five and twenty of us to share it. No, that would be no place for her! But I must try to make her acquaintance!" Then he lay down full length behind a snuffbox which stood on the table. From that point he could have a good look at the lady, who continued to stand on one leg without losing her balance.

Late in the evening the other soldiers were put into their box, and the people of the house went to bed. Now was the time for the toys to play; they amused themselves with paying visits, fighting battles and giving balls. The tin soldiers rustled about in their box, for they wanted to join the games, but they could not get the lid off. The nutcrackers turned somersaults, and the pencil scribbled nonsense on the slate. There was such a noise that the canary woke up and joined in, but his remarks were in verse. The only two who did not move were the tin soldier and the little dancer. She stood as stiff as ever on tiptoe, with her arms spread out; he was equally firm on his one leg, and he did not take his eyes off her for a moment.

Then the clock struck twelve, when pop! up flew the lid of the snuffbox, but there was no snuff in it, no! There was a little black goblin, a sort of Jack-in-the-box.

"Tin soldier!" said the goblin, "have the goodness to keep your eyes to yourself."

But the tin soldier feigned not to hear.

"Ah! You just wait till tomorrow," said the goblin.

In the morning when the children got up they put the tin soldier on the window frame, and, whether it was caused by the goblin or by a puff of wind, I do not know, but all at once the window burst open, and the soldier fell head foremost from the third story.

It was a terrific descent, and he landed at last, with his leg in the air, and rested on his cap, with his bayonet fixed between two paving stones. The maidservant and the little boy ran down at once to look for him; but although they almost trod on him, they could not see him. Had the soldier only called out, "Here I am," they would easily have found him, but he did not think it proper to shout when he was in uniform.

Presently it began to rain, and the drops fell faster and faster, till there was a regular torrent. When it was over two street boys came along.

"Look out!" said one, "there is a tin soldier! He shall go for a sail."

So they made a boat out of a newspaper and put the soldier into the middle of it, and he sailed away down the gutter; both boys ran alongside, clapping their hands. Good heavens! What waves there were in the gutter, and what a current, but then it certainly had rained cats and dogs. The paper boat danced up and down, and now and then whirled round and round. A shudder ran through the tin soldier, but he remained undaunted, and did not move a muscle, only looked straight before him with his gun shouldered. All at once the boat drifted under a long wooden tunnel, and it became as dark as it was in his box.

"Where on earth am I going now!" thought he. "Well, well, it is all the fault of that goblin! Oh, if only the little maiden were with me in the boat it might be twice as dark for all I should care!"

At this moment a big water rat, who lived in the tunnel, came up.

"Have you a pass?" asked the rat. "Hand up your pass!"

The tin soldier did not speak, but clung still tighter to his gun. The boat rushed on, the rat close behind. Phew, how he gnashed his teeth and shouted to the bits of stick and straw, "Stop him, stop him, he hasn't paid

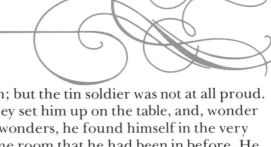

his toll; he hasn't shown his pass!" But the current grew stronger and stronger; the tin soldier could already see daylight before him at the end of the tunnel; but he also heard a roaring sound, fit to strike terror to the bravest heart. Just imagine! Where the tunnel ended, the stream rushed straight into the big canal. That would be just as dangerous for him as it would for us to shoot a great rapids.

He was so near the end now that it was impossible to stop. The boat dashed out; the poor tin soldier held himself as stiff as he could; no one should say of him that he even winced.

The boat swirled round three or four times and filled with water to the edge; it must sink. The tin soldier stood up to his neck in water, and the boat sank deeper and deeper. The paper became limper and limper, and at last the water went over his head—then he thought of the pretty little dancer, whom he was never to see again, and this refrain rang in his ears:

Onward! Onward! Soldier!
For death thou canst not shun.

At last the paper gave way entirely and the soldier fell through—but at the same moment he was swallowed by a big fish.

Oh, how dark it was inside the fish, it was worse than being in the tunnel even; and then it was so narrow! But the tin soldier was as dauntless as ever, and lay full length, shouldering his gun.

The fish rushed about and made the most frantic movements. At last it became quite quiet, and after a time, a flash like lightning pierced it. The soldier was once more in the broad daylight, and someone called out loudly, "A tin soldier!" The fish had been caught, taken to market, sold, and brought into the kitchen, where the cook cut it open with a large knife. She took the soldier up by the waist, with two fingers, and carried him into the parlor, where everyone wanted to see the wonderful man who had traveled about in the stomach of a

fish; but the tin soldier was not at all proud. They set him up on the table, and, wonder of wonders, he found himself in the very same room that he had been in before. He saw the very same children, and the toys were still standing on the table, as well as the beautiful castle with the pretty little dancer.

She still stood on one leg, and held the other up in the air. You see, she also was unbending. The soldier was so much moved that he was ready to shed tears of tin, but that would not have been fitting. He looked at her, and she looked at him, but they said never a word. At this moment one of the little boys took up the tin soldier and, without rhyme or reason, threw him into the fire. No doubt the little goblin in the snuffbox was to blame for that. The tin soldier stood there, lighted up by the flame, and in the most horrible heat; but whether it was the heat of the real fire, or the warmth of his feelings, he did not know. He had lost all his gay color; it might have been from his perilous journey, or it might have been from grief, who can tell?

He looked at the little maiden, and she looked at him, and he felt that he was melting away, but he still managed to keep himself erect, shouldering his gun bravely.

A door was suddenly opened, the draft caught the little dancer, and she fluttered like a sylph, straight into the fire, to the soldier, blazed up, and was gone!

By this time the soldier was reduced to a mere lump, and when the maid took away the ashes next morning she found him in the shape of a small tin heart. All that was left of the dancer was her spangle, and that was burned as black as coal.

Let us, then, try what love will do; for if men once see we love them, we should soon find they would not harm us. . . . Force may subdue, but love gains; and he that forgives first, wins the laurel.

William Penn

CHRISTMAS DAY IN THE MORNING

Pearl S. Buck

He waked suddenly and completely. It was four o'clock, the hour at which his father had always called him to get up and help with the milking. Strange how the habits of his youth clung to him still! Fifty years ago, and his father had been dead for thirty years, and yet he waked at four o'clock in the morning. He had trained himself to turn over and go to sleep, but this morning, because it was Christmas, he did not try to sleep.

He slipped back in time, as he did so easily nowadays. He was fifteen years old and still on his father's farm. He loved his father. He had not known it until one day a few days before Christmas, when he overheard what his father was saying to his mother.

"Mary, I hate to call Rob in the mornings. He's growing so fast, and he needs his sleep. If you could see how he sleeps when I go in to wake him up! I wish I could manage alone."

"Well, you can't, Adam." His mother's voice was brisk. "Besides, he isn't a child anymore. It's time he took his turn."

"Yes," his father said slowly. "But I sure do hate to wake him."

When he heard these words, something in him woke: his father loved him! He had never thought of it before, taking for granted the tie of their blood. Neither his father nor his mother talked about loving their children—they had no time for such things. There was always so much to do on a farm.

Now that he knew his father loved him, there would be no more loitering in the mornings and having to be called again. He got up after that, stumbling with sleep, and pulled on his clothes, his eyes tight shut, but he got up.

And then on the night before Christmas, that year when he was fifteen, he lay for a few minutes thinking about the next day. They were poor, and most of the excitement was in the turkey they had raised themselves and in the mince pies his mother made. His sisters sewed presents and his mother and father always bought something he needed, not only a warm jacket, maybe, but something more, such as a book. And he saved and bought them each something, too.

He wished, that Christmas he was fifteen, he had a better present for his father. As usual, he had gone to the ten-cent store and bought a tie. It had seemed nice enough until he lay thinking the night before Christmas, and then he wished that he had heard his father and mother talking in time for him to save for something better.

He lay on his side, his head supported by his elbow, and looked out of his attic window. The stars were bright, much brighter than he ever remembered seeing them, and one was so bright he wondered if it were really the star of Bethlehem.

"Dad," he had once asked when he was a little boy, "what is a stable?"

"It's just a barn," his father had replied, "like ours."

Then Jesus had been born in a barn, and to a barn the shepherds and the Wise Men had come, bringing their Christmas gifts!

The thought stuck him like a silver dagger. Why should he not give his father a special gift, too, out there in the barn? He could get up early, earlier than four o'clock, and he could creep into the barn and get all the milking done. He'd do it alone, milk

and clean up, and then when his father went in to start the milking, he'd see it all done. And he would know who had done it.

At a quarter to three, he got up and put on his clothes. He crept downstairs, careful of the creaky boards, and let himself out. The big star hung lower over the barn roof, a reddish gold. The cows looked at him, sleepy and surprised.

"So, boss," he whispered. They accepted him placidly, and he fetched some hay for each cow and then got the milking pail and the big milk cans.

He had never milked all alone before, but it seemed almost easy. He kept thinking about his father's surprise. His father would come in and call him, saying that he would get things started while Rob was getting dressed. He'd go to the barn, open the door, and then he'd go to get the two big empty milk cans. But they wouldn't be waiting or empty; they'd be standing in the milk house, filled.

The task went more easily than he had ever known it to before. Milking for once was not a chore. It was something else, a gift to his father who loved him. He finished, the two milk cans were full, and he covered them and closed the milk-house door carefully, making sure of the latch. He put the stool in its place by the door and hung up the clean milk pail. Then he went out of the barn and barred the door behind him.

Back in his room, he had only a minute to pull off his clothes in the darkness and jump into bed, for he heard his father up. He put the covers over his head to silence his quick breathing. The door opened.

"Rob!" his father called. "We have to get up, son, even if it is Christmas."

"Aw-right," he said sleepily.

"I'll go on out," his father said. "I'll get things started."

The door closed and he lay still, laughing to himself. In just a few minutes his father would know. His dancing heart was ready to jump from his body.

The minutes were endless—ten, fifteen, he did not know how many—and he heard his father's footsteps again. The door opened and he lay still.

"Rob!"

"Yes, Dad—"

His father was laughing, a queer sobbing sort of a laugh. "Thought you'd fool me, did you?" His father was standing beside his bed, feeling for him, pulling away the cover.

"It's for Christmas, Dad!"

He found his father and clutched him in a great hug. He felt his father's arms go around him. It was dark, and they could not see each other's faces.

"Son, I thank you. Nobody ever did a nicer thing—"

"Oh, Dad, I want you to know—I do want to be good!" The words broke from him of their own will. He did not know what to say. His heart was bursting with love.

"Well, I reckon I can go back to bed and sleep," his father said after a moment. "No, hark—the little ones are waked up. Come to think of it, son, I've never seen you children when you first saw the Christmas tree. I was always in the barn. Come on!"

He got up and pulled on his clothes again, and they went down to the Christmas tree; and soon the sun was creeping up to where the star had been. Oh, what a Christmas, and how his heart had nearly burst again with shyness and pride as his father told his mother and made the younger children listen about how he, Rob, had got up all by himself.

"The best Christmas gift I ever had, and I'll remember it, son, every year on Christmas morning, so long as I live."

They had both remembered it, and now that his father was dead he remembered it alone: that blessed Christmas dawn when, alone with the cows in the barn, he had made his first gift of true love.

Instead of allowing yourself to be unhappy, just let your love grow as God wants it to grow. Seek goodness in others. Love more persons more. Love them more impersonally, more unselfishly, without thought of return. The return, never fear, will take care of itself.

Henry Drummond

WHAT IS LOVE?

What is love?
  No words can define it,
It's something so great
  Only God could design it ...
Wonder of Wonders, beyond
    man's conception,
  And only in God can love find
  true perfection,
For love means much more than
    small words can express,
  For what man calls love is so
  very much less
Than the beauty and depth and
    the true richness of
  God's gift to mankind—His
  compassionate love ...
For love has become a word
    that's misused,
  Perverted, distorted and
  often abused,
To speak of "light romance" or
    some affinity for
  A passing attraction that is
  seldom much more
Than a mere interlude of
    inflamed fascination,
  A romantic fling of no lasting
  duration ...
But love is enduring and patient
    and kind,
  It judges all things with the
  heart, not the mind,
And love can transform the
    most commonplace

Into beauty and splendor and
  sweetness and grace ...
For love is unselfish, giving
  more than it takes,
  And no matter what happens
  love never forsakes,
It's faithful and trusting and al-
  ways believing,
  Guileless and honest and
  never deceiving ...
Yes, love is beyond what man
  can define,
  For love is Immortal and
  God's Gift is Divine!

Helen Steiner Rice

TURNING POINTS

A FRAGILE MOMENT...

Returning from my vacation, I shared my dining car table with a man of about 60, a minister. I don't remember what led us to talk about my life; perhaps it was the dissatisfaction I felt. I was 35 and life seemed nothing but gray routine.

My discontent must have been very obvious, because the minister remarked: "You seem to feel that you haven't got very much out of life. Why?"

"Well," I said, "I suppose I've always been too afraid of things. Afraid to try this, and afraid to do that."

My breakfast companion smiled. "I agree that you've missed a lot—but it's not because you've been, as you say, 'too afraid.' It's because *you haven't been afraid enough*.

"Fear isn't necessarily negative," he continued. "There's a positive way of being afraid—and that is to be so afraid of missing the really good things of life that nothing holds you back from trying to get them."

I've never forgotten that minister—I remember his words whenever the old fears of failure, disappointment, or the opinions of others threaten me. I can't say that I've succeeded at all the things I've tried since then, but I've certainly succeeded in many of them.

"*...you haven't been afraid enough*." It's meant a whole new life to me.

Robin James

Too often, people have felt Christianity was a miracle drug to make life miraculously easy, without suffering and pain. The purpose of Christianity is not to avoid difficulty, but to produce a character adequate to meet it when it comes. It does not make life easy; rather it tries to make us great enough for life. It does not give us escape from life's burdens, but strength for meeting them when they come.

James L. Christensen

From THE POSITIVE POWER OF JESUS CHRIST

Norman Vincent Peale

I have been most fortunate in life to have had as friends some very exciting people. One of them whose memory I revere was Grove Patterson, one-time editor of the *Toledo Blade*, a famous newspaper executive, great writer, and dynamic Christian. I worked for him as a reporter on the old *Detroit Journal* and he became a lifelong friend from whom I learned much.

When fresh out of college I went to work for him. "Have you had any experience in journalism?" he asked.

"Oh, yes," I replied. "I was associate editor of my college paper." Whereupon he told me to repeat after him the statement, "I know nothing at all about journalism," which I proceeded meekly to do. He then said he was going to give me a lesson in writing. With his pencil he put a dot on a sheet of white paper. "Know what that is?" he asked.

"It's a dot," I said.

"No, it is a period, the greatest literary device known to man. When you have finished a sentence—and always make it a short sentence—put down a period. Never run on and on. Always make your story interesting, factual, and honest. Tell only the truth. Be a reliable reporter and writer. Use short words, a simple yet graphic style, and be succinct. Let us say that you have two readers—one a digger of ditches and the other a university professor. To which will you write? To the less educated, of course; the better educated will understand.

"Now, son," he said one day, "I detect some self-doubt in you." Apparently my old inferiority complex was showing through. "You seem to come to this office rather dispirited from time to time, as though you were discouraged or even unhappy. For what it may mean to you, I have never had a low moment since one night years ago."

"What happened then?" I asked curiously, for I respected this man highly and grew to love him devotedly. His answer was simple and straightforward, as were all his comments. "I met Jesus Christ that night, and I've been happy and excited ever since. I have had plenty of ups and downs, but He lifted me up from the downs. He is a great Companion. You will never really be dispirited if you stick with Him." So saying, he got up out of his chair, came around the desk, and hit me a kindly whack on the back. "Get out there and enjoy being a reporter," he said, "and remember this: If you practice being excited you will be excited. Make it a habit. People will like you for it, and you will become a great newspaperman."

I explained that I, too, had experienced conversion and was a committed Christian. "It's a matter of depth," he declared. "Surrender to Christ and acceptance of Him as Lord and Savior can give you release from sin and weakness, but to get full joy and the excitement you must let Christ take over in every aspect of your life until no area is left unclaimed by Him, and then the deeper power will come. You apparently still have some fears and some inadequacy feelings. Let them all go by, putting yourself totally into the Lord's hands."

Throughout this period I was struggling within myself because I felt that God was calling me to the ministry. But I was resisting it. Under Mr. Patterson's guidance newspaper work was becoming a thrilling occupation. As a minister's son my memories of some of the unpleasant things about the ministry—ecclesiastical maneuvering, dictatorial laymen, the tendency of some ministers to compel you

to think as they did—had turned me off, at least partially. However, having committed myself to obey God's will and loving Jesus Christ deeply, I felt that, for whatever strange reason I was being called, it was my duty as a Christian to follow the leading of the Holy Spirit.

Accordingly, I went in to tell Mr. Patterson that I had decided, after much agonizing prayer, that God wanted me to preach the gospel and that henceforth his paper would have to struggle along as best it could without my valued service! I thought he bore up right well, but the fact remains that I had not been gone from the *Detroit Journal* but a year or so before it merged with another paper. Mr. Patterson always contended that the departure to the ministry of his young reporter had no connection with the paper's demise.

Mr. Patterson congratulated me upon what he seriously took to be a valid call from God, although he was kind enough to express regret that I was giving up newspaper work. "There will always be printer's ink on your fingers," he warned. Apparently he was right, for I have written twenty-four books, had a national magazine column, write two newspaper columns currently, as well as publish *Guideposts* magazine, now the fourteenth largest publication in the United States with eleven million readers monthly.

"Remember those principles I gave you for writing a newspaper story," Mr. Patterson advised. "Keep your sermon interesting, use words everyone can understand, be succinct, be factual and honest, and put down a period when finished. Those rules apply to sermons as well as to newspaper writing. There is one additional principle that is vital; always be excited—and why not, for you will be talking about the greatest truth in the world; you will be telling people that God loves them and Jesus saves them." In concluding he gave me this comfort: "If you

don't like the ministry or don't do very well at it, come on back to the paper. Your old job will always be waiting for you."

One Sunday early in my long service at Marble Collegiate Church in New York City I looked down from the pulpit and noticed Grove Patterson in the congregation. With my usual strong desire to persuade people about the things of God, I was excitedly talking about the greatness of Jesus and what He can do for anyone. Afterward, as I greeted people in front of the pulpit, along came my old editor. I felt that even if he had to stretch the point a bit he might say something nice about his erstwhile reporter's sermon. Instead, with a dour look he said, "Well, Norman, your old job is still waiting for you!"

Afterward in my study he sat back in an easy chair. "Norman," he said, "you moved me in that sermon by talking straight and simply about God and loving people and about how Jesus can take a surrendered life and make it wonderful. And you were sincere and honest. What you said is so practical, sensible, and down to where people live. You meant every word you said. You were excited and enthusiastic and as a result the power came through. I felt it deeply. Never lose that excitement."

The last time I ever saw this great human being was when we sat together one night on a platform which had been erected in the middle of the Cotton Bowl at Dallas, Texas. He presented me to the crowd of 75,000 persons. As he turned from the podium and I stepped forward to speak, he said, "Make the good old gospel exciting and the power will come down in this huge crowd." I learned much about the positive power of Jesus Christ from Grove Patterson, top newspaper editor, public speaker extraordinary, magnificent Christian, and beloved friend.

So nigh is grandeur to our dust,
So near is God to man,
When Duty whispers low, "Thou must,"
The youth replies, "I can."

Ralph Waldo Emerson

ANNIE SULLIVAN, A FRIEND

Margaret Chase Smith and H. Paul Jeffers

Annie Sullivan's family moved to America from Ireland in the 1860's in the hope of escaping poverty, but they discovered that they had simply moved from one place of poverty to another. To make matters worse, when Annie was three, she began having trouble with her eyes. "Trachoma," a doctor called the disease, an infection which spread rapidly through slum neighborhoods.

Annie was not the only member of the Sullivan family who was sick. Her mother died of tuberculosis and her little brother Jimmie was crippled by the same disease. After her mother's death, Annie's father looked to his relatives for help in caring for Annie, Jimmie, and baby Mary.

In spite of their good intentions the Sullivans couldn't cope with the two handicapped children. They decided to send them to the Massachusetts State Infirmary— the poorhouse. The little boy died there, leaving Annie the only child among many old people in the poorhouse.

A solitary little girl in a strange and older world, Annie grew more and more lonely as her eyes grew weaker. The women in the ward, realizing that Annie was going blind, shook their heads. "Poor little thing," they said, "if she can't see, she'll never learn anything."

Hearing the old women call her a poor little thing, Annie Sullivan threw herself onto her bed and cried. "I can't stay here," she thought. "I have to get away."

One day official investigators came to the poorhouse. As they passed her bed, Annie strained her eyes to make something out of the gray shapes in front of her. Suddenly, the shadowy figures moved away from her. They were leaving the ward. Annie screamed.

Startled, the men turned to see who was making such a noise. They saw Annie groping toward them, her small hands grabbing at the air, reaching for the gray shapes. "I want to go to school," she cried.

"Poor little thing," the voice said.

After that, Annie heard no more voices. The gray shapes went away. Again she was alone. Then, a few days later, there was a stir in the women's ward. "Where's Annie?" someone asked. "Tell her to get her things. She's leaving. She's going to school."

Annie could hardly believe her ears.

"One of the men who was here," a woman said excitedly. "He's fixed it so you can go to the Perkins School in Boston. A school for the blind!"

On October 3, 1880, Annie Sullivan started school. She learned to read with her fingertips. She learned the special system of writing for the blind—Braille. She learned how to spell, how to add, how to subtract. She learned as much as she could.

"I think we can do something about your eyes, Annie," a doctor said to her one day. "You need two operations. Your vision won't be perfect, but you should be able to see again."

Waking up in her hospital bed after the final operation, Annie was afraid. Layer after layer, the white gauze had been removed. Annie kept her eyes closed for a moment. Then, slowly, she opened them, waiting for the gray shapes.

A bright light! Brighter than anything she had seen in years! "I can see the window," she exclaimed. "And there's a tree outside. And the river, too."

They were blurred, as they would be if she were looking through a glass of water. But she could see.

TURNING POINTS

There was so much to see, so much to learn, so much to do. Suddenly, Annie was no longer a little girl but a young woman. She would soon be leaving the Perkins School. But what could a half-blind young woman do to earn a living?

Annie spent her last summer before leaving the Perkins School at a friend's beach house on Cape Cod. There she received a letter from the Director of the Perkins School.

Would Annie be interested in taking care of a little blind girl in Alabama? Would she like to try teaching the child?

"I hear this seven-year-old girl, Helen Keller, is a terror. She always gets her own way because her parents feel so sorry for her," the Director warned.

Annie smiled as she read the letter. She remembered what a brat she had been at seven. But she also remembered how lonely.

Arriving at Tuscumbia, Alabama, on March 3, 1887, Annie Sullivan was greeted by Mrs. Keller. "Thank God, someone's going to try to help the poor little thing," Mrs. Keller said.

Annie turned and angrily flared, "Don't let anybody call her a poor little thing anymore."

"I very soon made up my mind that I could do nothing with Helen in the midst of the family," Annie wrote in a letter to the Director of the Perkins School. She added that she and Helen were living in a little garden house about a quarter of a mile from the main house. "We had a terrific tussle, I can tell you," she wrote. "The struggle lasted for nearly two hours . . . but I am a little stronger and quite as obstinate when I set out."

At the same time, Annie was beginning the process of teaching Helen how to spell. By forming letters of the alphabet with her fingers placed against Helen's palm, Annie was able to teach how to imitate her and also spell the words. Helen, of course, did not know that the motions she was making with her fingers were letters and that the letters were words and that words have meaning. It was just another game. Annie was unable to straighten out the confusion until one bright, warm morning in April, 1887.

"This morning, while she was washing," Annie wrote, "she wanted to know the name for water. We went out to the pumphouse, and I made Helen hold her mug under the spout while I pumped. As the cold water gushed forth, filling the mug, I spelled 'w-a- t-e-r' in Helen's free hand. The word coming so close upon the sensation of cold water rushing over her hand seemed to startle her."

Helen was amazed. She dropped her mug. Reaching out for Annie's apron, she held out her hand. Annie spelled the word for her again. The little girl smiled and then dropped to the ground, pounded her fist on it, and then held out her hand to her teacher. Annie spelled the new word. The pump was next. Then a trellis. And, at last, Helen pointed to Annie herself. "T-e-a-c-h-e-r," Annie spelled with the sign language. "T-e-a-c-h-e-r," Helen responded.

The game of words was over. For the first time in her life, Helen Keller was no longer alone in a dark world. No one was happier at that moment than Annie Sullivan.

From THE ETERNAL GOODNESS

I see the wrong that round me lies,
    I feel the guilt within;
I hear, with groan and travail-cries,
    The world confess its sin.

Yet, in the maddening maze of things,
    And tossed by storm and flood,
To one fixed trust my spirit clings:
    I know that God is good!

John Greenleaf Whittier

From TO LIVE AGAIN

Catherine Marshall

When a deep injury to the spirit has been sustained, the tendency of the sorrowing is to shut the heart and bar the door lest hurt be heaped upon hurt. Yet isolation is not the way toward mental health. Of course, the newly bereaved person needs periods of stabilizing solitude both for physical rest and to gain perspective. But in between times, he needs to accept as fully as he can the love that flows from friends and family.

The truth is that this spontaneous sympathy from other human beings is only a small token, a pale reflection of the great heart of a compassionate and understanding Father. And God's love is always a healing love. The one who—almost involuntarily— shuts his heart against his friends and lets bitterness creep in is, in a tragic way, insulating himself against that reenergizing love of God.

When my own private crisis came, I certainly knew nothing about the way out of grief. I had never heard that psychologists and psychiatrists consider the matter of establishing new patterns of interaction with other human beings one of the most important laws for recovery.

Part of the miracle of God's direction was the fact that I was enabled immediately after my husband's death to open my heart wider than ever before. For the temperament with which I was born was that of a deep reserve; I was not naturally endowed with the gregariousness and outgoingness of my husband.

Yet on the fateful January 25, within an hour after I had returned home from the hospital, friends began dropping in. One couple, who had been particularly fond of Peter, sought me out in my bedroom. I remember that the young wife, her cheeks wet with tears, threw her arms around my neck. "Darling," she cried, "I love you so.

We're going to have to stick awfully close together now."

My split-second choice at the moment was made by instinct—not in my conscious mind at all. It was a choice of whether or not I would merely politely tolerate such an overflowing exuberance of love—or really accept it. In yielding to it, I found a oneness with all human beings, a kinship with all suffering in the world—an authentic glimpse of the Kingdom of God actually at work in a given community.

And so I opened wide the door of the Manse. People came with warm handclasps and tear-filled eyes. And somehow, they found in our home an atmosphere that dried their eyes. The gap of Peter's absence was sorely felt. But the love that flowed like a great tidal wave through the Christian community that was our church family, blessed us all.

It is God alone who can finally heal the brokenhearted. Grief is a real wound, a mutilation, a gaping hole in the human spirit. After all, the ties that bind parents to children, brothers to sisters, and husbands to wives are the deepest of bonds, as real as love is real. Some beloved person has been wrested, torn bodily from one's life. The hurt is none the less real because the family physician cannot probe it; Christ alone is Physician to the spirit.

CONSOLATION

There is never a day so dreary
 But God can make it bright,
And unto the soul that trusts Him,
 He giveth songs in the night.
There is never a path so hidden,
 But God can lead the way,
If we seek for the Spirit's guidance
 And patiently wait and pray.

There is never a cross so heavy
 But the nail-scarred hands are there

Outstretched in tender compassion
 The burden to help us bear.
There is never a heart so broken,
 But the loving Lord can heal.
The heart that was pierced on Calvary
 Doth still for his loved ones feel.

There is never a life so darkened,
 So hopeless and unblessed,
But may be filled with the light of God
 And enter His promised rest.
There is never a sin or sorrow,
 There is never a care or loss,
But that we may bring to Jesus
 And leave at the foot of the cross.

Author Unknown

THE DIAMOND NECKLACE

Guy de Maupassant

She was one of those pretty, charming young ladies, born as if through an error of destiny, into a family of clerks. She had no dowry, no hopes, no means of becoming known, appreciated, loved, and married by a man either rich or distinguished; and she allowed herself to marry a petty clerk in the office of the Board of Education.

She was simple, not being able to adorn herself; but she was unhappy, as one out of her class; for women belong to no caste, no race; their grace, their beauty, and their charm serving them in the place of birth and family. Their inborn finesse, their instinctive elegance, their suppleness of wit are their only aristocracy, making some daughters of the people the equal of great ladies.

She suffered incessantly, feeling herself born for all delicacies and luxuries. She suffered from the poverty of her apartment, the shabby walls, the worn chairs, and the faded stuffs. All these things, which another woman of her station would not have noticed, tortured and angered her. The sight of the little Breton, who made this humble home, awoke in her sad regrets and desperate dreams. She thought of quiet antechambers, with their Oriental hangings, lighted by high, bronze torches, and of the two great footmen in short trousers who sleep in the large armchairs, made sleepy by the heavy air from the heating apparatus. She thought of large drawing rooms, hung in old silks, of graceful pieces of furniture carrying bric-a-brac of inestimable value, and of the little perfumed coquettish apartments, made for five o'clock chats with most intimate friends, men known and sought after, whose attention all women envied and desired.

When she seated herself for dinner, before the round table where the tablecloth had been used three days, opposite her husband who uncovered the tureen with a delighted air, saying: "Oh! the good potpie! I know of nothing better than that—" she would think of the elegant dinners, of the shining silver, of the tapestries peopling the walls with ancient personages and rare birds in the midst of fairy forests; she thought of the exquisite food served on marvelous dishes, of the whispered gallantries, listened to with the smile of the sphinx, while eating the rose-colored flesh of the trout or a chicken's wing.

She had neither frocks nor jewels, nothing. And she loved only those things. She felt that she was made for them. She had such a desire to please, to be sought after, to be clever, and courted.

She had a rich friend, a schoolmate at the convent, whom she did not like to visit, she suffered so much when she returned. And she wept for whole days from chagrin, from regret, from despair, and disappointment.

One evening her husband returned elated bearing in his hand a large envelope.

"Here," he said, "here is something for you."

She quickly tore open the wrapper and drew out a printed card on which were inscribed these words:

"The Minister of Public Instruction and Madame George Ramponneau ask the honor of Mr. and Mrs. Loisel's company Monday evening, January 18, at the Minister's residence."

Instead of being delighted, as her husband had hoped, she threw the invitation spitefully upon the table murmuring:

"What do you suppose I want with that?"

"But, my dearie, I thought it would make you happy. You never go out, and this is an occasion, and a fine one! I had a great deal of trouble to get it. Everybody wishes one, and it is very select; not many are given to employees. You will see the whole official world there."

She looked at him with an irritated eye and declared impatiently:

"What do you suppose I have to wear to such a thing as that?"

He had not thought of that; he stammered:

"Why, the dress you wear when we go to the theater. It seems very pretty to me—"

He was silent, stupefied, in dismay, at the sight of his wife weeping. Two great tears fell slowly from the corners of his eyes toward the corners of his mouth; he stammered:

"What is the matter? What is the matter?"

By a violent effort, she had controlled her vexation and responded in a calm voice, wiping her moist cheeks:

"Nothing. Only I have no dress and consequently I cannot go to this affair. Give your card to some colleague whose wife is better fitted out than I."

He was grieved, but answered:

"Let us see, Matilda. How much would a suitable costume cost, something that would serve for other occasions, something very simple?"

She reflected for some seconds, making estimates and thinking of a sum that she could ask for without bringing with it an immediate refusal and a frightened exclamation from the economical clerk.

Finally she said, in a hesitating voice:

"I cannot tell exactly, but it seems to me that four hundred francs ought to cover it."

He turned a little pale, for he had saved just this sum to buy a gun that he might be able to join some hunting parties the next summer, on the plains of Nanterre, with some friends who went to shoot larks up there on Sundays. Nevertheless, he answered:

"Very well, I will give you four hundred francs. But try to have a pretty dress."

The day of the ball approached and Mme. Loisel seemed sad, disturbed, anxious. Nevertheless, her dress was nearly ready. Her husband said to her one evening:

"What is the matter with you? You have acted strangely for two or three days."

And she responded: "I am vexed not to have a jewel, not one stone, nothing to adorn myself with. I shall have such a poverty-laden look. I would prefer not to go to this party."

He replied: "You can wear some natural flowers. At this season they look very *chic*. For ten francs you can have two or three magnificent roses."

She was not convinced. "No," she replied, "there is nothing more humiliating than to have a shabby air in the midst of rich women."

Then her husband cried out: "How stupid we are! Go and find your friend Mrs.

Forestier and ask her to lend you her jewels. You are well enough acquainted with her to do this."

She uttered a cry of joy: "It is true!" she said. "I had not thought of that."

The next day she took herself to her friend's house and related her story of distress. Mrs. Forestier went to her closet with the glass doors, took out a large jewel case, brought it, opened it, and said: "Choose, my dear."

She saw at first some bracelets, then a collar of pearls, then a Venetian cross of gold and jewels and of admirable workmanship. She tried the jewels before the glass, hesitated, but could neither decide to take them nor leave them. Then she asked:

"Have you nothing more?"

"Why, yes. Look for yourself; I do not know what will please you."

Suddenly she discovered, in a black satin box, a superb necklace of diamonds, and her heart beat fast with an immoderate desire. Her hands trembled as she took them up. She placed them about her throat against her dress, and remained in ecstasy before them. Then she asked, in a hesitating voice, full of anxiety:

"Could you lend me this? Only this?"

"Why, yes, certainly."

She fell upon the neck of her friend, embraced her with passion, then went away with her treasure.

The day of the ball arrived. Mme. Loisel was a great success. She was the prettiest of all, elegant, gracious, smiling, and full of joy. All the men noticed her, asked her name, and wanted to be presented. All the members of the Cabinet wished to waltz with her. The Minister of Education paid her some attention.

She danced with enthusiasm, with

passion, intoxicated with pleasure, thinking of nothing, in the triumph of her beauty, in the glory of her success, in a kind of cloud of happiness that came of all this homage, and all this admiration, of all these awakened desires, and this victory so complete and sweet to the heart of woman.

She went home toward four o'clock in the morning. Her husband had been half asleep in one of the little salons since midnight, with three other gentlemen whose wives were enjoying themselves very much.

He threw around her shoulders the wraps they had carried for the coming home, modest garments of everyday wear, whose poverty clashed with the elegance of the ball costume. She felt this and wished to hurry away in order not to be noticed by the other women who were wrapping themselves in rich furs.

Loisel retained her: "Wait," said he. "You will catch cold out there. I am going to call a cab."

But she would not listen and descended the steps rapidly. When they were in the street, they found no carriage; and they began to seek for one, hailing the coachmen whom they saw at a distance.

They walked along toward the Seine, hopeless and shivering. Finally they found on the dock one of those old, nocturnal *coupes* that one sees in Paris after nightfall, as if they were ashamed of their misery by day.

It took them as far as their door in Martyr Street, and they went wearily up to their apartment. It was all over for her. And on his part, he remembered that he would have to be at the office by ten o'clock.

She removed the wraps from her shoulders before the glass, for a final view of herself in her glory. Suddenly she uttered a cry. Her necklace was not around her neck.

Her husband, already half undressed,

asked: "What is the matter?"

She turned toward him excitedly:

"I have—I have—I no longer have Mrs. Forestier's necklace."

He arose in dismay: "What! How is that? It is not possible."

And they looked in the folds of the dress, in the folds of the mantle, in the pockets, everywhere. They could not find it.

He asked: "You are sure you still had it when we left the house?"

"Yes, I felt it in the vestibule as we came out."

"But if you had lost it in the street, we should have heard it fall. It must be in the cab."

"Yes. It is probable. Did you take the number?"

"No. And you, did you notice what it was?"

"No."

They looked at each other utterly cast down. Finally, Loisel dressed himself again.

"I am going," said he, "over the track where we went on foot, to see if I can find it."

And he went. She remained in her evening gown, not having the force to go to bed, stretched upon a chair, without ambition or thoughts.

Toward seven o'clock her husband returned. He had found nothing.

He went to the police and to the cab offices, and put an advertisement in the newspapers, offering a reward; he did everything that afforded them a suspicion of hope.

She waited all day in a state of bewilderment before this frightful disaster. Loisel returned at evening with his face harrowed and pale; and had discovered nothing.

"It will be necessary," said he, "to write to your friends that you have broken the clasp of the necklace and that you will have it repaired. That will give us time to turn

around." She wrote as he dictated.

At the end of a week, they had lost all hope. And Loisel, older by five years, declared:

"We must take measures to replace this jewel."

The next day they took the box, which had inclosed it, to the jeweler whose name was on the inside. He consulted his books:

"It is not I, Madame," said he, "who sold this necklace; I only furnished the casket."

Then they went from jeweler to jeweler seeking a necklace like the other one, consulting their memories, and ill, both of them, with chagrin and anxiety.

In a shop off the Palais-Royal, they found a chaplet of diamonds which seemed to them exactly like the one they had lost. It was valued at forty thousand francs. They could get it for thirty-six thousand.

They begged the jeweler not to sell it for three days. And they made an arrangement by which they might return it for thirty-four thousand francs if they found the other one before the end of February.

Loisel possessed eighteen thousand francs which his father had left him. He borrowed the rest.

He borrowed it, asking for a thousand francs of one, five hundred of another, five louis of this one, and three louis of that one. He gave notes, made ruinous promises, took money of usurers and the whole race of lenders. He compromised his whole existence, in fact, risked his signature, without even knowing whether he could make it good or not, and, harassed by anxiety for the future, by the black misery which surrounded him, and by the prospect of all physical privations and moral torture, he went to get the new necklace, depositing on the merchant's counter thirty-six thousand francs.

When Mrs. Loisel took back the jewels to Mrs. Forestier, the latter said to her in a frigid tone:

"You should have returned them to me sooner, for I might have needed them."

She did open the jewel box as her friend feared she would. If she should perceive the substitution, what would she think? What should she say? Would she take her for a robber?

Mrs. Loisel now knew the horrible life of necessity. She did her part, however, completely, heroically. It was necessary to pay this frightful debt. She would pay it. They sent away the maid; they changed their lodgings; they rented some rooms under a mansard roof.

She learned the heavy cares of a household, the odious work of a kitchen. She washed the dishes, using her rosy nails upon the greasy pots and the bottoms of the stewpans. She washed the soiled linen, the chemises and dishcloths, which she hung on the line to dry; she took down the refuse to the street each morning and brought up the water, stopping at each landing to breathe. And, clothed like a woman of the people, she went to the grocer's, the butcher's, and the fruiterer's, with her basket on her arm, shopping, haggling to the last sou her miserable money.

Every month it was necessary to renew some notes, thus obtaining time, and to pay others.

The husband worked evenings, putting the books of some merchants in order; and nights he often did copying at five sous a page.

And this life lasted for ten years.

At the end of ten years, they had restored all, all, with interest of the usurer, and accumulated interest besides.

Mrs. Loisel seemed old now. She had become a strong, hard woman, the crude woman of the poor household. Her hair badly dressed, her skirts awry, her hands red, she spoke in a loud tone, and washed the floors in large pails of water. But sometimes, when her husband was at the office, she would seat herself before the window and think of that evening party of former times, of that ball where she was so beautiful and so flattered.

How would it have been if she had not lost that necklace? Who knows? Who knows? How singular is life, and how full of changes! How small a thing will ruin or save one!

One Sunday, as she was taking a walk in the Champs-Elysées to rid herself of the cares of the week, she suddenly perceived a woman walking with a child. It was Mrs. Forestier, still young, still pretty, still attractive. Mrs. Loisel was affected. Should she speak to her? Yes, certainly. And now that she had paid, she would tell her all. Why not?

She approached her. "Good morning, Jeanne."

Her friend did not recognize her and was astonished to be so familiarly addressed by this common personage. She stammered:

"But, Madame—I do not know— You must be mistaken—"

"No, I am Matilda Loisel."

Her friend uttered a cry of astonishment: "Oh! My poor Matilda! How you have changed—"

"Yes, I have had some hard days since I saw you: and some miserable ones—and all because of you—"

"Because of me? How is that?"

"You recall the diamond necklace that you loaned me to wear to the Commissioner's ball?"

"Yes, very well."

"Well, I lost it."

"How is that, since you returned it to me?"

"I returned another to you exactly like it. And it has taken us ten years to pay for it. You can understand that it was not easy for

us who have nothing. But it is finished and I am decently content."

Madame Forestier stopped short. She said:

"You say that you bought a diamond necklace to replace mine?"

"Yes. You did not perceive it then? They were just alike."

And she smiled with a proud and simple joy. Madame Forestier was touched and took both her hands as she replied:

"Oh! my poor Matilda! Mine were false. They were not worth over five hundred francs!"

VICTORY IN DEFEAT

Defeat may serve as well as victory
  To shake the soul and let the glory out.
When the great oak is straining in the wind,
  The boughs drink in new beauty, and the trunk
Sends down a deeper root on the windward side.
  Only the soul that knows the mighty grief
Can know the mighty rapture. Sorrows come
  To stretch out spaces in the heart for joy.

Edwin Markham

JOY OF LIFE

The joy of life is living it and doing things of worth,
In making bright and fruitful all the barren spots of earth.
In facing odds and mastering them and rising from defeat,
And making true what once was false, and what was bitter, sweet.
For only he knows perfect joy whose little bit of soil
Is richer ground than what it was when he began to toil.

Author Unknown

INTERVIEW WITH AN IMMORTAL

Arthur Gordon

The month was June, the English weather was blue and gold. The world was young, and so was I. But, driving down from Oxford in the old Sunbeam I had borrowed for the occasion, I felt my assurance deserting me.

The great man was almost a recluse now, and it was said that he did not care for Americans. Through a mutual friend I had managed to secure permission to visit him. Now as I neared the little village of Burwash, where he lived, I began to experience something like stage fright. And when I found the sombre seventeenth-century house and saw my host walking down to the gate to meet me, I grew so flustered that I hardly knew whether to shake hands or turn and run.

He was so small! The crown of the floppy hat he wore was not much higher than my shoulder, and I doubt if he weighed 120 pounds. His skin was dark for an Englishman's; his mustache was almost white. His eyebrows were as thick and tangled as marsh grass, but behind the gold-rimmed glasses his eyes were as bright as a terrier's. He was sixty-nine years old.

He saw instantly how ill at ease I was. "Come in, come in," he said companionably, opening the gate. "I was just going to inspect my navy." A Scottie came bounding down the path and stopped short when he saw me. "Now, this," his master said, "is Malachi. He's really quite friendly. But of course, being a Scot, he hates to show it."

He led me, still speechless, to a pond at the end of the garden, and there was the so-called navy: a six-foot skiff with hand-cranked paddle wheels. "You can be the engine room," he said. "I'll be the passenger list."

I was so agitated that I cranked too hard. The paddle wheel broke and there I was,

marooned in the middle of a fishpond with Rudyard Kipling. He began to laugh, and so did I, and the ice was broken.

A gardener finally rescued us with a long rake. By then my host had me talking. There was something about him that drove the shyness out of you, a kind of understanding that went deeper than words and set up an instantaneous closeness. It was odd; we couldn't have been more different. He was British; I was American. He was near the end of an illustrious road; I was at the beginning of an obscure one. He had had years of ill health and pain; I was untouched by either. He knew nothing about me—there was nothing to know. I knew all about him, and so to me he was not just a fragile little man in a toy boat. He was Kim and Fuzzy-Wuzzy and Gunga Din. He was Danny Deever and the Elephant's Child. He was the dawn coming up like thunder on the road to Mandalay; he was the rough laughter of the barrack room, the chatter of the bazaar and the great organ tones of "Recessional." To me he was, quite simply, a miracle, and no doubt this showed in my dazzled eyes, and he felt it and was warmed by it.

I had had an ulterior motive in coming, of course. I wanted to meet him for himself, but I was also a puzzled and unsure young man. I had in my pocket a letter offering me a job as instructor in an American university. I didn't really want to be a teacher; I knew I didn't have the selflessness or the patience. What I wanted to be, ultimately, was a writer. But the teaching job was the only offer I had. I had no other prospects, no money at all. At home, the dead hand of the Great Depression still lay heavy on the land. Should I play it safe, and say yes to the offer?

What I wanted desperately was for someone of great wisdom and experience in the field of letters to tell me what to do.

But I knew this was a preposterous responsibility to thrust upon a stranger. And so I waited, hoping that somehow the heavens would open and the miracle of certainty would descend upon me.

While I waited, he talked. And, as he talked, I began to forget about my problems. He tossed words into the air, and they flashed like swords. He spoke of his friendship with Cecil Rhodes, through whose generosity I had gone to Oxford. "They say we were both imperialists," said Kipling a little grimly. "Well, maybe we were. The word is out of fashion now, and some Englishmen are weak enough to be ashamed of it. I'm not." He questioned me almost sharply about some poets of prominence: Eliot, Stein, Cummings. I said I thought they were good.

"Do you?" he asked guilelessly. "Quote me a few lines."

I sat there, helpless, and he laughed. "You see," he said, "that's the trouble with verse that doesn't rhyme. But let's not be too harsh where poets are concerned. They have to live in no-man's land, halfway between dreams and reality."

"Like Mowgli," I said impulsively, thinking of the brown-skinned boy torn between village and jungle.

He gave me a look with his blue eyes. "Like most of us," he said.

He talked of ambition, of how long it took fully to master any art or craft. And of secondary ambitions: the more you had, he said, the more fully you lived. "I always wanted to build or buy a 400-ton brig," he said reflectively, "and sail her round the world. Never did. Now, I suppose, it's too late.

"Do the things you really want to do if you possibly can. Don't wait for circumstances to be exactly right. You'll find that they never are.

"My other unrealized ambition," he went on, "was to be an archaeologist. For sheer,

gem-studded romance, no other job can touch it. Why, right under our feet here in Sussex...."

He described how he had decided to sink a well. A few feet down, they found a Jacobean tobacco pipe. Below that, a Cromwellian latten spoon. Still farther down, a Roman horse bit. And, finally, water.

We went back to his study, a large square room lined with bookcases on two sides. There were his desk, his chair, an enormous wastebasket and his pens—the kind you dip in ink. At right angles to the fireplace was a small sofa. "I lie there," he said with a smile, "and wait for my daemon to tell me what to do."

"Daemon?"

He shrugged. "Intuition. Subconscious. Whatever you want to call it."

"Can you always hear him?"

"No," he said slowly. "Not always. But I learned long ago that it's best to wait until you do. When your daemon says nothing, he usually means no."

Mrs. Kipling called us to lunch, and afterward I felt I should take my leave. But Kipling would not hear of it. "I'm still full of talk," he said. "You've eaten my salt, so now you must be my audience."

So we talked. Or rather, he talked while I made super-human efforts to remember everything. He had a way of thrusting a harsh truth at you and then, in the next breath, beguiling you into a wry acceptance of it. "If you're endowed," he said at one point, "with any significant energies or talent, you may as well resign yourself to the fact that throughout your life you will be carrying coattail riders who will try to exploit you. But instead of fuming and fretting about this you'd better thank God for the qualities that attract the parasites, and not waste time trying to shake them off."

We talked of friendship; he thought young ones were best and lasted longest.

"When you're young," he said, "you're not afraid to give yourself away. You offer warmth and vitality and sympathy without thinking. Later on, you begin to weigh what you give."

I said, somewhat diffidently, that he was giving me a lot, and his eyes twinkled. "A fair exchange. You're giving me attention. That's a form of affection, you know."

Looking back, I think he knew that in my innocence I was eager to love everything and please everybody, and he was trying to warn me not to lose my own identity in the process. Time after time he came back to this theme. "The individual has always had to struggle to keep from being overwhelmed by the tribe. To be your own man is a hard business. If you try it, you'll be lonely often, and sometimes frightened. But no price is too high to pay for the privilege of owning yourself."

Suddenly the shadows were long on the grass. When I stood up to go, I remembered the letter in my pocket and the advice I had thought I wanted. But now there was nothing to ask. *Do the things you really want to do.... Don't wait for circumstances to be exactly right.... When your daemon says nothing, he usually means no.... No price is too high to pay for the privilege of owning yourself.*

I knew, now, that I would refuse the teaching job and wait for my daemon to speak clearly to me.

We walked to the gate, Malachi scampering ahead of us. My host held out his hand. "Thank you," he said. "You've done me good."

The thought that I could have done anything for him was beyond my grasp. I thanked him and climbed into the old Sunbeam. I looked back once. He was still standing there in his floppy hat, a great little man who forgot his own illness and his own problems and spent a whole day trying to help a troubled and self-conscious boy from across the sea.

He had a gift for young friendships, all right. He gave me much more than advice. He gave me a little bit of himself to carry away. After all these years, I feel the warmth of it still.

LEAD, KINDLY LIGHT

Lead, Kindly Light, amid th' encircling
    gloom,
    Lead thou me on!
The night is dark, and I am far from home;
    Lead thou me on!
Keep thou my feet; I do not ask to see
The distant scene; one step enough for me.

I was not ever thus, nor prayed that thou
    Shouldst lead me on;
I loved to choose and see my path; but now
    Lead thou me on!
I loved the garish day, and, spite of fears,
Pride ruled my will. Remember not past
    years!

So long thy power hath blest me, sure it still
    Will lead me on
O'er moor and fen, o'er crag and torrent,
    till
    The night is gone,
And with the morn those angel faces smile,
Which I have loved long since, and lost
    awhile.

John Henry Newman

THE ANCIENT CRY

Long centuries have passed, yet still this
    morning
    The ancient cry sounds on the startled
    air,
Crystal-clear it rings: "The Christ is risen!"
    And hurt hearts are rejoicing
    everywhere.
After last Friday's tragedy and sorrow,
    After our many doubts and blinding
    fears,

To hear the glad cry sounding down the
    ages
    Should lift grief's bondage, and should
    dry our tears.

"The Christ is risen!" four brief words so
    vital
    To bewildered mankind in this hour of
    need!
He said: "Because I live ye shall live also."
    And truly the Christ is risen, is risen
    indeed.
Cry out the message to earth's farthest
    outpost,
    Let none believe the blessed Christ is
    dead.
Make it a joyous hallelujah chorus:
    "He is risen! He is risen as He said."

Grace Noll Crowell

FAMILY

A FRAGILE MOMENT...

A gap is just a space between two points. That's how the dictionary might put it. Our gap is supposed to be between the point of view of our young people and the point of view of middle-aged or old people. Right? It is a *generation* gap. It's nothing new. It has been around for a long, long time. We are all born as babies; we all become children; we all become adults. That's been fact for thousands of years. It didn't just pop up in the last five or ten years—or since rock music was born! As a teen- ager I used to rock and roll mightily to the tune of "St. Louis Blues"; my mother would hold her ears and say, "Do you call *that* music?" I thought she didn't understand me—that she was an old fogey. When I got to be twenty-one, I wondered how she got so smart so quick!

Dale Evans Rogers

A PARENT'S PRAYER

Abigail Van Buren

Oh, God, make me a better parent. Help me to understand my children, to listen patiently to what they have to say and to understand all their questions kindly. Keep me from interrupting them, talking back to them, and contradicting them. Make me as courteous to them as I would have them be to me. Give me the courage to confess my sins against my children and ask them forgiveness when I know that I have done wrong.

May I not vainly hurt the feelings of my children. Forbid that I should laugh at their mistakes, or resort to shame and ridicule as punishment. Let me not tempt a child to lie and steal. So guide me hour by hour that I may demonstrate by all I say and do that honesty produces happiness.

Reduce, I pray, the meanness in me. May I cease to nag; and when I am out of sorts, help me, O Lord, to hold my tongue. Blind me to the little errors of my children as those of their own age, and let me not exact of them the judgments and conventions of adults. Allow me not to rob them of the opportunity to wait upon themselves, to think, to choose, and to make their own decisions.

Forbid that I should ever punish them for my selfish satisfaction. May I grant them all their wishes that are reasonable and have

the courage always to withold a privilege which I know will do them harm.

Make me so fair and just, so considerate and companionable to my children that they will have genuine esteem for me. Fit me to be loved and imitated by my children. Oh, God, do give me calm and poise and self-control.

LEAD HER LIKE A PIGEON

Jessamyn West

It was deep in May. Fingers had lifted the green strawberry leaves and had found fruit beneath them. Wheat was heading up. Cherries, bright as Christmas candles, hung from the trees. The bees had swarmed twice. The wind was from the south and sent a drift of locust blossoms like summer snow—Mattie thought—through the air.

She left her churn on the back porch and stood for a minute by the spring house with uplifted face to see how locust-snow felt; but the wind died down and no more blossoms fell, so she went back to her churning.

She counted slowly as she moved the dasher up and down. She was keeping track of the least and most strokes it took to bring butter. This at any rate was not going to be a least-time. "Eighty-eight, eighty- nine . . ." Little Jess was putting horsehairs in the rain barrel to turn into worms. Enoch stuck his head out of the barn door, saw her and directly pulled it in again.

"Mattie," called her mother, "get finished with thy churning and ride over the Bents' with some rocks."

Mattie could smell the rocks baking: raisins and hickory nuts all bedded down together in sweet dough.

"Lavony Bent's as queer as Dick's hatband," her mother called above the slap and gurgle of the dasher, "half Indian and a newcomer. She needs a token to show she's welcome."

Listening, Mattie slowed her churning. "Bring that butter humping," her mother said. "Thee'll have to get a soon start or it'll get dark on thee." She came to the kitchen door, rosy from the oven's heat, bringing Mattie a new-baked rock. "Day fading so soon," she said.

Mattie looked at her mother because of the sadness in her voice, and felt uncertainty and sorrow herself.

"There'll be another to match it tomorrow," her mother promised. "Its equal or better, Mattie. That red sky's a sure sign."

The butter was slow coming, only five strokes short of the most she'd ever counted. "Thee'd best go as thee is, Mattie."

"In this?" said Mattie.

"Who's to see?" asked her mother. "None but Bents and hoot-owls at this hour."

Mattie wouldn't've named them together—hoot-owls and the black-haired, brown-faced boys she'd watched walking riverward with fishing poles over their shoulders.

"Once thee starts combing and changing it'll be nightfall."

So Mattie rode as she was to the Bent's, barefooted and in her blue anchor print which had faded until the anchors were almost as pale as the sea that lapped about them.

She carried the rocks in a little wooden box her mother was fixing to make into a footstool. So far, it was only painted white, with cranes and cattails on each side. The brown cattails were set onto the box with so much paint that they curved up plump as real ones beneath Mattie's exploring thumb.

Old Polly walked like a horse in a dream . . . slow . . . slow . . . with forever to arrive. Tonight, a short way on the pike and then across the wood lot. Mattie ate a rock, pulled down a limb to see it spring back in place . . . remembered what she'd heard about the Bents . . . .

"Never seen a more comfortable sight in my life," her father called one day, and there on a padded chair was Jud Bent riding down the pike in his manure wagon sitting and reading like a man at ease in his parlor. "Wonderful emancipation," her father said. "Thee mark it, Mattie. The spirit of man's got no limitations."

Jud Bent read and farmed. His boys, all but Gardiner, fished and farmed. "Gardiner's a reader like his pa," said Mattie's father, "off to Normal studying to be a teacher. He figures on getting shut off the manure wagon and having just the book left."

But the day she rode through was more to Mattie than her destination. In the woods it was warm and sheltered and the sun, setting, lay like butter on the new green leaves.

At the far edge of the woods she stopped for a minute at the old Wright place. A little white tumbling-down house, empty for years, stood there. A forgotten house, but flowers still came up about it in the patterns in which Mrs. Wright had planted them. It was a sad, beautiful sight, Mattie thought, to see flowers hands had planted, growing alone in the woods with not an eye to note whether they did well or not: the snowball bush where the front gate had been, gold-powdered now at sunset, by the ruined upping-block. A pair of doves, as she watched, slid down from the deep shadows of the woods and wheeled about in the sunlit clearing as if coming home.

Mattie stretched a hand to them. "You don't act like wildings," she said.

She slipped down from fat old Polly and carrying her box of cookies went to pick some flags. These flowers and buildings have known people for too long, she thought, to be happy alone. They have grown away from their own kind and forgotten the language of woods and doves and long to hear household words again. To hear at bedtime a woman coming to the door for a sight of stars and saying, "There'll be rain before morning. A circle round the moon and hark to that cock crowing. It's a sure sign."

Or a man at morning, scanning the sky as he hitches up his suspenders, "A weather breeder. Have to hustle the hay in."

Mattie talked for the house and flowers to hear as she gathered the flags and laid them across the top of the cookie-filled footstool.

"If it's a dry summer I'll bring you some water," she said. "I couldn't bear to lie abed a hot night, and you parching here. I'll carry buckets from the branch if the well's dry, and some night I'll come and light a candle in the house so it'll look like olden times. I'll sing a song in the house and it'll be like Mrs. Wright playing on her melodeon again."

"Sing now, why don't you?"

She was bending over the flags, but she wasn't frightened—the voice was so quiet. It was a young man's voice though and she dropped the flags in her hand onto her bare feet before she turned to face him.

"No human would enjoy my singing . . . only maybe an old house that can't be choosy."

"I'm not choosy, either."

"No, I'm on an errand to take some rocks to Lavony Bent. I only stopped to pick some flags."

"Well, I'm Gard Bent," the boy said, "and I'll walk along home with you. What's your name?"

"Martha Truth Birdwell. Only I'm mostly called Mattie."

"Martha Truth Birdwell. That's as pretty as any song. If he'd a known you," and Gardiner Bent held up the book he was carrying, "he'd written a poem called Martha Truth."

Mattie saw the name on the book. "He mostly writes of Jeans and Marys," she said. Now maybe this Bent boy wouldn't think she was a know-nothing, barefooted and

talking to herself. "Thee take the rocks on to thy ma. I've dallied here so long it'll be dark going home through the wood lot."

"No, I'll walk back with you to the pike. Ma'd never forgive me if I let you go home with your box empty. The boys've been on the river this afternoon. They'll have a fine mess of catfish. Can I help you onto your horse?"

Mattie would dearly have liked being handed onto her horse had she been rightly dressed and old Polly saddled, but that would have to wait for another time. She would not be hoisted like a sack of meal, plopped barefooted onto a saddleless horse. She stood stock still, the flags covering her feet, and said nothing.

"I'll get the rest of my books," the boy said.

While he was gone Mattie led old Polly to the upping-block and settled herself as sedately as if she were riding sidesaddle, one bare foot curled daintily beneath her.

Old Polly stepped slowly along in the dusk down the back road that led to the Bents' and Gard walked beside her. There wasn't much Indian about him, Mattie thought, unless it was his black hair and his quiet, toed-in walk. But his hair wasn't Indian straight, and his eyes weren't black at all but the color of the sandstone in a go-to-meeting watch fob. It was a pleasing face, a face she did not tire of regarding. Her eyes searched its tenderness and boldness in the May dusk.

"I thought thee was away at Vernon, studying at the Normal."

"I was—but it's out. Now I'm studying to take the teacher's examinations. I've got the promise of the school at Rush Branch when I pass. That's why I come to Wright's—to study where it's quiet. If it gets dark on you, you could see your way home by the fireflies, they're so thick," he finished, as if ashamed of telling so much of himself.

"Fireflies. Is that what thee calls lightning bugs?"

"Elsewhere they're known as fireflies."

It was full sunset before they reached the Bent place. Lavony Bent was cleaning fish on a stump at the edge of the yard. Jud Bent was on the back steps getting the last of the light on to the book he was reading. Two black-haired boys were rolling about on the ground wrestling; a third was trying to bring a tune from a homemade-looking horn. There weren't any flowers or grass about the Bents' house, but the yard was trodden flat and swept clean as a plum.

Gard called out, "Ma, this is Martha Truth Birdwell come to bring you some cookies."

Mrs. Bent didn't stop her fish cleaning, but looked up kindly enough. "Light down, Martha Truth, light down. I knowed your folks years ago when we's all younger than you are now."

Jud Bent closed his book on his finger and walked over to Mattie. He was a little plump man with a big head of red hair and a silky red mustache. "If it isn't Spring," he said. "Spring riding a white horse and with flowers in her hands."

Mattie was too taken aback to answer, but Gard laughed. "She's got a box of cookies under the flowers, pa."

Mattie handed the box of cookies and the white flags to him. "Spring for looks and Summer for gifts," said Jud Bent and took a rock in two bites, shaking the crumbs from his mustache like a water-drenched dog.

Mattie was afraid to talk to this strange man who carried a book as if it had been a pipe or a jack-knife, and spoke of her as though she were absent, or a painted picture.

Mrs. Bent took the head from a still quivering catfish with a single, clean stroke.

The boy with the horn started a tune she knew, but he couldn't get far with it. "Lead her like a pigeon . . . Lead her like a pigeon . . ." he played over and over. Mattie's ears ached to hear the next notes, have the piece played through to its ending, not left broken and unfinished. "Lead her like a pigeon . . ." Mattie's mind hummed the tune for him . . . "Bed her like a dove . . . Whisper when I'm near her . . . Be my only love . . ." but the horn could not follow. "Lead her like a pigeon," it said once more, then gave up.

The wrestlers groaned and strained. They turned up the earth beneath them like a plow. A catfish leaped from the stump and swam again, most pitifully, in the grass.

"I'll have to be turning homewards," Mattie spoke suddenly. "Could I have my box? Ma's fixing to make a footstool of it."

Mrs. Bent sent Gard into the house to empty the cookies, then she lined the footstool with leaves and filled it with fish.

"There's a mess of fish for your breakfast," she said. "Tell your ma she's so clever at sharing I can't hope to keep pace with her."

As they went out of the yard, Mattie once more on old Polly and Gard walking beside her, Jud Bent called after them, "Persephone and Pluto. Don't eat any pomegranate seeds, Martha Truth."

"What does he mean?" asked Mattie. What Mr. Bent had said didn't sound like English to her.

"Persephone was a girl," Gard said. "The goddess of Spring, and Pluto, another god, stole her away to live underground with him. And while she was gone it was winter on earth."

"She's back on earth now, isn't she?" Mattie asked, watching the fireflies light themselves like candles among the dark leaves.

"Yes, she's back again," Gard said.

They parted at the edge of the woods where Mattie could see the lights of home glimmering down the road. Supper was over when she brought her box of catfish into the kitchen, and the dishes half washed.

"Sit down, child," her mother said, "and have thy supper. What kept thee?"

"The Bents all talk a lot," said Mattie. "It didn't seem polite to go and leave them all talking."

"They'll not be hindered by thy leaving . . . never fear. Eat, eat. Thy food will lose its savor."

"I can't eat," Mattie said. "I don't seem to have any relish for victuals." She got the dishtowel from the rack and started drying.

"Was thee fanciful," asked her mother, who never attributed fright to aught but fancy, "crossing the wood lot?"

"No. Gardiner Bent came with me."

"The Normal School boy?"

"Yes," said Mattie. "He's learned. Flowers. Fireflies. Poetry. Gods and goddesses. It's all one to him," she declared ardently. "He can lay his tongue to anything and give thee a fact about it. Oh, he's full of facts. He's primed for an examination and knows more than he can hold in."

Mattie made the plates she dried fly through her hands like thistledown—as if they were weightless as thistles and as imperishable. Her hands were deft but they had not her mother's flashing grace, and they were silent; they could not play the tune she envied, the tinkling bell-like song of her mother's wedding ring against the china; the constant light clatter of gold against glass and silver that said, I'm a lady grown and mistress of dishes and cupboards.

Behind were the dark woods, shadows and bosky places and whatever might slide

through them when the sun was set. Here, the kitchen, the stove still burning, sending a wash of light across the scrubbed floorboards, the known dishes in her rightful stacks, and ma's ring sounding its quick song of love.

Mattie hummed a little.

"What's thee humming?" her mother asked. "Seems like I've heard it."

" 'Lead Her Like a Pigeon,' " Mattie, smiling, said.

"Play-party tune." Her mother held her hands above the soapy water and looked far away. " 'Weevily Wheat.' Once I was tempted to lift my foot to that."

Lift her foot . . . Mattie looked at her mother . . . the Quaker preacher, whose foot now never peeped from beneath her full and seemly skirts. Once tempted . . . the wedding-ring music began again, but Mattie was watching, not drying. A long time ago tempted, yet there was something in the way her mother'd bury her face in a cabbage rose, or run to the door when father's spring wagon turned off the pike that showed her the black-haired girl who once listened to that music.

"Who's the Bent boy favor, Mattie?"

"His mother, I reckon. But handsomer. He's got a face to remember," Mattie said earnestly. "A proud, learned face. He's got eyes the color of sandstones. When he walks there isn't any up and down. It's a pleasure to watch him walk."

Mattie's mother put a washed skillet on the still warm stove to dry. "After a good heart," she said, "the least a woman can do is pick a face she fancies. Men's so much alike and many so sorry, that's the very least. If a man's face pleasures thee, that doesn't change. That is something to bank on. Thy father," she said, "has always been a comely man."

She turned back to her dishpan. "Why, Mattie," she said, "what's thee crying about?"

Mattie would not say. Then she burst out. "Pushing me off. Pushing me out of my own home. Thee talking about men that way . . . as if I would marry one. Anxious to be shut of me." She cried into her already wet dishtowel. "My own mother," she sobbed.

"Why, lovey," her mother said and went to her, but Mattie buried her face more deeply in her dishtowel and stumbled up the back stairs. "My own mother," she wailed.

"What's the trouble? What's Mattie taking on about?" Mattie's mother looked up at her husband, filling the doorway from the sitting-room like a staunch timber.

"Well, Jess," she said. "I think Mattie got a sudden inkling of what leaving home'll be like."

"Leaving home?" asked Jess. "Getting married? Thee think that's a crying matter, Eliza?"

Eliza looked at the face that had always pleasured her. "Thee knows I don't, Jess," she said.

Jess smiled. "Seems like," he said, "I have a recollection of some few tears thee shed those first . . ." But Eliza would have none of that. "Tsk, tsk," she said, her wedding ring beating a lively tattoo against the last kettle, "tsk, tsk, Jess Birdwell."

"Thee happy now?" Jess asked, smiling.

Eliza wouldn't say, but she hummed a little raveling of a song.

"Seems as if I know that," Jess said. "A long time ago."

"Like as not," Eliza agreed and handed him the pan to empty.

Jess went out with it, trying the tune over. "Tum-te-tum-te-tum. I can't name it," he said when he came back, "but it runs in my mind I know it."

"Thee know it, Jess, never fear," Eliza said. She took the empty pan from him, her wedding ring making one more musical note.

SCULPTURE

I took a piece of plastic clay
And idly fashioned it one day.
And as my fingers pressed it, still
It moved and yielded to my will.

I came again when days were past:
The bit of clay was hard at last.
The form I gave it still it bore,
But I could change that form no more!

I took a piece of living clay,
And gently pressed it day by day,
And molded with my power and art
A young child's soft and yielding heart.

I came again when years had gone:
It was a man I looked upon.
He still that early impress bore,
And I could fashion it no more!

Author Unknown

THE FLOOD

Conrad Richter

It's gone now, receded and dried up, so that amid all the peace and plenty long since dwelling on its shores, you can hardly find a living trace of it, save in the history books, the war colleges and in the Gettysburg words of Abraham Lincoln. And yet once not so long ago that flood flowed like a tide of blood two thousand miles across the country, dyeing rivers, engulfing farms, climbing mountains and penetrating the quiet valleys between. It even reached its long red arm across the endless plains of Texas, and if you look sharp, you may still see it there as it was then, sweeping from saddle to saddle, and from remote ranch house to ranch house, pulling men from horses and lonely pallets and starting them toward the distant front.

That's what it had done to Coe Elliot. Rigged out in his newly sewn suit of gray, he stood in this Texas town room with the alien young woman at his side, and in front of them the gaunt circuit preacher with a fierce look on his face and the open Book in his veined hands.

The preacher's voice grew sterner. "Coe Ellyit, do you take this lady, Bethiah Todd, as your lawful wife till death do you part?"

Now he was in for it, Coe thought. He would ride a thousand miles to get at those fool Yankees who reckoned they could tell the South what it had to do. He would leave his herd of longhorns scattered over the Nogal plain and his half dugout in the little Mexican settlement on the flat between the river and his spring. But riding the ninety miles into town yesterday and the day before, he had wished he had a woman to leave behind, somebody to think of him when he was away and to come back to when the war was over. And that was a funny thing to wish, for white women were scarce as prairie chicken's teeth out in this new Texas country.

"I do," he said, and anybody, knowing Coe or not, could have told from that hard, tanned face that he would keep his word.

The gaunt Texas preacher turned to the girl. The blight of his eyes was on her. You could see he had nothing for this marriage. He might have Christian pity on her for her plight, but that was as far as his religion bade him go.

"Bethiah Todd, do you take this man, Coe Ellyit, as your lawful husband till death do you part?"

That's the way she had looked, Coe told himself, when they had brought her to town with the oxen and wagon after the Comanches had ambushed her father. They had got him at the river, with a cedar pail in one hand and a tin cup in the other, and they had nigh split his head open with their scalping. He was a plowman from Kentucky, out here for free land. He was big and shut-mouthed and dark, they said,

and his daughter was little and slight and white as milk in her red dress against those jetty-black oxen. But now she was shut-mouthed too. Her little wisp of a face was set and her lips tight at what had overtaken her. Her eyes were dead and hopeless.

She had no place to go, Coe Elliot had thought with pity when he saw her, and he had spoken before he had weighed it.

"I can give you a home at the ranch," he had told her. "The Mexican women will look after you till I get back from the wars. And if I don't come back, everything I got is yours as my widow."

Bitterly she had looked at him then, and in bitter silence consented. And that was the way she answered the preacher now. If she gave him ever a plain word, like "yes" or "sir," it was too low for him to hear it. The preacher looked at her, and finally at Coe, who nodded him to go on.

"Then, with the authority invested in me by the Church of Christ," he declared, "and by the Confederated States of America, I declare you man and wife."

It was mighty quiet in that room now. Nobody made a move to kiss the set little face of the bride.

"All I got to say, Miz Ellyit, you got a mighty fine man," the preacher told her. It was plain that was all he intended to say. He turned away as if in disapproval of the whole business.

"Well, I reckon Miz Ellyit and me'll start for the ranch," the groom took hold of things to say. "We got only five hours till sundown, and steers are mighty slow."

The room kind of froze like the first skim of ice on a slough. The preacher turned around with the half-written marriage paper in his hand. "You're going up there today?"

"I ain't got much time," Coe said pleasantly. "I got to get back or they'll have those Yanks licked before I get a chance at 'em."

Nobody said anything for a little. At the end, the preacher spoke for all. "Couldn't you get there quicker and safer with a team and buggy, Coe?"

"I take it Miz Ellyit wants her fixens along," the bridegroom said. "She has too much in that wagon for a buggy to pack. And anything my wife wants, Reverend, she can have."

"Certainly, Coe, certainly," the preacher boomed in his great voice, but his eyes looked sad and dull. "May you move in the protecting shadow of the Lord's wing all the way."

Coe stole a quiet look at his wife. She stood there like she was deaf to what was being said, and if she wasn't, she was too slight to do anything about it one way or the other. Her eyes never changed when the women wished her a safe journey. And when he hoisted her up to the wagon seat, she felt small and light in his hand as a cured calfskin. But he reckoned it might please her to have some creatures she could call by name around the ranch while he was away. Now those ponderous beasts started, hard of horn and soft of eye and muzzle. Some oxen, their owners claimed, were mighty smart walkers, but to Coe the best were like these, slow as land turtles, moaning a little as they let their shoulders into the pull, moving first one foot, then the other. Up the dusty street they went, the wagon lumbering after, the wheels dragging, the spokes turning slow as clock hands. He could see the town folk in their doors and windows, waiting to see the Kentucky plowman's daughter go by, fresh-orphaned and as fresh-married, setting out in a hard and savage world, sitting alone on her high seat while her cowman groom in his spurred boots walked

the ground. But Coe didn't mind. He was in no great hurry to get there, for this was his wedding trip, the only time with his bride he'd get. Soon as he landed her at the ranch, he'd have to light out for Houston. Let folks wonder at him if they would. This was his honeymoon. You did queer things when you took a woman. He just hoped no Confederate soldier would happen along to see him plodding on foot in his short-cut cavalry jacket.

A prettier spot for a bride and groom you hardly could find than what he picked for the night. This was no camp along the trail for late travelers to stop and join them. He had turned the oxen off the wheel tracks. Down in a basin behind a long butte, he halted them. The land spread around like a saucer, soft and green with grass, while all the rolling knolls in the distance were stained with violet mist. Quickly he picketed the mare, unyoked the oxen, hobbled them and turned them loose. In a shake he had a fire of low cedar snapping, and the scent of his bacon and coffee stung the crystal-clear evening air. This was nothing. Men always cooked for their womenfolk out on the range. But she never came down from the wagon seat.

"You want to eat up there?" he asked gravely, and passed up the tin plate and cup.

He turned his back with a plainsman's politeness. The tin cup was half empty when it came down, but the plate had hardly been touched.

"You ought to had eat something," he told her sternly, like a husband should, but she only sat on her wagon seat, staring out over the wild land. He stood there, stiff and clumsy, holding the cup in one hand and plate in the other.

"If you don't want to eat, couldn't you drink the rest of the coffee?"

Her lips moved no more than when the K-town preacher had put the solemn

question. But she turned her head. And that was all he got from her—a turn of that slight head for "no," and a nod of that white face for "yes."

"Anything special I can get for you?" he persisted.

A slow turn of the head.

"You feeling all right?"

Not a move from her, neither yes nor no, just a long look at that wide horizon.

"You like this country out here?" he asked hopefully.

She turned on him such a suddenly bitter and terrible face that he felt all his hopes go out of him.

"Well, you better take a little walk before it gets too dark on you," he said kindly. "I'll fix up your bed this end of the wagon. You don't need to be scared of me. I'll have my bed on the ground."

But when he looked again, all the bright mist had gone from the distant hills, and a grayness from a low bank of clouds was creeping over the broad land.

Before closing his eyes, he could smell the rain coming. More rain. It had been raining most of the week. All night he heard the heavy drops pelting wagon top and sideboards. When he looked out along the tongue, he could see heavy lightning playing far ahead. It seemed to hang in that one spot all night. It was too far away to hear the thunder. Just before daylight, he crawled out and rolled up his bed. He didn't want any stray rider to come along and carry the news back to town that the groom had slept under the wagon.

That was a mighty strange day for a bridegroom, he told himself, driving a span of oxen through the rain, walking beside them through mud and puddles, with your bride sitting on the seat above you and

never a spoken word between. Sometimes he fell a little behind, so his eyes could study her. What kind of a "creetur" had he married, sitting there with a face white as gyp rock, in a bright red dress above those jetty-black oxen?

What was the name of the place she hailed from, he wondered, and had she brother or sister back there? Why, he didn't even know how old was his bride. Neither would she eat and neither talk. He heard that women were mighty hard to brand. Now he knew that you might brand them, but they were a long sight harder to break or gentle.

Halfway to noon he remembered the ox hobbles left behind, and he rode back on his mare to find them. The hobbles were gone, but he found where fresh hoofs of two unshod ponies had cut this way and that across the wet camping ground. More than once he took to the mare that day, to sit gravely in the saddle and scan the four horizons. Behind them, K-town had already vanished behind the mesa. Ahead, the nester settlement along the river was still too far away to see. And if any red Comanche pair still followed the wagon, they kept themselves in some arroyo hidden in that blue expanse of sun and rain-streaked plain.

The river had looked much higher when they had come back to it that morning. Last night's rain in the upland country was starting to come down, bringing the Texas earth with it. And it was still raining. All the time they stopped at noon, while the mare cropped and the oxen grazed greedily side by side, as if still in the yoke, looping up the tufts of buffalo grass with their long tongues, the river kept steadily rising. It rained again that night, and next morning, when they started out, the river ran bankfull beside them.

They entered the long *cañada* about noon. For an hour or two they crawled

along with higher mesa land on either side and the river winding like a dark snake between. The sun was halfway down the western sky when something made Coe look around. Back where they had passed on dry land only a few minutes before, a thin, dirty stream was spilling over the bank, lapping a little farther as he watched, trickling into the wheel tracks and running down the trail.

"Come on! Buck and Berry! Step up!" he called, swinging his dead father-in-law's whip.

They had only a mile or two to go until the steep escarpment softened and a draw led up to the mesa. But the great plodding beasts never hurried. You could add ton after ton to their load, and they would pull it as long as the wagon would hold it. They would moan softly and lean their stout shoulders into the bows, their tails would twitch and the wheels would be dragged through hell and damnation. But they wouldn't move any faster. Not for flies or whiplash.

The river was still rising. From every upcountry arroyo, wash and fork came the dark tide that could get through the wide cañada intake above faster than it could get out of the narrows below. Each time Coe looked around, he could see behind them a chocolate lake spreading, backing up, pushing ever closer to their heels. In the end, the water spread out on the trail ahead, widening and deepening until the team was in it, moving in one continual splash.

Up to now, those stolid, heavy-footed beasts had made little of the water, save to look down at it with their soft, wondering eyes. But once surrounded by it, a change came over them. They had waded many a

ford. But they could always see the trail rising up the bank on the other side. Now they moved through an endless lake, and there was no trail to see either here or ahead. Their pace slowed, their great horned heads swung cautiously from side to side, and when the water at last touched their bellies, they stopped dead. No shouting or beating could stir them. There they stood, immovable except for their swaying horns, while the flood slowly rose to engulf them, first their dewlaps, then their gaunt black thighs, and finally the bows of the yoke itself. The water began pouring through the cracks of the wagon. Coe climbed in and piled his wife's goods to the rear, the most valuable on top out of reach of the wetness.

All the while his mare at the tailboard stood covered to her breast. Her eyes were rolling, and now and then she threshed about, backing as far as she could with her neck outstretched, trying to slip her halter. He would have to watch her or she might hang or drown herself.

He looked around for his wife. In all this waste of muddy water, she was drawn up tight as a jackknife. She had clutched her red skirts from below, so they wouldn't be fouled by the water, and now she sat there, small and rigid, her petticoats held between her knees. Her cheeks were like tallow and her small neck mighty hollow and thin. She was sure showing the long strain. With the little she ate and all she went through, it didn't seem like she could go it much longer.

"It ain't safe for you on shore alone, Bethiah," he told her. "But if you get on the mare behind me, I'll ride you to the Sugareet till I get your wagon there."

She was staring at the oxen. She shook her head. She wouldn't leave her dead pap's jetty-black span, you could tell that. It showed how much he knew about women. A girl could be little and slight as if the wind would blow her away. She could be worn thin to a frazzle, and just when you figured she would go to pieces, she stiffened up and you couldn't break her.

Well, his wife couldn't sit there on the seat all night, he told himself. When he saw a board or plank coming down on this side, he waded the mare out, caught it with his hands or rope and laid it across the front end of the wagon box. By early dusk he had enough, and on this ill-assorted frame he threw down her bed and unrolled it.

"You better get some rest while you can," he told her.

That was a night he wouldn't forget easy, black as pitch, with the rain coming down and the unseen flood all around them. He tried his bed on the narrow seat, but it wouldn't lay right, and he sat there most of the time, listening to the water lapping at the wagon box, feeling with his hand to see how high it had risen. Now and then, some floating object struck the wagon softly and went on. When it was quiet, he could hear the oxen moving their heads in the bows, this way and that, this way and that, all the night through.

When dawn broke, he looked out on a wide and lonely scene. The cañada swam from escarpment to escarpment, while out in the center the current rolled with such power that it lifted in riffles above the rest of the flood. It had risen during the night. His mare's neck was nearly covered. She seemed exhausted and half-drowned. Her wild eyes rolled toward either shore, but the oxen stood unchanged. The water flowed over their jetty-black backs. All you could see of them was their rhythmically-moving heads sticking out of the water, and that's the way they stood the whole day, without grass or grain, refusing to budge, although

from time to time the heavy wagon seemed to lift from the ground and float of itself in the tide.

It rained fitfully most of the time, but the water rose little higher. This was the crest, Coe told himself. An endless assortment of flotsam was coming down now—posts, gates, loose clapboards, drowned cattle and sheep, and pole roofs from adobe walls that had become mud and collapsed. A nester's chicken coop went by in the current, and what looked like a buckboard with the top of its seat bobbing out. He stood out on the tongue and roped a cedar tub, which he hauled into the wagon. It was a very pretty tub, handmade, with alternate red and white cedar staves, but his bride showed it no interest.

At the very top of the flood, a nester's cabin came down. It was made of pine logs that could be cut on the big mesa above Sugareet. He saw it first far up the river. Now it sank, partly covered by water, and now it reared up like it was on springs. He studied hard at it when it came close, but he couldn't make out whose it was, for a cabin sure looked different standing at its home place than floating down the river. It went on by, and at the sharp bend swept so wide with the current, it stuck on the shallow wagon side. Coe took his dead pappy-in-law's Kentucky rifle from its buckskin loops on the wagon bows. He'd carry it with him down the river, just in case. He could see back to the wagon all the time.

When his mare waded out, he found it wasn't the whole cabin. It had broken off three or four logs from the ground. The door was still there. The water had swelled the puncheons fast, and that was what had grounded the cabin. He couldn't budge the door, only the little loft shutter. He stood on his saddle and stuck his head in. That was a mighty strange sight in a cabin, to look down from the loft hole into gurgling water, with shelves and stools floating around inside. The flood had eaten out the

mud chinking, and the current flowed through the logs like it was cribbing.

A bolster lay across one loft corner, with a pile of clothing beyond, and he reached out a hand to rummage through it. Then he saw all had been laid to keep something from rolling to the loft hole. It was a white baby, a couple of months old.

Must be the Cartwright cabin, he told himself. The babe lay flat on its back, its pinched face toward the roof. Coe studied it a long time before he saw the mite of a mouth twitch.

Now what did he have to come down here for and stick his nose in this cabin, he told himself. He had enough trouble on his hands without a babe. Now he couldn't go off and let it lay! Nor could he ride it on to some woman in Sugareet, for his wife wouldn't go. How he hated to go back and give it to her! She was miffed at him enough, without knowing he had a sick and starved babe to give her, a nameless orphan to tend, one that couldn't lift a finger to wait on itself and would likely die on her hands. Then she'd sulk toward him sure. But what could a man do? He could only break it to her easy as he could.

He covered up the bundle so she couldn't see what it was, rode back to shore, up and out to the wagon.

"That was the Cartwright cabin went by, Bethiah," he started in, mighty sober. "Jim's off to the Army. His woman must have tried to get out for help and was drowned. I can't see no other way, or she'd have been down the river with a posse after what she left behind."

"Drowned?" his wife whispered, and that was almost the first word she had said to him. Her face was bitter, as if this was just another proof of the horror of this wild Texas land.

"I reckon you better ride along behind me now. I got to get this to Sugareet sure," he said gravely.

Her dull eyes rested on the bundle.

"It's her babe," he said.

"Drowned too?" she whispered.

"Mighty near," he agreed.

Her face twisted and grew cruel. "You mean it's still alive?"

"It was a little while ago."

"Coe Elliot!" she cried, sitting up. "Give it here to me!"

He handed over the bundle, staring at her. Now what do you suppose got into her? You never could make out women. About the time you figured you knew how they'd take to something, they'd take it a different way. He watched her lift the cloth off that small face. Those tiny eyes squinted from the daylight, the peaked face screwed up and the pale lick of a mouth started to cry.

"It's suffocated and most starved!" she cried at him. "Coe Elliot, go out and get it some fresh milk!"

Now wasn't that just like a woman, he told himself. Why, a cowman never got a taste of milk, unless he had a family and his wife kept a tame cow in the corral. He rode grimly up to the mesa on this side, where he had seen some Bar Cross T calves with their mammies not far off. He could tackle a cow here and still keep his eye on the wagon. Those cows looked peaceful enough grazing there in a bunch like a V, heads all one way, but he felt glad no cowhand was around to watch him.

Oh, he roped his cow easy, and his mare did what she could to keep the rope tight, but the mare had to dodge when a longhorn made a rush for her. And when the cow wasn't after his mount, she was swinging at him. He couldn't get a drop till he took a couple of dallies around a cedar with his rope and snubbed the cow fast. Then, while it bawled and jerked and kicked, his hands manfully did their bidding. The canteen mouth was mighty small, but he got what precious white wetness he could and hustled back to the wagon with it.

His young wife shook the canteen. "Is that all you got?" she cried.

"Ain't that enough?" he stammered.

It was the look she gave him, he told himself, that sent him across the river—a provoked, exasperated, belittling look for him as a milker. Anything bad that came out of this now was her fault, for he had nothing to say. Already that bunch of cows he had tackled on this side had drifted out of sight of the wagon. But a few grazed on the other side. They looked like grains of sand up on the escarpment. He could keep an eye on the wagon from there. She told him to take a tin cup along. He could milk into it better, she said, and pour from that into the canteen. He took it silently from her hand, but the rifle he left behind. It would be mighty unhandy swimming the deep channel.

Once out in the swift current, his eyes swept the rim of the escarpment ahead. The cap rock above him dipped with arroyos and was tufted with cedars. He had seen no fresh sign on the wagon side of the river, and if that pair of red devils that followed them lay up there with their ponies picketed in some hidden draw, he couldn't help it. He hadn't wanted to come to this side. He had no choice. It might be too far for a good shot from up there to the wagon, but it was mighty close range to where he was putting himself now.

Even then he wouldn't make like he cared when it first happened. All he heard above the snorts and splashes of his swimming mare was a noise like the breaking of a distant corral bar. At the same time, he saw, just a little ahead of him, a gush of water raise from the river. It stood up for a moment, spinning like a top.

He had his cap-and-ball pistol in his belt, twice looped around his neck to keep it from the water, but all he could make out

was a puff of black smoke floating away from the rim of the mesa. Then, nearer on the escarpment, another puff came. He could see the smoke before he heard the report. Almost at once, his mare sank and was gone, leaving him struggling in the water.

Well, it had happened like he thought, he told himself, and tried to swim back to the wagon. But the river bore him away. The main current ran as if something had given way in the narrows below, and all the water was going out. He kept his head above with difficulty. He hung to a piece of floating gatepost with one hand and worked for the wagon side of the river with the other all the time, but he was being swept downstream. When he saw it was hopeless, he raised up in the water as far as he could and tried to see Bethiah. He couldn't see her. Last thing he made out before the current swept him around the bend was two red riders swimming their ponies for the wagon. After a little, he heard what he never wanted to hear. The shots rang loudly several times along the bed of the water and echoed from escarpment to escarpment.

Far below and very far spent, he dragged himself out and stood in the shadow of a rock, blowing. All he could hear when he got his breath was the low gurgle of water and a curlew calling dismally as it flew over the flood in the dusk. Once he thought that he heard a horseman climbing the dim mesa. His pistol lay at the bottom of the river, but he still had his knife. He took the benefit of every shadow and bush as he made his way up the river. He could now see the wagon in the deepening gloom, a lone, desolate dot surrounded by the wide water. Save for the specks of oxen, it hadn't a sign of life about. But when he grew closer, he thought he smelled smoke, and as he came abreast on the shore, there rose a faint, sinister glow of red in the wagon.

Wading out in the darkness, he could tell the river was definitely lower. Now that the worst had happened to him, the flood was going down. The oxen must be still alive, he reckoned, for he could hear the constant creak of yoke and coupling ring. Once he felt sure he saw the moving shadow of someone against the wagon sheet. It looked like a woman.

He splashed loudly, so if Bethiah were there she might be warned of his coming. Instantly, a rifle cracked from the wagon and a bullet sang near him.

"Bethiah!" he called.

"Why didn't you say who it was?" she called back sharply. In a little while he pulled himself up over the front wheel.

That was a picture under the wagon sheet he reckoned he'd never see in this life, Bethiah and the babe big as life and kicking. His wife had set a dutch oven on a plank and had a low fire of wagon wood going in it. She must have opened her trunk, for she had changed her red dress for a blue homespun one. As he climbed in, she knelt there by her pappy's rifle while she boiled coffee and fried bacon. Her bedroll had been spread on the boards. In it a tin cup and plate for him had evidently just been laid. And down there in the water, a-watching everything, was the babe. She had bedded it in the cedar tub. And now that tub kept floating around the wagon box, rocking like a cradle in every little wave their movements in the wagon made.

"I might 'a' killed you like I did that red devil!" she scolded.

He looked at her. Her slight little face with its black hair parted in the middle and pulled down on both sides didn't look like she could take her part or stand her ground. But he knew better now.

"What happened to the other one?"

"He didn't stay," she said briefly.

Little by little, as he put out the fire, she told him how she stood behind her pile of barrels and boxes to fire out of the wagon. She vowed she was going to get that other devil, for he had put an unsightly bullet hole in her trunk, and that meant through some of her best fixens. She'd have done it, too, for she could reload faster than he could. She had often done it for her pappy. But he turned tail and ran.

Coe sat there mighty quiet while they ate their supper, hardly daring to look at her, lest she see the respect in his eyes. Mostly he watched the babe in the tub swimming around the wagon. He had left a small, lone coal for light. So this was how a man felt when he was married, he told himself, with his wife cooking for him and setting beside him to eat while their young one drooled to itself close by. This was something to come back to afterward. And if she could take care of a ranch like she could a wagon, he'd have something to come back to when it was over. "Water's goin' down fast," he told her when they finished. "That young one's tub'll ground in a minute. If this keeps on, the trail will be free by midnight. Maybe then we can get your oxen a-goin'."

The moon was just coming up as she washed the dishes and fed the babe for the night.

"You might as well get some sleep till the water's down," he told her. "I don't expect that long-haired feller to bother you any more tonight."

She didn't say anything right then. But when he went to get his bed, she said he needn't bother. She said it, looking the other way. It was mighty narrow for a bed out there on the wagon seat. He could sleep better here on the platform, if he wanted to. Her bed, she allowed, was wide enough for two.

Four things in any land must dwell,
   If it endures and prospers well;
One is manhood true and good;
   One is noble womanhood;
One is child life, clean and bright;
   And one an altar kept alight.

Author Unknown

DADDY CAN FIX IT
Marjorie Holmes

Father can fix it. Or Daddy, as little folks call him. Or, as they get older, Pop or Dad.

Whatever his title, there's nothing like that remarkable do-it-yourself but do-it-for-everybody-else male parent.

Often his ingenuity surges to the front even before his offspring arrive, as he fashions a crib, a feeding table. More, today's dad enjoys bathing and feeding his babies sometimes, rocking them, telling them stories. And when they come running in with a broken toy, how many a lucky wife can console, "Don't cry. Wait till Daddy gets home. Your father can fix it."

Daddy can fix it. Anything, everything. Radios, clocks, a bike, a pair of roller skates. A doll, a leaky boat, an eyeless stuffed rabbit. Or those antiques his wife is always dragging home from auction sales. Patiently, cleverly, with glue and tape and nails, and paint and love and imagination—whatever the object, if it's dear to its owner, somehow, some way, he'll devise the means of its salvation.

Father can fix it. Often he will even build it. A playhouse, a picnic table, a fireplace, a wall, a patio in the yard.

Handyman—yes, he's usually that, but more important, he's the family handyman in matters of the heart. Report cards. Budding romances. Times of illness, worry, family strain. That complication in the Cub Scouts, that looming problem at church, at school—don't worry, talk it over with Dad.

Dad will analyze the whole thing wisely, come up with the proper solution, make you realize it's not so grave a complication, after all. Or if it proves to be—well, your father will be standing by.

Daddy can fix it. Dad will get it for you. That costume for the play, though it means a trip clear across town. The supplies you need for the bazaar. That last-minute birthday present. Those pretzels and cold drinks for the teen-age party. And regularly, with the car crammed with little folks, groceries at the supermarket on Friday night.

Father can fix it. Find it, get it, pay for it, help you figure it out. Here's to him, bless him—the one who lives at our house, and at yours. The American dad!

From SOMETHING MORE

Catherine Marshall

Most of us feel no need of facing the question, "Does God heal directly today?" until we are personally confronted with some physician's blunt finality: "There's nothing more we can do."

Those were the precise words my friend Sandra was hearing so incredulously that night—February 8, 1966. I did not learn of this sequence of events until later when Sandra Ghost (now a close friend. Yes, her name really is Ghost) shared it with me. Arriving at the hospital room where her little son lay, Sandy had encountered Dr. Gallo.

"Mrs. Ghost, there's been no improvement in Kent's condition since this afternoon," the distinguished-looking, dark-haired doctor told her. "No question of the diagnosis—a cerebral hemorrhage. He's still in deep coma."

Over his shoulder Sandra could see the slight form of her two-year-old son, usually unable to stay still for an instant. Now there wasn't a flicker of movement anywhere—from his toes to his blond head.

Dr. Gallo asked gently, "You did call your husband in Louisville?"

"Yes, I did. Bill caught the first plane possible. He should be here at ten o'clock."

"I must warn you . . . Kent may not hold on until your husband gets here. Mrs. Ghost, you may go in now." He paused. "There's nothing more we can do."

The words spoken so slowly for emphasis struck Sandra like a physical blow. Their impact detached some part of her mind and sent her thoughts spinning backward to that first day when she and Kent, his hand clinging so tightly to hers, had walked through the front door of the National Institute of Health on the outskirts of Washington, D.C. What relief she had felt! To think that this great research arm of the United States Government had been willing to take on their son's case of acute lympho-cytic leukemia. Why, this place was one of medicine's frontiers. In these vast governmental buildings they were finding answers. Surely, she told herself, only God could have made the connection between the Ghost family in Louisville, Kentucky, and NIH. Therefore, the fine and compassionate doctors on Two-East (the leukemia unit) would discover the key to the healing of Kent's leukemia.

And in the two months since, the doctors had indeed proved themselves compassionate. In fact, the warmth of everyone around NIH—laboratory technicians, housekeeping detail, clean-up crews, and Mr. Botts, the gentle black elevator operator who "God-blessed" all his passengers—had steadily reassured her.

So how could Dr. Gallo be saying so seriously, "There's nothing more we can do?" For what he meant was, "Kent is going to die and I can't prevent his death. Medicine, science, the best we know, has no further resources to give you."

Her thoughts reeled and staggered. "But

that can't be! This is the twentieth century. I—Sandra Ghost—am a twentieth-century woman. I have relied on science. Science can do *anything*."

But she only stared at the doctor, nodded her head, and murmured, "Thank you, Doctor." For an instant she watched the physician's back retreating down the long corridor almost at a trot, as though eager to be away. Then she hurried into Kent's room.

This was Intensive Care with Di-Gi on duty, a nurse whom Sandra had learned to know well during the two months. Every ten minutes Di-Gi was taking vital signs: Would Kent respond to the beam of light flashed directly into his eyes? Any sign of consciousness by grip or response? Any change in temperature? Blood pressure?

But there was no visible response—none at all. Her child was so still and so white, his legs so limp. Almost the smell of death was in this room. Was Sandra imagining it? No, this was no illusion; she saw it in the nurse's eyes.

Sandy kept a grip on her emotions through two of the ten-minute periods. Then she broke down, sobbing quietly.

Di-Gi understood. "Some black coffee would help," she suggested, "help me too. Why don't you go down to the Snack Shop for two cups?"

The distraught mother realized the nurse was using psychology on her, but she also knew that some activity would help. "Sure," Sandra agreed, "good idea."

On Sandy's return from the Snack Shop, she was surprised to see Mr. Botts running the elevator; it was rare to see him on night duty, rarer still for her to be the only passenger. As the doors slid shut and the elevator mounted, Mr. Botts asked as he always did, "And how's my little man?"

This time the question brought quick tears to Sandra's eyes. She shifted the sack with its two steaming cartons of coffee to her left hand in order to grope for her handkerchief. "Mr. Botts, Kent's bad. He's—not expected to live." Then from deep inside her came a request that she was surprised to hear herself making. "Will you—would you pray for Kent?"

At that moment they arrived at the second floor and the elevator doors opened. Sandra was no more than three steps into the hallway when she heard Mr. Botts's voice behind her. "Get back on the elevator, would you? Let's pray *now*. Please get back on."

Wordlessly, Sandra obeyed. The elevator doors shut, only this time Mr. Botts left the elevator stationary at the second floor.

"Lord Jesus," he prayed, "I ask You to heal this child as You healed me when the doctors told me I would never walk again. The Church prayed and You heard their prayers, and there's nothing wrong with me now. I ask You to do for this child what You did for me since the Good Book says, 'God is no respecter of persons.'

"Lord, enter this little boy's body. Heal Kent, Lord, and let him walk again. And Lord Jesus, give Kent's mother here Your strength. She needs it so much. . . . "

Was there more of the prayer? Sandy could never remember, only that she was aware of God's love in that elevator as she had never before felt it. And wasn't it odd that during what had seemed to her a long stretch of time, no one had rung for the elevator? Fumbling for words, she tried to thank Mr. Botts. Then she ran left down the corridor and through the double swinging doors to Kent's room. As she went, she glanced at her wristwatch—six minutes before nine.

"Any change?" she asked the nurse.

Di-Gi shook her head. "No change."

As the two women sipped coffee, Di-Gi talked. Sandra discovered one reason for this nurse's special depth of compassion. She had been through trouble too: Her

mother and her younger sister had died in an automobile wreck just two months before. Sandra wondered why Di-Gi was not angry with God or bitter. She had the feeling that the nurse knew Him.

As they talked, two sets of vital signs were taken. At the third, Di-Gi seemed startled and made no attempt to hide it. "His blood pressure! Coming down fast, toward normal."

Almost immediately, Kent stirred in the bed. His eyes fluttered open. Recognizing his mother, he turned toward her, "Mommy, I'm thirsty."

Di-Gi restrained her excitement long enough to finish taking all the vital signs and recheck them, then she ran for the doctor on duty. He made it to Kent's room in record time.

By the time Bill Ghost arrived from the airport, Kent was fully conscious, sitting up in bed, sipping a soft drink through a straw, anticipating his Daddy's coming.

During the night hours Kent continued to improve. The next day, February 9, Dr. Robert Gallo appeared to be in sharp disagreement with a battery of neurologists. Though the parents at NIH are always considered a part of the "medical team" for their own child, the Ghosts were surprised to hear the physicians openly discussing their differences: Dr. Gallo could not possibly have been correct in his diagnosis, the neurologists insisted; no patient could recover from a cerebral hemorrhage as quickly as Kent Ghost had.

Dr. Gallo stood his ground. Yes, he reiterated, his diagnosis had been correct. He had performed the requisite spinal tap. Nor had a vein been punctured during the tap, thus accounting for blood in the test tube.

Finally the neurologists would not be appeased unless they performed another spinal tap, so Kent was wheeled away to a treatment room. There Dr. Gallo was

vindicated: Yes, the little boy had had a brain hemorrhage.

Two days later, Kent was riding the rocking horse in the playroom at NIH, unaware of the doctors and nurses who kept drifting by the playroom door, staring at him. . . . "Can you believe that's Kent Ghost?" Between his turns on the rocking horse, he would ride Mr. Botts' elevator up and down, down and up, and each time a jubilant Mr. Botts would pat "his little man's" head, make gleeful remarks or hum under his breath, all the time looking as though he possessed a secret too marvelous to contain.

THE FREEDOM OF LOVE

Eugenia Price

Repeatedly, I have written of the creative liberty I have been given in my own life through the freeing love offered me for all my years by my mother. By my father too, when he was alive. I must have often perplexed them both during the years in which I was not a Christian. But always, their love came toward me, reminding me of their faith in me, of their generosity, of their expectations for me. I was never permitted to stop believing in myself. To this day, I am convinced that their love, the quality of their love, ultimately did this for me. My own belief in myself bent often and broke once or twice. Theirs never wavered. As with every family, mine had its share of good times and bad times. Not once, through either, did they try to force their problems upon me by insisting (as they had every right to do because they supported me much of the time) that I "come home" in order to make things easier for them for one reason or another. They believed in me and believed that I would make my goal of becoming a professional writer more quickly in a big city, so through my

vicissitude or theirs, I was left free.

The results in my life were slow to appear. I still marvel at their patience. But one example of how their unselfish, freeing love got through to me at perhaps the most self-centered period of my life shows the creative effect of their love on me in a rather concrete way. It may sound unimpressive. It may seem what any ordinarily considerate daughter would have done anyway. Not this one. At a time when my career was just beginning to focus my mother fell ill and required serious surgery. It was putting definite financial pressure upon them to keep me in Chicago in my own apartment. Mother needed me with her. My father needed me with him. But they did not intimate even by so much as a look that they expected me to do anything but go on living in the big city "on them ." Result? Of my own accord, not because I thought I *had* to, but with all my heart because I *wanted* to, I went home to stay out the year. I was nineteen, and although I didn't do anything else noticeably unselfish until I became a follower of Jesus Christ at the age of thirty-three, I began to like myself a little once I stopped pushing aside obstacles and people in order to protect myself.

The quality of the love I have always received from Mother and Dad conditioned me for quick, rather natural belief in the love of God. They had made it utterly possible for me to believe that God loved me. I admit to some problems with accepting His discipline, but never His love. My parents were, like yours, not perfect. I'm sure I needed more discipline at their hands. But human love at its very highest will always make mistakes in its action. It is the *reaction* of love that counts.

My parents have loved me freely and in the process conditioned me to love. Even at the first moment of conscious faith in God, I felt at home. I had grown up in the very atmosphere of giving love. Love that left me free to seek my own fulfillment. Love that did not choke my particular personality. Love that did not bend me to the image of anyone. Love that never put me in competition with my brother, nor my brother with me.

A FAMILY FOR FREDDIE
Abbie Blair

I remember the first time I saw Freddie. He was standing in his playpen at the adoption agency where I work. He gave me a toothy grin. "What a beautiful baby," I thought.

His boarding mother gathered him into her arms. "Will you be able to find a family for Freddie?" she asked.

Then I saw it. Freddie had been born without arms.

"He's so smart. He's only ten months old, and already he walks and talks." She kissed him. "Say 'book' for Mrs. Blair."

Freddie grinned at me and hid his head on his boarding mother's shoulder. "Now, Freddie, don't act that way," she said. "He's really very friendly," she added. "Such a good, good boy."

Freddie reminded me of my own son when he was that age, the same thick dark curls, the same brown eyes.

"You won't forget him, Mrs. Blair? You will try?"

"I won't forget."

I went upstairs and got out my latest copy of the Hard-to-Place list.

Freddie is a ten-month-old white Protestant boy of English and French background. He has brown eyes, dark-brown hair and fair skin. Freddie was born without arms, but is otherwise in good health. His boarding mother feels he is showing signs of superior mentality, and he is already walking and

saying a few words. Freddie is a warm, affectionate child who has been surrendered by his natural mother and is ready for adoption.

"He's ready," I thought. "But who is ready for him?"

It was ten o'clock of a lovely late-summer morning, and the agency was full of couples—couples having interviews, couples meeting babies, families being born. These couples nearly always have the same dream: they want a child as much like themselves as possible, as young as possible, and—most important—a child with no medical problem.

"If he develops a problem after we get him," they say, "that is a risk we'll take, just like any other parents. But to pick a baby who already has a problem—that's too much."

And who can blame them?

I wasn't alone in looking for parents for Freddie. Any of the caseworkers meeting a new couple started with a hope: maybe they were for Freddie. But summer slipped into fall, and Freddie was with us for his first birthday party.

"Freddie is so-o-o big," said his boarding mother, stretching out her arms.

"So-o-o big," said Freddie, laughing. "So-o-o big."

And then I found them.

It started out as it always does—an impersonal record in my box, a new case, a new "Home Study," two people who wanted a child. They were Frances and Edwin Pearson. She was 41. He was 45. She was a housewife. He was a truck driver.

I went to see them. They lived in a tiny white frame house in a big yard full of sun and old trees. They greeted me together at the door, eager and scared to death.

Mrs. Pearson produced steaming coffee and oven-warm cookies. They sat before me on the sofa, close together, holding hands. After a moment Mrs. Pearson began: "Today is our wedding anniversary. Eighteen years."

"Good years." Mr. Pearson looked at his wife. "Except—"

"Yes," she said. "Except. Always the 'except.'" She looked around the immaculate room. "It's too neat," she said. "You know?"

I thought of my own living room with my three children. Teen-agers now. "Yes," I said. "I know."

"Perhaps we're too old?"

I smiled. "You don't think so," I said. "We don't either."

"You always think it will be this month, and then next month," Mr. Pearson said. "Even when you begin to guess the truth, you don't want to accept it."

"We've tried everything," Mrs. Pearson said. "Examinations. Tests. All kinds of things. Over and over. But nothing ever happened. You just go on hoping and hoping, and time keeps slipping by."

"We've tried to adopt before this," Mr. Pearson said. "One agency told us our apartment was too small, so we got this house. Then another one said I didn't make enough money. We had decided that was it, but this friend told us about you, and we decided to make one last try."

"I'm glad," I said.

Mrs. Pearson glanced at her husband proudly. "Can we choose at all?" she asked. "A boy for my husband?"

"We'll try for a boy," I said. "What kind of boy?"

Mrs. Pearson laughed. "How many kinds are there? Just a boy. My husband is very athletic. He played football in high school; basketball, too, and track. He would be good for a boy."

Mr. Pearson looked at me. "I know you can't tell exactly," he said, "but can you give us any idea how soon? We've waited so long."

I hesitated. There is always this question.

"Next summer maybe," said Mrs. Pearson. "We could take him to the beach."

"That long?" Mr. Pearson said. "Don't you have anyone at all? There *must* be a little boy somewhere."

"Of course," he went on after a pause, "we can't give him as much as other people. We haven't a lot of money saved up."

"We've got a lot of love," his wife said. "We've saved up a lot of that."

"Well," I said cautiously, "there *is* a little boy. He is 13 months old."

"Oh," Mrs. Pearson said, "just a beautiful age."

"I have a picture of him," I said, reaching for my purse. I handed them Freddie's picture.

"He is a wonderful little boy," I said. "But he was born without arms."

They studied the picture in silence. He looked at her. "What do you think, Fran?"

"Kickball," Mrs. Pearson said. "You could teach him kickball."

"Athletics are not so important," Mr. Pearson said. "He can learn to use his head. Arms he can do without. A head, never. He can go to college. We'll save for it."

"A boy is a boy," Mrs. Pearson insisted. "He needs to play. You can teach him."

"I'll teach him. Arms aren't everything. Maybe we can get him some."

They had forgotten me. But maybe Mr. Pearson was right, I thought. Maybe sometime Freddie could be fitted with artificial arms. He did have nubs where arms should be.

"Then you might like to see him?"

They looked up. "When could we have him?"

"You think you might want him?"

Mrs. Pearson looked at me. "Might?" she said. "*Might?*"

"We want him," her husband said.

Mrs. Pearson went back to the picture. "You've been waiting for us," she said.

"Haven't you?"

"His name is Freddie," I said, "but you can change it."

"No," said Mr. Pearson. "Frederick Pearson—it's good together."

And that was it.

There were formalities, of course; and by the time we set the day Christmas lights were strung across city streets and wreaths were hung everywhere.

I met the Pearsons in the waiting room. There was a little snow on them both.

"Your son's here already," I told them. "Let's go upstairs, and I'll bring him to you."

"I've got butterflies," Mrs. Pearson announced. "Suppose he doesn't like us?"

I put my hand on her arm. "I'll get him," I said.

Freddie's boarding mother had dressed him in a new white suit, with a sprig of green holly and red berries embroidered on the collar. His hair shone, a mop of dark curls.

"Going home," Freddie said to me, smiling, as his boarding mother put him in my arms.

"I told him that," she said. "I told him he was going to his new home."

She kissed him, and her eyes were wet.

"Good-by, dear. Be a good boy."

"Good boy," said Freddie cheerfully. "Going home."

I carried him upstairs to the little room where the Pearsons were waiting. When I got there, I put him on his feet and opened the door.

"Merry Christmas," I said.

Freddie stood uncertainly, rocking a little, gazing intently at the two people before him. They drank him in.

Mr. Pearson knelt on one knee. "Freddie," he said, "come here. Come to Daddy."

Freddie looked back at me for a moment. Then, turning, he walked slowly toward them; and they reached out their arms and gathered him in.

The happiest moments of my life have been the few which I have passed at home in the bosom of my family.

Thomas Jefferson

A SHARING OF WONDER

Arthur Gordon

Many summers ago a small boy lived in a tall house by the sea. The house had a tremendous peaked roof made of weather shingles that towered above all the surrounding cottages. In this roof, near the top, was a trapdoor that could be reached only by a ladder propped up on the attic floor. Children used to play in the attic sometimes, but no one ever climbed up to the trapdoor. It was too high and forbidding.

One sunny day, however, when the boy's father was storing some boxes in the attic, he glanced up at the underside of the great roof. "Must be quite a view from up there," he said to his son. "Why don't we take a look?"

The boy felt his heart lurch with excitement and a touch of fear, but his father was already testing the shaky ladder. "Up you go," he said. "I'll be right behind you."

Up they went through the mysterious darkness, each step a terror and a delight. Up through the tiny sunbeams lancing through the cracks, up until the boy could smell the ancient heat-soaked shingles, up until the trapdoor, sealed with cobwebs, touched the top of his head. His father unhooked a latch, slid the trapdoor back ... and a whole new universe burst upon his dazzled eyes.

There lay the sea—but what a sea! Gigantic, limitless, blazing with splintered sunlight, it curved away to infinity, dwarfing the land, rivaling the sky. Below him, queerly inverted, were the tops of trees and—even more unimaginable—the backs of gulls in flight. The familiar path through the dunes was a mere thread where heat waves shimmered; far away a shrunken river with toy boats coiled into the sea. All this he saw at a glance from the protective circle of his father's arm, and the impact of such newness, of such violently expanded horizons, was so great that from that moment the world of his childhood was somehow altered. It was stretched; it was different; it was never quite the same again.

Decades have passed since then; most of the minor trials and triumphs of childhood have faded from my mind. But I remember that moment on the roof as if it had happened yesterday. And I think of it sometimes when the day set aside as Father's Day comes round; because it seems to me that the real Father's Day is not this sentimentalized, over-commercialized occasion at all. The real Father's Day is the day that exists only in memory, in the mind of some happy child or nostalgic adult, the magical day when—just for a moment or perhaps simply by accident—a chord was struck, a spark jumped the gap between generations, a relationship was suddenly achieved so warm, so intense, that it was caught and held in the meshes of the mind, impervious to time.

My father has been dead for many years now, but he left so many Father's Days behind him that he doesn't seem to have gone very far. Whenever I want to feel close to him, all I have to do is choose one from the assortment in my mind labeled "the time we...." Some are little-boy memories like the day on the roof; some are teen-age recollections; some no doubt would seem trivial to anyone else, but all have the same quality: a sense of exploration, a discovery of newness, a sharing of wonder.

There was the time we went to see a captured German U-boat that our navy had brought into the harbor. We climbed down into the maze of machinery smelling coldly of oil and war and claustrophobia and

death. Another visitor asked my father bitterly if he did not consider the German sailors murderers who struck without warning from the depths of the sea. I remember how he shook his head, saying that they, too, were brave men caught like their adversaries in the iron trap of war. The answer did not please his questioner, but somehow brought relief and pride to me, as if a sudden test had been met and mastered.

Or the time we explored a cave, and at one point far underground snapped off our flashlights and sat there in darkness and silence so profound that it was like being in the void before the beginning of time. After a while Father said, in a whisper, "Listen! You can hear the mountain breathing!" And such is the power of suggestion that I did seem to hear, in the ringing silence, a tremendous rhythm that haunts me to this day.

Did my father deliberately set out to manufacture Father's Days for his children? I doubt it. In the episodes I remember so vividly I don't think he was primarily seeking to instruct or inspire or enlighten us. He was satisfying his own curiosity— and letting us in on his discoveries. He was indulging his own sense of wonder—and letting us share it.

This is the stuff of which *real* Father's Days—and Mother's Days also—are made. Sometimes, when the formula works, the parents may not even know it. But sometimes you do know, and when this happens there is no satisfaction in the world quite like it.

Not long ago our family visited one of those marine establishments where trained porpoises—and in this case a small whale— put on a marvelous show. I was so fascinated by the whale that I lingered after the performance to ask the trainer how it was captured, what it was fed, and so on. He was an obliging fellow who not only

answered the questions but summoned the whale herself to the side of the pool. We patted her back, smooth and hard and gleaming like wet black rubber. This evidently pleased her, for suddenly she raised her great barrel of a head out of the water, rested it on the coping and gazed with friendly, reddish eyes at our eight-year-old daughter, who was nearest.

"Apparently," I said, "she wants to rub noses with you."

Our daughter looked both interested and aghast.

"Go ahead," the trainer said good-naturedly. "She won't mind."

There was an electric pause, then the briefest of damp contacts, then both participants hastily withdrew. And that seemed to be the end of it, until bedtime that night. Then, staring pensively at the ceiling, my daughter said, "Do you think any other third-grader in the whole wide world ever rubbed noses with a whale?"

"No," I said, "I'm pretty sure you're the only one."

She gave a deep, contented sigh, went to sleep, and hasn't mentioned it since. But thirty years from now, when her nose tingles, or when she touches wet black rubber, or sometimes for no reason at all, maybe . . . just maybe . . . she will remember.

A PRAYER FOR PARENTS

Build me a son, O Lord, who will be strong enough to know when he is weak, and brave enough to face himself when he is afraid; one who will be proud and unbending in honest defeat, and humble and gentle in victory.

Build me a son whose wishbone will not be where his backbone should be; a son who will know Thee—and that to know himself is the foundation stone of knowledge.

Lead him, I pray, not in the path of ease

and comfort, but under the stress and spur of difficulties and challenge. Here, let him learn to stand up in the storm; here, let him learn compassion for those who fail.

Build me a son whose heart will be clear, whose goal will be high; a son who will master himself before he seeks to master other men; one who will learn to laugh, yet never forget how to weep; one who will reach into the future, yet never forget the past.

And after all these things are his, add, I pray, enough of a sense of humor, so that he may always be serious, yet never take himself too seriously. Give him humility, so that he may always remember the simplicity of true greatness, the open mind of true wisdom, the meekness of true strength. Then I, his father, will dare to whisper, "I have not lived in vain."

General Douglas A. MacArthur

Little Bobby, scolded for being naughty, was asked by his mother, "How do you expect to get into Heaven?"

He thought for a moment, then replied:

"I'll just run in and out and keep slamming the door until they say, 'For goodness' sake, come in or stay out!' Then I'll go in."

C. J. Papara

HOME, SWEET HOME

'Mid pleasures and palaces though we may
    roam,
Be it ever so humble, there's no place like
    home;
A charm from the sky seems to hallow us
    there,
Which, seek through the world, is ne'er met
    with elsewhere.
Home, home, sweet, sweet home!
There's no place like home! There's no
    place like home!

How sweet 'tis to sit 'neath a fond father's
    smile,
And the caress of a mother to soothe and
    beguile!
Let others delight 'mid new pleasures to
    roam,
But give me, oh, give me, the pleasures of
    home!
Home, home, sweet, sweet home!
There's no place like home! There's no
    place like home!

John Howard Payne

DEATH AND THE DAWN

Pearl S. Buck

"There's no place to put him, Doctor," the nurse said. "The wards are full."

"Put him in a private room," the surgeon said, stripping off his white coat.

"Private rooms are full, too, except that semiprivate where old Mr. MacLeod is. And he's under an oxygen tent—not expected to live through the night. His family is standing by."

"This kid won't bother him. He'll not be waking tonight," the surgeon said. He had his topcoat on now and his hat. It was midnight, he was tired, and he slammed the door after him.

If ever he wakes, the nurse thought, looking at the kid. He was the reckless type, blond hair worn too long, sharp thin face, long thin body, thin to the bone, the kind that was always getting smashed up in car accidents. Under the heavy white bandages the young face was somber. Nobody knew who he was. There had been nothing on him to tell who he was. The car was stolen—at least the owner had not yet been identified, except that he was not this eighteen-year-old boy. Eighteen—seventeen—maybe only sixteen, he could be any age. He was unconscious when they brought him in, and bleeding. Lucky for

him the town had a hospital—not every small town had one.

"Put him in twenty-three," the nurse said to the orderlies.

They wheeled him away and she followed. The hospital was quiet at this time of night. Not even a baby cried. In an hour or two and before dawn the calls would begin, bells ringing, sick people sighing and moaning and babies waking each other up.

Twenty-three was quiet, too, except for the hissing of the oxygen. The small night light was on and she could see old Mr. MacLeod lying there. She'd take a look at him before she went out.

"Be careful of the boy's head," she told the orderlies.

"We know," the older one said. "We saw him brung in."

"Nothing left of the car," the other one said.

They lifted him on the bed with big gentle hands and straightened his arms and legs.

"Anything more, Miss Martin?" the older one asked.

"Nothing, thanks," she said.

They went away and she pulled the sheet and the thin cotton blanket over the boy. He was breathing but not too well. She took his pulse. It was fluttering but that was to be expected. No sedatives, the doctor had directed, after the last injection.

The telephone rang in the hall and she went to answer it. One nurse on the floor wasn't enough at night but that was the way it was. There weren't enough nurses. Mr. MacLeod ought to have a nurse with him. And now this boy—

"Hello," she said softly.

"Miss Martin?" A clear, carefully calm voice and she recognized it.

"Yes, Mrs. MacLeod."

"I can't sleep, of course. None of us can. Would you just see if—"

"Certainly."

She put down the receiver and went back to the room. The boy's breathing was a little better, but she did not look at him. Mr. MacLeod was lying perfectly still. She was not sure about him. Was he breathing, this old, old man? She felt for his pulse and could not find it. She ran back to the telephone.

"Mrs. MacLeod?"

"Yes?"

"You'd better come."

"Immediately."

She called then on the house telephone for the intern on duty.

"Doctor, I've sent for the MacLeod family."

"Oh—it's the end, is it?"

"I'm afraid so."

"I'll be over. Have the hypodermic ready."

"Yes, Doctor."

She arranged the small tray, the needles on the white sterile cloth. None of it was any use except perhaps to bring an old man back for a moment to say goodbye. But it was the rule, and only a doctor could break it. She carried the tray to the room and set it down noiselessly. The old man had not moved. Neither had the boy. But the boy was breathing better.

She adjusted the oxygen tent and increased slightly the flow of oxygen. She turned on a side light and brought in two extra chairs. When Mrs. MacLeod had been told yesterday, in the doctor's office, that her husband could not live beyond the next day, her face had turned as white as her hair. Then she said, "I ask only one thing—that when the end is near you call me. I shall not leave the house."

These had been the instructions from doctor to nurse. "When you see the end is near, you are to send for Mrs. MacLeod."

The intern came in, a short, stout young man with a round, kind face.

"Ready, Doctor," Miss Martin said.

"Good. I'll just check. Take the tent off."

The nurse took away the tent and the doctor checked quickly.

"He's very nearly gone. As soon as they come I'll give him the hypodermic."

"It's here," Miss Martin said.

"Not that it will stay him much," the doctor went on. "Half an hour—maybe an hour. Who's the other patient?"

"Accident case."

"Hm—too many of those nowadays."

"Yes."

It was commonplace talk, concealing the knowledge of death—death of the young, death of the old.

"Shall I come in?" It was Mrs. MacLeod at the door.

"Come in," the intern said. "I'm just about to give him a shot—a boost, you know. You'll be able to talk."

"Thank you, Doctor."

She was composed, an aging figure, short but strong, her face controlled. Only Miss Martin noticed that her small, compact hands were trembling as she took off her hat.

"Sit down, Mrs. MacLeod."

"We're all here," Mrs. MacLeod said.

"Come in, come in—it can't hurt him," the intern said.

They came in, the son, a tall young man, his plain face anguished, his wife a slender blond woman who was crying behind her handkerchief, and the daughter, pretty and young, and dark like her father. Miss Martin knew them all, George, Ruth and Mary. It was a close family, anyone could see. The children had come every day to visit their father. They had decided together for the operation. It had been successful—that is, it had prolonged his life for three months in this narrow room.

"What about that fellow?" George asked, nodding toward the other bed.

"He's unconscious," Miss Martin said. "There's no other place to put him. Hospital's full. You can just forget him."

She was rubbing Mr. MacLeod's skeleton arm with alcohol. The intern plunged the needle into the loose skin.

"You should have as much as a half hour, Mrs. MacLeod. I'll be just outside the door."

"Thank you, Doctor," Mrs. MacLeod said.

She waited until doctor and nurse were gone and then, at her look, George and Ruth sat down near the bed. Mary came and knelt by her side.

"We're all here, Hal," Mrs. MacLeod said in her clear voice. "George and Ruth came over for supper tonight. We had lamb stew, the way you like it. The garden is coming in nice now. I pulled some little carrots this afternoon for the stew. It was good."

"We had lemon pie for dessert, Dad," George said. "Ruth is learning to make pie like Mom's. I didn't tell her she had to, either, did I, hon?"

"Sure not," Ruth said. She had stopped crying, but her lips were quivering.

"Ruth is one good little cook," George went on.

"Better than I was at her age," Mrs. MacLeod said. "You remember the first pie I ever made, Hal? Burned on top and raw on the bottom! It was cherry, too—your favorite. I could have cried. But you laughed and said you hadn't married me for a pie maker."

"The cherry tree will be full of cherries again this year, Dad," Mary said. She leaned her elbows on the bed, her eyes fixed on her father's face. "When they're ripe George must spread the net over it for you. The starlings are already waiting."

George laughed. "Those starlings, Dad! They never learn. Remember how they come every year and sit on the net and stare down at the cherries inside? You said you could almost hear them cuss. Well, it'll be

the same this year as ever."

Mary spoke, her voice very soft. "Cherry pie and picnics. That's when summer begins for me."

"I like picnics, too," Mrs. MacLeod said. "Old as I am, there's something about a picnic. We got engaged at a Sunday school picnic—your father and I."

"Dad, remember the time we had a Fourth of July picnic at Parson's Lake?" It was George again. "You showed me how to cast and the very first time I caught a bass. I yelled for everybody to come and see it."

"I love the summers," Mary said, in the same dreaming voice, "but when autumn comes I am glad, too. Remember the hickory nut tree, Dad? And I liked school, I really did. Don't make a face at me, George, just because you didn't!"

"Now you two," Mrs. MacLeod said, trying to laugh. "Can't you ever quit arguing?"

On the other bed, the boy's eyelids quivered, but no one noticed. He did not know himself that his eyelids quivered. Deep in the caverns of his brain he heard voices echoing.

"We had such good times when we were little," Mary said. "Sometimes I wish I were back there again, Mom, with you and Dad."

"Hush," Mrs. MacLeod said. "He wants to say something."

They leaned forward, their faces etched in the light, their eyes fixed upon the old man's grave face. His lips moved, he sighed, he opened his eyes and gazed at them, one face and then another.

"Dear," Mrs. MacLeod said, "it's lonesome at home without you. When the dishes were washed tonight we thought we'd come over."

She stopped to listen. He turned his head toward her.

"Martha . . ." It was his voice, a sigh, a whisper.

"Yes, Hal, I'm here, we're all here, the children wanted to come too, just to talk."

She nodded toward them.

"Little Hal and Georgie said to tell you hello, Dad," Ruth said quickly. "They're in bed. I have Lou Baker sitting with them. She's the girl next door, a nice girl. Little Hal said as soon as you come home he wants you to see his new tricycle you told us to get him for his birthday."

"He's thinking about Christmas already," George said. "He asked me yesterday if you'd get him a horn to put on the tricycle."

"I love Christmas." It was Mary's voice dreaming again. "Every Christmas I think about all the other Christmastimes that I can remember—our stockings hanging up on the mantel, yours and Mother's at the end, Dad, and George's and mine between. And the carol singers in the night—oh, how lovely the music was outside the window when I was warm in bed!"

She sang softly, "What child is this, who, laid to rest . . ."

In the other bed the boy's eyes were half open. He turned his head, not seeing, but the voices were clear now. He heard singing.

"I remember . . . everything," Mr. MacLeod said.

"Christmas Day," Mrs. MacLeod said, her yearning eyes upon his face. "It's always pure happiness. I never believe in company at Christmas. It's enough to have us all together. And now we have little Hal and Georgie."

"Mary will be getting married one of these days," George said. "And there'll be more of us."

"But we'll not be changed," Mary said. "Dad and Mother are our parents, forever and ever. We're your family, Dad. Even our being grown up can't change that."

"I hope I can be as good a father as you

are, Dad," George said.

The boy could see now. His eyes were open. He saw the other bed. An old, old man was lying there, and around him—people.

"Good children," the old man said drowsily. He seemed half asleep.

"How you two always knew exactly what we wanted!" Mary's voice was tender. "I remember the doll I had when I was nine, and the ring I found on the tree when I was fifteen—my first ring, but how did you know I wanted an emerald?"

"It was a very small one," her mother said.

"It had a little diamond on either side, and I still have it, and I still love it."

"I had skis when I was twelve," George said, "but I don't know how you knew I wanted them, Dad, for I never told you. I was afraid they'd cost too much. That was the year I had my appendix out."

"Dad always listens, especially around Christmas," Mrs. MacLeod said.

"But how did you know that for graduation I wanted a shockproof watch almost more than I wanted my diploma?" George asked.

"Or that I wanted a trip to California?" Mary asked.

"We . . . knew," Mr. MacLeod said. His voice trailed off. His eyelids fluttered.

The boy on the other bed turned to see the people better. That hurt, that hurt something awful. Where had he been going when he hit the truck? Nowhere, nowhere at all. He just couldn't stand anything anymore. He was running away from nobody, from nowhere to nowhere. Loafing around the streets, because nobody cared what he did—he couldn't remember anybody who had ever cared. Christmastime—he couldn't remember.

"Next Sunday is Easter," Mrs. MacLeod was saying. "The daffodils are up and the Easter lily is in bloom. It has six flowers on it

this year. I think the most it ever had before was three, wasn't it?"

Mr. MacLeod made an effort. "Five," he said distinctly.

"There now," Mrs. MacLeod said proudly. "He remembers better than I do. It did have five, one year."

The boy on the other bed listened. Easter. He knew the word. People dressed up and went to church. But what for?

Mr. MacLeod's eyelids fell. Mrs. MacLeod nodded and George went to the door.

"Come in, please, Doctor."

The intern came in on tiptoe and bent over Mr. MacLeod. He felt his pulse. It was still. Then he felt a few wavering beats. He shook his head.

Mrs. MacLeod's face went white but her voice was still clear. "You'd better be getting home to bed, children," she said. "You need your sleep—you're young. I'll stay a while with your dad."

They looked at each other, knowing. Ruth tried not to cry again. "Wait till you get out of the room, honey," George had told her.

"Good night, Dad," George said. "We'll see you in the morning."

"In the morning, darling Dad," Mary said. She leaned over her father, all her tenderness in her face. "In the bright, bright morning," she said.

Her father's eyes opened, but he did not speak.

They were gone then, the three children. The intern, hesitating, followed them.

From the other bed the boy watched the two old people. Gosh, they were old. What would happen now? He felt like crying but not about them. He felt like crying about himself because he had never had a father, because his mother had died when he was

little, because he had no family. That was the trouble with him—he had no family. You could be born and grow up with a lot of other kids in an orphanage and you thought you were all right but you weren't. The old woman was talking to the old man.

"Hal, all this remembering—and you and I have more to remember than the children. You've been a good husband, Hal. A good husband makes a happy wife. I don't mean just a good provider. You're that, of course. But the man you are, you've made me a happy woman, Hal. And out of our happiness together, the two of us, we've made happy children."

She paused, controlled her voice and went on. "I never pass by that little piece of woods where you asked me to marry you that I don't see us two standing there, you taking my hand." His hand was searching for hers and she clasped it in both of hers.

"Here I am. Oh darling—darling— darling—"

Her voice broke at last but she bit her lips. "Oh, God, help me—"

Then, her voice strong again, she went on. "I'll always see us standing there in the woods together. I'll never pass by without seeing us—"

"Martha." Her name scarcely broke the stillness, but she heard.

"Yes, Hal? I'm here. I shall stay right here."

He opened his eyes suddenly, he saw her and he smiled. "A good—life . . ." His voice trailed into silence and his hand loosened upon hers. His eyelids closed.

Now anyone could see the old man was dying. The boy wanted to cry. He hadn't cried since he was a kid and a big boy had hit him on the head. He didn't mind being hit, he was used to it, but not from that boy. And he had cried because he had liked to think the boy was maybe like a brother if he'd had one.

Mrs. MacLeod was crying, too. Tears rolled down her cheeks. After a few seconds she put down her husband's hand. She opened her bag and took out a small book with a leather cover, and she began to read aloud in a low voice, while the tears kept rolling down her cheeks.

"The Lord is my Shepherd, I shall not want . . ."

The boy heard the words. It was something in the Bible. In the orphanage Sunday school he'd heard that. But it hadn't meant anything. It was just words. People said words and it didn't mean anything. Now suddenly he knew what it meant. It meant the old man needn't be afraid, even though he had to die.

"Yea, though I walk through the valley of the shadow of death, I will fear no evil."

You don't need to be afraid, that's what the old woman was saying to him. You have a family, she was saying, and we love you. She would always remember that piece of woods, she told him, and how they stood there, he and she long ago, and he'd asked her to marry him, and she did, and they loved each other and that's how the family was made, he and she and then the children, and George's children—and Mary's, some day. . . .

The boy lay back on his pillow. His head was hurting him but it didn't hurt too bad. He didn't feel like crying anymore.

"And I shall dwell in the house of the Lord forever," Mrs. MacLeod was saying.

She closed the book and sat for a long, long moment. Then she got up and leaned over her husband and kissed him on the lips.

"Goodbye, my love," she said, "until we meet again."

She went to the door. "I'll go home now, Doctor," she told the intern.

He came in. "It's all over. You've been

very brave, Mrs. MacLeod."

"I haven't been brave," she said. "And it isn't over. The life we began together will go on and on—eternal life."

"Yes, indeed," the intern said without listening.

She went away then. But the boy knew what she meant. He lay thinking, staring up at the ceiling. He had never before known what life was for or what it was about, but now he knew. It was simply to love someone so much that you wanted to live together and make a family. It didn't matter any-more that he'd never had anyone to love him or to love. He could make his own family.

"Hey, young man!" The intern leaned over him. "How long have you been awake?"

"Not too long," the boy said, "maybe half an hour—"

He smiled a big smile but the intern was upset. "It's too bad, your seeing all this."

He pressed the bell and the nurse came in.

"Get a screen here, nurse!"

"Yes, doctor."

So they put up the screen and soon two men came with a stretcher and took the old man away and the boy said nothing. He knew just what was going on anyway. The family was together in the house that was their home and they'd be getting some breakfast, likely, and George would tell his mother not to mind for she still had them and the little kids. But all the same she'd never forget the old man—never, never. That was sure, because they loved each other and always would.

Peace came into the boy's heart. So now he knew why he had been born. And he wasn't going to die . . . only sleep. . . .

He woke late. The room was clean, the screen was gone. The other bed was empty and made up with fresh sheets. The sun was shining through the window. He was alone but for the first time in his life he was not lonely. He didn't have to live alone ever again. He could make a family, now that he saw how it was done. He'd get a job, find a girl, a nice girl. A girl could be nice. The old woman must have been a nice girl. He could see the old man, too, when he was young—a tall, skinny kid, standing there in the woods, asking the girl to marry him. And she'd said right away she would. He'd find a girl like that, someone who would be good to the kids, someone who would know how to cook and how to trim a Christmas tree. A tricycle! He'd wanted a tricycle something awful when he was a kid. It was the first thing he could remember about the orphanage—the tricycle he never got. You had to have parents for things like that. And kids—you could have kids of your own. Lucky old man, dying comfortable like that with all his kids there to see him off! You wouldn't mind dying when you'd had everything to live for—

The nurse came in, looking starched and clean. "How about some breakfast, young man?" she said in a bright voice.

He laughed and stretched himself.

"I feel *good*." he said. "Give me a real meal, will you? I'm plenty hungry!"

COMFORT

A FRAGILE MOMENT...

During the war a boy was brought into the hospital badly wounded. Word was sent to the mother that the boy was dying. She came to the hospital and begged to see him, but the doctors said that he was just hovering between life and death and that the slightest excitement might kill him. Besides, he was unconscious and would not know her. She promised that she would not speak to him or make the slightest noise, but begged to sit by the side of his bed and be with him. The doctor relented and gave permission for her to sit there without a word. She sat by her boy with her heart bursting. His eyes were closed. She gently put her hand upon his brow. Without opening his eyes the boy whispered, "Mother, you have come." The touch of that mother's hand was self-verifying to the boy. He knew it. When Christ puts His hand upon the fevered brow of our souls, we know the meaning of that touch and say from the inmost depths, "My Saviour, You have come."

E. Stanley Jones

THE SEASONS OF THE SOUL

Why am I cast down and despondently
   sad
When I long to be happy and joyous and
   glad?
Why is my heart heavy with unfathomable
   weight
As I try to escape this soul-saddened state?
I ask myself often—"What makes life this
   way,—
Why is the song silenced in the heart that
   was gay?"

And then with God's help it all becomes
   clear,
The Soul has its Seasons just the same as
   the year—
I too must pass through life's autumn of
   dying,
A desolate period of heart-hurt and crying,
Followed by winter in whose frostbitten
   hand
My heart is as frozen as the snow-covered
   land—
Yes, man too must pass through the seasons
   God sends,

COMFORT

Content in the knowledge that everything
   ends,
And oh what a blessing to know there are
   reasons
And to find that our soul must, too, have its
   seasons—
Bounteous Seasons and Barren Ones, too,
Times for rejoicing and times to be blue,
But meeting these seasons of dark
   desolation
With strength that is born of anticipation
That comes from knowing that
   "autumn-time sadness"
Will surely be followed by a "Springtime of
   Gladness."

Helen Steiner Rice

A MORNING PRAYER

Through the night Thine angels kept
Watch around me while I slept.
Now the dark has gone away,
Lord, I thank Thee for the day.

Anonymous

God shall be my hope,
My stay, my guide and lantern to my feet.

William Shakespeare

OUT IN THE FIELDS WITH GOD

The little cares that fretted me
   I lost them yesterday
Among the fields, above the sea,
   Among the winds at play,
Among the lowing of the herds,
   The rustling of the trees,
Among the singing of the birds,
   The humming of the bees.

The foolish fears of what might happen,
   I cast them all away,
Among the clover-scented grass,
   Among the new-mown hay,
Among the husking of the corn,

Where drowsy poppies nod.
Where ill thoughts die and good are
   born—
Out in the fields with God.

Elizabeth Barrett Browning

ON SUFFERING

Colleen Townsend Evans

Persecution . . . what a grim word. I don't
even want to think about it. I flinch from it
. . . it reminds me of the early Christians
and the suffering they endured.

But persecution still exists, and many of
us later Christians suffer for our faith. The
acts of torment are more subtle than those
the Romans used, but they can be very
painful . . . the social stigma we're given
when we refuse to join organizations that
exclude certain people . . . the looks of
guests at a dinner party when we don't
laugh at their dehumanizing jokes . . . the
ridicule a young person gets when he
refuses to go along with the group in
unhealthy experiments. Love itself disturbs
some people.

Chip, chip, chip—that's the way it goes
these days . . . hundreds of little
persecutions that chip away at our spiritual
complacency, reminding us that we are not
our own. We belong to Jesus, and there is a
price we must pay. . . .

If we're humble—the proud and
arrogant will call us foolish.

If we're tamed by God—those who are
self-made will call us weak.

If we're transparently honest—we will
irritate those who feel uncomfortable with
the truth.

If we're generous, and those around us
seek revenge—we'll be known as a soft
touch.

If we believe that God's ways are the best
ways for mankind—we'll be called prudes.

If we're peacemakers when others want
war—we'll be called weaklings, even
traitors.

Just as Jesus was persecuted, His followers will meet with opposition along the Way. Unavoidably the Christian life will be a rebuke to some—and people don't take kindly to being rebuked. . . .

But why does anyone have to suffer? Is it God's way of reprimanding us when we do something wrong? And if we do all the right things, will we automatically be exempt from this pain? . . .

Suffering is a stubborn fact of human life. It comes to everyone, without discrimination. But not all suffering has value—what we suffer *for* can make a difference. Jesus didn't say, *Happy are you when you suffer*—period. He said, *Happy are you when you suffer for right causes*.

If I were to tally the score, I'm sure I'd find that most of my suffering has come from doing something wrong to my brothers and sisters in life and not from doing something right for God. I have goofed more often than I like to admit . . . I've been thoughtless . . . I've hurt people . . . I've been selfish . . . and when I realize what I've done, I suffer. There is no joy in this kind of pain.

But even when I make careless mistakes I can feel God at work in me . . . showing me my weaknesses . . . pushing me to admit I was wrong . . . stretching me . . . and then finally giving me the grace to forgive myself. So there is some good in this kind of suffering, after all—yet it's not the kind Jesus is describing in this final Beatitude. When He says we will find joy through our pain, He is speaking about the kind of suffering we will know only when we stand with Him and walk His Way. It is the outcome of *living* the Beatitudes.

How easy it is for me to nod my head and say, "Yes, that's right!" Making it part of my life is something else. I find it very hard. When Jesus tells me not only to anticipate trouble but to "jump for joy" when it comes—that's hard. It will mean far more than nodding my head.

I think of Joachim, a man we met in a work camp in Europe some years ago. . . . He and his family suffered the loss of many material things because he was determined to fulfill his call to preach the gospel. . . .

I think of the martyred Stephen in the Book of Acts. . . . Yes, even today some Christians are giving their lives for Jesus Christ . . . and good things *do* come out of suffering when He is present.

I think of Corrie ten Boom and her sister, Betsie, imprisoned in the terrible concentration camp, Ravensbruck, during World War II . . . two young Dutch girls enduring inhuman brutality and coming through it spiritually triumphant. . . .

God invaded Corrie ten Boom's time of persecution, and He will do the same for us—*whenever our cause is right*. Few of us will ever go to prison for our faith, but at some point in our lives persecution will present us with a choice—do we enter in or back away? do we say *yes* or *no*? do we live or die? And by that, I don't mean only physical death, for there are other ways to die.

If we believe that the cause is right, if we are willing to suffer for the moment because God has given us eyes to see beyond now to what will follow, what then? What help will there be? What guarantee do we have that we will find strength, peace and joy at the end of the road?

A very good friend who has known more than a little suffering in life says, "We all will suffer persecution if we follow Jesus—but we must choose our hill wisely." In other words, we must be sure in our hearts that the cause we are willing to suffer for is His. For without His presence, there can be no joy in suffering.

But if we believe that the cause is God's—what then? How can we be sure He'll stand with us?

COMFORT

At this point I feel a little inadequate to write about this Beatitude. So many others could speak with depth of their experiences, while mine seem shallow. But Jesus doesn't tell us to *seek* suffering and persecution—only to expect it, accept it, and find joy in it when it comes. The portion that has come to me is small, and couldn't really be called persecution, but in my times of suffering God *has* brought me a strange kind of joy, and this is what I want to share. . . .

One day, without warning, it happens—you're not looking for trouble . . . you don't want to make waves . . . but all of a sudden you have to put your faith where your mouth is. . . . You do something that seems simple, uncompromising—and the world turns upside down. . . .

A few years ago we moved to a new church in a very beautiful, very affluent town. The town was changing . . . research centers were popping up all over the area, and the University of California had built a campus there. New industry brought new people, new ideas, new life-styles. Clearly, the town was on the growing edge of a changing American society. Its newness was part of what drew us there . . . it was also what repelled many of the established residents. That's the *where* of the situation. Add to this the *when*—the year of a bitter debate concerning open housing in California which wasn't the most welcome subject in a town where there were reports of a so-called gentlemen's agreement to keep "certain elements" out. And the *who*? The new minister and his wife, who didn't have the sense to do as they were told and stay away from controversy.

Within a short time after our installation Louie preached a group of sermons that applied the gospel to life—to *our* life in *our* town! In one sermon he read from Colossians 3:11: *In Christ there is no Jew or Greek, male or female—we are all one*. And

then he ended with a question. . . . If we believed in this oneness, could we actually deny *anything*—housing, jobs, education—to *anyone*?

A few weeks earlier I had been asked to join an Open Housing committee, and of course I did. I worked with some of our most dedicated citizens—dowagers, domestics, faculty wives, realtors, and just plain *hausfraus* like me. I had no idea I was headed for trouble until one day there was a picture of our committee in the newspaper. Immediately a member of our congregation took me aside and said, "No minister's wife should ever get involved in such a controversial thing!"

Well, Louie did, and I did, and now the repercussions began. First there were phone calls from friends who felt sorry for us . . . then there were angry callers who wanted to put us in our place. On the Sunday Louie preached on Colossians 3:11 I just got back to the house when the phone rang—it was my first obscene call! I guess I'm pretty "cream cheese" because I was so shocked, all I could say was, "Why, sir! God bless you!" and hung up. Then there was the message telling us, "Go back to Harlem where you belong" . . . and the endless stream of hate literature, parts of it underlined especially for us. . . .

In the beginning, when Louie became aware of the hostility, he was angry. I remember walking the beach with him for hours . . . we were asking ourselves—and God—if this was one of those times when we were to shake the dust from our feet and move on. There were places to move on to, and certainly we were tempted, but always the sense of call and the urgency to do a job right where we were won out. Our decision was simply to do as the gospel says—and take the consequences.

Then I saw something happen in Louie's life . . . Something was coming in from the outside. His times of quiet and prayer were

rewarded with peace and love . . . peace regarding what had happened, love for the opposition. It didn't seem natural—that's what I mean by "Something from outside." It was Christ's own Spirit.

I knew then that the cause was right. There would be no turning back. . . .

And through all these glad-sad years, many exciting things were happening—the Greater Parish Ministry, born of our Minister of Missions' dream of churches working together to meet the human needs of *our* people in *our* city . . . lay people trained and sent out as evangelists in our own congregation and community . . . new classes to make the mind stretch . . . a new contemporary worship service added to the two traditional Sunday-morning services . . . on Friday nights a chapel service of prayer and praise led by laymen . . . a youth program that makes your spirit zing, as young people from the church and from the streets of our town come together in the Sun House, getting to know each other and their Lord . . . the choirs growing in all ways, young people encouraged and trained to use their talents for God—their flutes, recorders, violins, bells, trumpets and guitars—surprising us with joy in our services . . . and best of all—*love* . . . love being felt and expressed, love touching and healing lives . . . a true baptism of love through the Holy Spirit.

Yes, during all these years God has been at work, and probably more in us than anywhere else. We have been pulled and pushed and made to grow, and He has been more than faithful. He has never left us without help.

During our most difficult days, help came in many forms, most of them unexpected. God was telling us that we weren't alone.

One Sunday a visiting minister came to speak at our church. He was a man everyone loved and respected. Although I had never met him, it took all of two

minutes after our introduction to make me feel he and I had been friends for a long time. He was old enough to be my father, widely traveled, and very charming.

Our guest was easy to talk to and as we lingered over Sunday dinner Louie and I told him about the crisis in our lives. If we were looking for sympathy—and I suppose we were—we didn't get any from him. Instead, this urbane, sophisticated man lifted our wounded spirits with words spoken quietly, almost to himself. He said, "In all my years of ministry, whenever the going gets rough because of preaching and living the gospel, I just turn my mind to my Lord. And when I think of *Him*, and all He went through—the ridicule, the misunderstanding, the betrayal, and then the cross—for *me*, for old me, I can't get too worked up about what I may be going through at the moment. I just think of my Lord—and it helps."

Our friend left town that evening and we didn't see him again, but his words stayed with us. They were like good seed in our hearts. Help had come gently, but unmistakably. Thinking of our Lord during our time of suffering made the wounds easier to bear. Looking at Him got our eyes off ourselves and gave us perspective.

We had lived through a difficult time—no, more than lived through it. We felt not only alive but strong . . . and very much at peace.

While that particular phase seemed over, and a beautiful new work of the Spirit was begun, the experience had left scars deep inside me. I wasn't aware of them until much later.

It happened on a rare quiet afternoon at our house. Everyone else was off somewhere, and I was about to splurge on an afternoon to myself. I was savoring the time to read . . . about five books I had already begun stared at me from my bed stand. I reached for the smallest one, a slim

volume on praise, hoping I would have the satisfaction of finishing it. I read for most of the afternoon and I was almost at the end of the book when a feeling of excitement came over me. I was expectant, eager, as if something important was about to happen. As I read I came to a quote from 1 Thessalonians 5:16-18: "Rejoice evermore. Pray without ceasing. In every thing give thanks: for this is the will of God in Christ Jesus concerning you." (KJV)

The words seemed to speak directly to me, and in response I began thanking God for all the beautiful and happy things in my life:

For my husband. . . . What do you say when, after twenty-two years of sharing life, you feel more love than when you first began—not *less*, but *more*! And not just love, but its handmaidens: Honesty and freedom of expression . . . the things that stretch a relationship and allow the soul within to grow. I thanked my God for Lou.

For our children, each one so unique, so full of his and her own special brand of joy and potential. I almost ached with love as I thought of Dan, Tim, Andie and Jim. . . .

For my mother's healing . . . because now this wonderful woman who had worked so hard—and alone—to raise a daughter would have a chance to enjoy her retirement years with her good husband. . . .

For Louie's parents—so incredibly active and used by God in their "retirement" ministry. . . .

For our special friends, the ones we call our "warm fuzzies," the ones with whom we share our life and ministry. . . .

For our congregation . . . if our first years among these people were hard, the recent years more than made up for them. We were among a loving, ministering core of believers, sharing their faith and trying to live the gospel we all believed in. . . .

There were so many things to thank God

for . . . they kept coming to my mind, one after another. I had never known such a full heart. But when I thought I was through, the Spirit let me know that He was not through with me . . . I heard no words, but the feeling was very clear—*There is more!*

In my mind I answered, "But, Lord, I've thanked You for *everything*—for *all* the good and lovely things in my life— honestly!"

Again there was that feeling—*There is more!*

I went back to I Thessalonians 5:16-18— ". . . In every thing give thanks: for this is the will of God in Christ Jesus concerning you." And again the words seemed to speak directly to me. They weren't telling me to thank God for all the beautiful and lovely things in my life. They said, ". . . In *every* thing give thanks. . . . " *All things* . . . did that mean even the hard, the painful things? Was I to thank God for the times of suffering, too? Yes—that was the "something more." The Spirit seemed to confirm it in my heart.

Now, if you were like me, you'd be thinking, "Wait a minute—that would be insincere. It doesn't make sense." To thank God for the good that comes out of suffering is realistic—but to thank Him for the suffering itself—well, I just didn't understand. Yet I knew that there were times when I had to respond to God in a simple, childlike way, or my faith wouldn't work. This was one of those times.

And so I began—thanking God for all the hard and bitter experiences of the past years. One by one, I relived them, and as I named them aloud they seemed so petty . . . the letters, the phone calls, the looks. As God brought them into my mind I was able to let go and give them to Him—with thanks. Then it was finished, and I was spent. But I felt whole. Deep inside me something tender had been touched by a gentle, loving, healing Hand. While I still

didn't understand what had happened, I knew that thanking God in all things had done something for me that I wasn't able to do for myself. Yes, I felt a kind of joy. . . . I knew then that this final Beatitude was as real, as practical, as right for today as all the others.

As the burden was lifted from my heart, I felt love replacing it . . . love for those who had helped, forgiveness and love for those who had hurt . . . understanding for their motives, compassion for their prejudices. I was free . . . and the kingdom of heaven was mine.

Sweet are the uses of adversity;
Which, like the toad, ugly and venomous,
Wears yet a precious jewel in his head;
And this our life, exempt from public haunt,
Finds tongues in trees, books in the running
 brooks,
Sermons in stones, and good in every thing.

William Shakespeare

When it is dark enough, men see the stars.

Ralph Waldo Emerson

More things are wrought by prayer
Than this world dreams of. Wherefore let
 Thy voice
Rise like a fountain for me night and day.
For what are men better than sheep or
 goats
That nourish a blind life within the brain,
If, knowing God, they lift not hands of
 prayer
Both for themselves and those who call them
 friend?
For so the whole round earth is every way
Bound by gold chains about the feet of God.

Alfred, Lord Tennyson

FLOWER CHORUS

O such a commotion under the ground,
 When March called "Ho, there! ho!"
Such spreading of rootlets far and wide,
 Such whisperings to and fro!

"Are you ready?" the Snowdrop asked,
 "'Tis time to start, you know."
"Almost, my dear!" the Scilla replied,
 "I'll follow as soon as you go."
Then "Ha! ha! ha!" a chorus came
 Of laughter sweet and low,
From millions of flowers under the ground,
 Yes, millions beginning to grow.

"I'll promise my blossoms," the Crocus said,
 "When I hear the blackbird sing."
And straight thereafter Narcissus cried,
 "My silver and gold I'll bring."
"And ere they are dulled," another spoke,
 "The Hyacinth bells shall ring."
But the Violet only murmured, "I'm here,"
 And sweet grew the air of spring.
Then "Ha! ha! ha!" a chorus came
 Of laughter sweet and low,
From millions of flowers under the ground,
 Yes, millions beginning to grow.

Oh, the pretty brave things, thro' the
 coldest days
 Imprisoned in walls of brown,
They never lost heart tho' the blast
 shrieked loud,
 And the sleet and the hail came down;
But patiently each wrought her wonderful
 dress,
 Or fashioned her beautiful crown.
And now they are coming to lighten the
 world
 Still shadowed by winter's frown.
And well may they cheerily laugh,
 "Ha! Ha!"
 In laughter sweet and low,
The millions of flowers under the ground,
 Yes, millions beginning to grow.

Ralph Waldo Emerson

A single sunbeam is enough to drive away many shadows.

St. Francis of Assisi

LIKE A SHEPHERD

Don Ian Smith

I have a fine saddle horse named Nellis. She is rather high-strung, and temperamental, and has some very definite likes and dislikes about people. In fact, she is so temperamental that I have to be careful who rides her lest someone should get bucked off. The horse is well trained, and I think she resents people who ride her as if she were a pack mule. My eldest daughter, Heather, is very fond of Nellis, and because of the mutual regard involved Heather seems to be the favorite with Nellis. I am sure Nellis likes Heather better than she likes me. And one who has never seen the affection that a girl can have for a horse has missed something very beautiful.

A few years ago Nellis was frightened by something, probably a bolt of lightning or a bear, and jumped into a barbed-wire fence. She was about a mile from our house up on a grassy hillside where she often grazed. It was Heather who first found her—weak from loss of blood, stiff and crippled from the deep, nasty wire cuts in her front legs. With tears of compassion streaming down her cheeks, Heather spent two hours leading the injured horse down the hill and into the barnyard. I don't think I could have done it. I doubt if the horse would have followed anyone less sensitive to her suffering. The pain in those crippled legs must have been intense, especially while Nellis was getting down the steep part of the trail. When I came home that evening and saw the horse I felt sure she would never run again; never again would she and Heather proudly bring home a ribbon from the horse show.

But I underestimated my daughter's care of the horse. Every morning and every night for several months, regardless of weather and other activities, Heather devoted herself to the needs of Nellis. She disinfected, washed and anointed with oil—soothing oil, healing oil. Nellis runs now as well as she ever did, and I will never again read the words "thou anointest my head with oil" without seeing in my mind a crippled, suffering horse and a little teen-age girl; a girl who day after day was up at daylight or before and out the door in rain, snow, or sub-zero weather because she cared. Our God is like that!

Kind words toward those you daily meet,
   Kind words and actions right,
Will make this life of ours most sweet,
   Turn darkness into light.

Isaac Watts

LORD, TEACH US TO PRAY

Pray *humbly*, never proudly. The prayer of the haughty Pharisee never got beyond the roof, but the prayer of the humble publican reached and touched the heart of God the instant it was uttered. We must pray not in pride of what we are, but in hope of what we may be, with the help of His Spirit.

Pray in *confession*; tell God all of it. Let it be even painfully honest. The least little cover-up will smother all the rest of it. Since Eden, God has never once been deceived by any of His human creatures, nor by the insincerity of any prayer.

Pray in complete *unselfishness*, for others as well as for ourselves, asking not what we can get but what we can give. Prayer is no "gimme game" to be played with God; He

gives what we need, not what we may selfishly want. It might be good to thank Him occasionally for not answering some of our prayers with a "Yes."

Pray in *expectancy*. Why pray at all, if we doubt that He is listening? Prayer in vague hope is nothing better than vague wishing; pray in faith, and He will hear.

Frank S. Mead

Be strong!
We are not here to play, to dream, to drift,
We have hard work to do, and loads to lift;
Shun not the struggle—face it; 'tis God's
    gift.

Be strong!
Say not, "The days are evil. Who's to
    blame?"
And fold the hands and acquiesce—oh
    shame!
Stand up, speak out, and bravely, in God's
    name.

Be strong!
It matters not how deep intrenched the
    wrong,
How hard the battle goes, the day how
    long;
Faint not—fight on! Tomorrow comes the
    song.

Maltbie D. Babcock

HOW TO BE HAPPY

Ruth Stafford Peale

Quite often, after I have given a talk to some church group or women's club, there is a question-and-answer period in which anyone can bring up anything that's on her mind. The other day a young woman in her late twenties or early thirties stood up and fired a direct and uncompromising question. "Mrs. Peale," she said, "are you a happy person?"

Fortunately, I didn't have to hesitate. "Yes," I said, "I am."

"Well," she said, "how do you do it? What makes you that way? I'm not a really happy person. Oh, I pretend to be most of the time. But this thing called happiness eludes me. I think it eludes most of my friends, too, although some will deny it. I know very few happy people, if any. There are just too many problems and tensions and frustrations in the average person's life these days. So if you are happy, I wish you'd tell us how you got that way, and how you stay that way, and how we can be happy too."

The audience grew very quiet and expectant, the way an audience does when a topic deeply interests people. I drew a deep breath, said a quick silent prayer and then talked for five or six minutes. To the best of my recollection, what I said went something like this:

I can't offer you any absolutely foolproof formula for happiness. I doubt if anyone can. But I can tell you a few things that I have found out about it, things that have been useful to me.

First of all, I'd advise you to stop struggling to be happy. Happiness isn't something that you can deliberately set out to achieve for yourself, like skill at typing or a college degree. In fact, the more you focus on your own happiness, or lack of it, the more it will continue to elude you. This is because preoccupation with self seems to be the enemy of happiness. The more concerned you are with your own pleasures and successes—or your own problems and failures, for that matter—the less contented you are going to be.

As wiser people than I have pointed out for centuries, the best way to get happiness is to give it. I've heard my husband quote Emerson—something to the effect that it's impossible to sprinkle perfume on another person without having some of it come

wafting back to you. I don't know why more women who are idle and restless and basically bored don't grasp this fundamental fact. Playing bridge or playing golf is fine—as a diversion. But in terms of deep-down happiness that sort of activity can't begin to compare with volunteer work in a hospital, or leading a Girl Scout troop, or helping underprivileged people in some direct and personal way. How many such outlets do you have in your life right now? If you'll double them, you'll be quadrupling your chance for this thing called happiness.

And it may sound strange, but I have found that solving problems, really solving them, can give a good, happy feeling. We all have the problems and tensions and frustrations of everyday living; no one is immune. But there are useful techniques for dealing with problems, and ways of minimizing tensions. For instance, in my husband's life there are dozens of problems to be faced, endless writing deadlines to be met, scores of administrative details to handle. I found out long ago that Norman is brilliantly capable of dealing with these successfully so long as they come at him one at a time. If they're all dumped in his lap at once, if they all come clamoring for attention together, he gets harassed and irritable—as well he might.

So I give myself the task of shielding him from the avalanche as much as I possibly can, of seeing to it that the problems are presented one at a time so that he can really concentrate on each one and dispose of it before the next one comes along. That way, he works along smoothly and efficiently and happily.

In my own case, too, when I'm faced by some big, ugly, complicated problem, instead of just staring at it in gloom and despair, I've learned to make myself analyze it, break it down into less formidable fragments, fragments that I can tackle right away with some hope of success.

I've found that if you chip away at a problem, piece by piece, you can often whittle it down to a size you can manage. And getting a problem under control will add to anyone's happiness.

This was dramatized for me years ago up at our farm when one of our maples died. We were afraid that if a strong wind came up, it might fall against the house and damage it. So we had to have the tree taken down.

Norman and I thought that the tree expert would just saw through the trunk and let the whole thing crash to the ground. But he didn't do it that way at all. First he trimmed off the small upper branches. Then, one by one, he sawed through the great limbs and lowered them with ropes and pulleys. Then he began taking down sections of the huge trunk, piece by piece, until there was only about twenty feet left. Finally he sawed this down, and the whole tree was gone. "We always tackle the easy part first," he said. "That way, the rest of the problem gets simpler and simpler as we go along." Norman was so impressed that he used the story as an illustration on problem solving in one of his sermons. And I've been using it myself with good results ever since.

I think, also, I'm a genuinely happy person because I am fortunate in being really quite free from disturbing inner conflicts. Norman says I'm well-organized. The fears and anxieties that seem to bother so many people are no problem to me. And for this I'm very thankful, having observed what fear does to some.

We all have problems, and there's no doubt that problem-solving may remove specific causes of unhappiness. But this alone won't provide the peace of mind, the quiet sense of joy and fulfillment that I think you're talking about. This is a gift that life bestows when you live a certain way and observe certain rules. Religion has always

known this, and the Bible has a great deal to say about it. That's why some of the happiest people I know are those who have a strong religious faith—and some of the unhappiest are those who have none. After all, if you believe that the Power that runs the universe loves you, is concerned about you, cares for you and will help you, how can you be anything but happy, no matter what difficulties you may be facing?

Long ago I put my life in God's hands and I simply trust Him: trust His love; trust His watchful care. Because I've always tried to grow spiritually, I believe I have no resentments. I don't hate anybody and I try to take my disappointments graciously. If a plan doesn't work out I simply ascribe it to God's guidance and ask what He desires to teach me. Now don't get the idea that I'm perfect. Ask Norman. He will tell you.

I'll give you one example of the kind of happiness that comes through faith. Some years ago my husband was speaking at a convention of businessmen in Chicago. It was in the ballroom of one of the big hotels, and I noticed that as he spoke some of the waitresses who had served us were standing along the wall listening. We had a plane to catch right after the talk. We had said our good-byes and were walking through the lobby when we heard someone calling our name. We turned and saw one of the waitresses in her uniform hurrying after us. She had one of the sweetest, happiest faces I ever saw on anybody. She rushed up to Norman and cried, "Oh, Dr. Peale, I just love you!"

"Well," laughed Norman, "I love you too. But what has happened to make us love each other so much?"

"I'll tell you," she answered. "I have a little boy. His father deserted us soon after

he was born, but I thanked God all the more that He'd given me this wonderful baby boy. Then when my boy was five years old, he got sick. The doctor told me it was very serious. He said, 'Mary, you've got to be strong. I don't know whether we can save your boy or not.' He was preparing me for the worst. I was in despair. I felt that my whole world would collapse if I lost my boy. He was all I had, and I loved him so.

"Then a neighbor gave me one of your sermons to read. In it you said, 'If you have a loved one who is ill or about whom you are worried, don't hold this loved one too closely. Surrender him to God. God gave him to you. He isn't yours, really, he is God's. So give him to God, for God is good. He's a great, kind, loving Father who holds each of His children in His love.'

"Well," she continued, "I'd never heard anything like that before. And it seemed awfully hard to do, but something inside me told me that it was right. So I prayed the way you said, and put my boy in God's keeping." And she held out her hands as if she were lifting up a child into the great arms of God.

"And what happened?" Norman gently asked.

Smiling through tears of joy, she said, "Isn't God good! He let me keep my boy. And now God and I are raising him together."

A number of other waitresses, Mary's friends, joined us and stood listening. There were tears in everybody's eyes, including mine. I guess there are always tears when you come into the presence of that kind of happiness.

You can't demand it. You can't buy it. You can't even earn it. It's a gift. But you have to want it. You have to accept it. You have to reach out for it. If I were you, that's what I'd do.

COMFORT

GOD BE IN MY HEAD

God be in my head,
And in my understanding;
God be in my eyes,
And in my looking;
God be in my mouth,
And in my speaking;
God be in my heart,
And in my thinking;
God be at my end,
And at my departing.

Old Sarum Primer

From SNOWFLAKE

Paul Gallico

The Snowflake was born on a cold, winter's day in the sky, many miles above the earth.

Her birth took place in the heart of a grey cloud that swept over the land driven by icy winds.

It came about from one moment to the next. At first there was only the swollen cloud moving over the tops of the mountains. Then it began to snow. And where but a second before there had been nothing, now there was Snowflake and all her brothers and sisters falling from the sky.

As gently as lying in a cradle rocked by the wind, drifting downward like a feather, blown this way and that, Snowflake found herself floating in a world she had never known before. Snowflake could not think when it was she had been born, or how. It had seemed almost like waking up from a deep sleep. An instant before she had been nowhere; now she was here, turning, gliding, sailing, falling, down, down.

She thought to herself: "Here I am. But where did I come from? And what was I before? Where have I been? Whither am I going? Who made me and all my brothers and sisters all about me? And why?"

There was no answer to these questions.

For the wind in the sky blows without sound, the sky itself is still; the very earth below is hushed when the snow begins to fall.

Looking about her, Snowflake could see hundreds upon hundreds of other flakes tumbling down as far as the eye could reach. And they were silent too.

It was strange, Snowflake thought, to see so many of her brothers and sisters, newborn like herself, and yet to feel so alone.

No sooner had she thought this when she became aware that all about her there was a kind of dear and tender love, the feeling as of some one caring, that filled her through and through with warmth and sweetness.

And now Snowflake no longer felt lonely. Secure and happy she gave herself up to the comfort and joy that came with the knowledge that she was loved.

Yet, she was no nearer the secret of her being, or Who it was had created her, or for what purpose, and whence came this deep and comforting affection. She wished she knew so that she could return some of the love she felt flowing from Him to her and which made her feel so content and safe at this moment. Perhaps she would find out more about Him when she came to the end of her journey.

As dawn began to come to the dark world through which Snowflake was tumbling on her long journey to the earth, the sky turned first the blue colour of steel, then grey, then pearl, and looking at herself as she tumbled over and over, fragile and airy as the wind that blew her, Snowflake knew that she was beautiful.

She was made up of pure, shining crystals, like fragments of glass or spun sugar.

She was all stars and arrows, squares and triangles of ice and light, like a church window; she was like a flower with many

shining petals; she was like lace and she was like a diamond. But best of all, she was herself and unlike any of her kind. For while there were millions of flakes, each born of the same storm, yet each was different from the other.

Snowflake felt grateful to the One who had given her such beauty and wished she knew how it came about that in an instant He was able to create them all, each one as lovely as a jewel and yet no two of them alike. How great a One must He be to devote such love and patience to perfect one and at the same time so many snowflakes.

It had been bitterly cold high up where she had been born, blown by the freezing wind, but after she had been falling for what seemed like a long time, Snowflake felt that it was growing warmer and the air more still.

She was no longer tossed and tumbled but instead dropped more slowly and softly. And this was a lovely feeling, a gentle, dreamy sinking, always slower and slower as though her long journey might be about to come to an end.

Which indeed it was.

Soon Snowflake could make out objects below her, dark tops of mountains and slopes of snow, forests of tall pine trees and on the side of a hill a village with houses and barns and a church with a round steeple shaped like an onion.

Her brothers and sisters clung to whatever they touched, rocks, branches, rooftops, fences and even the ragged eyebrows of an old man out for an early walk. But Snowflake landed gently with hardly a jar in a field on the mountainside just outside the village, and the journey was over.

A few moments later the storm came to

an end and it began to grow light, so that Snowflake, looking eagerly about her, could see where she was.

She lay on the side of a slope overlooking the village and the church with the curious steeple shaped like an onion and below this was a school and a number of little houses with peaked roofs, many with pictures in gay colours painted beneath the eaves and balconies with carved railings running around the second story.

Here and there a yellow light showed in the upper windows and wisps of smoke began to emerge from the chimneys and rise into the still air.

Nearby there was a signpost crowned with a hat of white where some of Snowflake's brothers and sisters had fallen upon it, and the snow came down hiding part of the sign so that all she could read was "..IESENBERG."

Whatever the name of the village was, Snowflake was glad she had fallen there and not higher on the mountain where there were only dark rocks and a few trees and it looked cold and lonely.

The wind blew the clouds away. The sky became brighter. And then a miracle began to happen.

First the very tip of the snow-capped mountain peak across the valley was touched with delicate rose. Slowly it spread to the next summit and then the next. The sky, the rocks and the trees became tinged with pink, the river winding far below reflected the colour; the snow everywhere was touched with it and soon even the air itself was glowing as though the whole world were but the mirror of a rose petal.

And Snowflake too saw that she was no longer white but bathed like everything else in this soft and beautiful colour.

Then the pink on the mountain tops turned to gold and orange and lemon and the blue shadows on the slopes melted and fled before the light that spilled down like

paint from the crests until soon every peak and range within sight gleamed yellow in the morning sun. From somewhere in the distance came the sound of sleigh bells. Snowflake thought it was so beautiful it made her want to cry. It was her first sunrise.

Later in the morning, Snowflake had a surprise.

Down the hill on a high wooden sled with steel runners came a little girl with flaxen pigtails, bright blue eyes and red cheeks like two rubber balls.

She was the merriest little girl, who sat bravely upright on her sled wearing a red cap with a tassel and red mittens on her fingers. Her schoolbag was strapped to her back, she carried her lunch in a paper box, and steered the sled cleverly with her feet, this way and that, sending up great clouds of snow as she whizzed by.

As she passed over, the steel runner cut deeply into Snowflake's heart and hurt her cruelly so that she gave a little cry.

But the child did not hear her. She was quickly gone and only her joyous shouts drifted back in the cold morning air, until she arrived at the school at the bottom of the hill where she stopped her sled at the front door and went inside.

Snowflake found herself wishing that she would come back, for she was so gay and pretty, prettier even, Snowflake thought, than the sunrise.

There were so many things that Snow-flake did not understand and wanted to know.

She thought how beautifully she had been greeted by the sunrise soon after she had been born. How simply some One had expressed His love for all the things He had created by painting for them such a glorious picture in the morning sky.

And what a splendid thing to do to make a little girl with yellow pigtails, blue eyes and red cheeks who rode bravely on a sled to school and laughed all the time.

But what was the purpose, and who was meant for whom?

Had Snowflake been born only to be there beneath the steel runner when it came by to speed sled and child along so that they would not be late for school?

Or had the Creator made the girl with her sweet face and silver laugh but to delight the heart of Snowflake? How could one ever know the answers to these problems?

There were so many new and exciting things going on all around that soon Snowflake forgot the questions that were troubling her.

From the barn just below the hill came a peasant wearing a stocking cap with a tassel and smoking a large pipe with a curved stem. He was leading a grey cow by a rope and had a small black and white dog with rough fur and a wise, friendly face who frisked at his heels. Around the neck of the cow was fastened a square bell that gave forth a gentle and musical "tonkle-tonkle" when she moved.

They passed close to where Snowflake was lying and the grey cow paused for a moment. The peasant cried "Heuh!", the dog barked and made believe to snap at her hooves, the bell tonkled sweetly and Snowflake looked for an instant into her face and saw the great, tender, dreamy eyes filled with patience and kindness and framed by long, graceful lashes.

Snowflake thought: "How soft and beautiful they are." And then she wondered: "What is beauty? I have seen the sky, the mountains, the forest and a village. I have seen the sunrise and a little girl and now the eyes of a grey cow. Each was different and yet they all made me happy. Surely they must have been created by that

same unknown One. Could it be that beauty means all things that come from His hands?"

Now that the storm was over and the day had come, everybody in the village went about his business again. But first one had to shovel a path from one's door to the road, piling up the snow on either side like miniature ranges of mountains.

Then the woodcutter carried out his sawhorse and big, bowed saw and began to cut the logs that lay in his yard into lengths for the stove. His son came to help him and with a glittering axe split some of the pieces into kindling.

Next door the carpenter went to work, planing and hammering on a window frame he was making.

In another house the tinsmith applied his heavy shears and mallet to shining sheets of metal and cut and bent them to the sizes and shapes he desired.

On the farm just above the road, the farmer's wife came out carrying a basket of scraps on each arm to feed the chickens and the pigs. The pigs squealed and crowded to the door of their pen. The chickens shook the snow from their wings and hurried over.

The cold, clear winter's day was filled with the sound of sawing, chopping, hammering and planing, with snuffling and grunting and crowing and clucking.

When the little girl with the red cap and mittens returned that afternoon from school two boys were at her side, each trying to see who could make her laugh the loudest. When they reached the place where Snowflake lay, one of them cried: "Let us make Frieda a snowman!"

No sooner said than done. They rolled together a huge ball for the body and a smaller one for the head. Two bits of charcoal served for the eyes and a piece of wood for the mouth.

"We will give him a long nose, just like Herr Hüschl, the teacher," cried one of the boys, and with that he bent over, scooped up snow in each hand, and began to pack the flakes firmly.

And, alas, Snowflake was amongst them.

How it hurt when she was squeezed until she could hardly breathe. All her beautiful design of which she had been so proud was crushed. When the nose was finished the boy planted it squarely in the middle of the face of the snowman. Then they put a ruler in his hand and said it looked exactly like Herr Hüschl.

The little girl Frieda laughed and laughed and screamed with delight and then she and the boys ran off still laughing and left Snowflake a part of the nose of the snowman who was like Herr Hüschl, the schoolmaster.

At first, Snowflake was sad, for she could not think why this had happened to her.

Always her thoughts came back to why, and what was the purpose of it all? Why had He who had taken such care in the beautiful design He had made for her high up in a cloud let her be squeezed all out of shape to be the nose of a snowman?

Why, indeed, had He made her a snowflake instead of a little girl with blue eyes, flaxen pigtails, red mittens and lunch in a paper bag? What fun it must be to ride downhill on a sled, go to school and have friends.

But soon Snowflake became more cheerful, for everybody who passed the snowman on the hill stopped and either smiled or laughed at the nose which was so exactly like that of the schoolmaster, even to the drop of water hanging from the end of it.

And Snowflake felt comforted. It seemed to be good for people to laugh and be happy. Perhaps it was for this that she had been created and sent to earth. Whenever

someone came by she waited eagerly for the laughter to begin.

Then came a day that was not at all like the others had been. To begin with it was quiet and solemn. The children did not come to the school. No one did any work. Even the barnyard animals seemed to make less noise. Only the bells from the belfry of the church steeple that was shaped like an onion rang out loudly and clearly and with a new kind of authority.

Thereupon Snowflake saw a most wonderful sight. All the people of the village appeared in the square below by the church, dressed up in their best clothes. The women wore long skirts with many petticoats beneath and had their hair done up in braids. All the men were clad in black suits with buttons of silver or horn on the coats, and many of them had fine gold or silver watchchains. They wore round black hats with green bands and a *gamsbart* like a small brush sticking up behind.

The children, too, had on their best ski suits and prettiest frocks, and all the little girls had gay ribbons and bows tied into the straw-coloured plaits of their hair.

Everyone was washed and scrubbed and shined and primped. They all stood in little knots in the square before the church as though they were waiting for something. Snowflake wondered what it could be.

She was soon to find out. For now occurred an even more exciting and wonderful thing.

Down the side of the mountain, on every path and slope, as far as the eye could see, little black dots appeared. They were moving and growing larger and Snowflake saw that there were whole families on sleds, fathers, mothers and children. They were all the people who lived on the farms high up above the village and who were now coasting down to church.

And they too were dressed in their best

clothes, for this was Sunday. The dark suits showed up bravely against the white snow. The coloured ribbons of the girls stood out like pennants. Converging from all directions they came whizzing down the hill to land in the square, amidst laughter and greeting. When the last family had arrived, they all went inside the church, leaving the square quite empty.

Then Snowflake heard the music of the organ and the sound of the voices of young and old lifted in song. And as she listened, she felt that her heart was deeply touched, though she did not know why.

Afterwards, when the service was over and the people went home, the sky clouded over and it grew colder. An old gentleman in a black frock coat and carrying a big stick walked by the snowman and paused to look. He had a long nose and angry eyes. He did not laugh as the others had. It was Herr Hüschl, the schoolteacher himself.

No, Herr Hüschl did not laugh at all. Instead he became red in the face and very angry, especially when he compared the nose of the snowman with his own and saw that they were exactly the same even to the drop of water at the end of it.

He gave a cry of rage, raised his stick and began to beat the snowman until it was broken into pieces and lay scattered on the hillside.

But he was not content with this. He sought out what was left of the head that contained his long nose and with a loud shout of "So!" he ground the offending piece beneath the heel of his muddy boot until there was no longer even the smallest bit of it left to suggest the length or shape of his nose.

Or, until there was very little left of Snowflake, either.

"Help!" she called out. "Won't someone help me?"

But there was no answer and she lay there, broken, dirtied, heavy-hearted and

full of pain, listening to Herr Hüschl stumping off mumbling angrily to himself. And a short while later, it began to snow again.

The new snowstorm lasted all day and all night, and when it was over, Snowflake was buried under many feet of the new fall.

It was quite dark and she could no longer see anything.

But although she could not see, she could still hear, and, listening, she tried to guess the things that were happening above her.

Snowflake knew, for instance, that the peasant must be leading the grey cow home to milk, for she heard her soft moo, and the gentle tonkling of the square bell around her neck.

Thus she strained eagerly for all the well-known sounds that told her that even while she lay buried and forgotten, life in the village was going on. She heard the church clock strike the hours and the bells ring out to come to service. There were the sounds of wood being sawed, nails being hammered and roosters crowing.

Dogs barked, cats meowed. There were footsteps and people hailed one another with "*Gruess Gott!*" as they passed. She even thought that once she heard the laughter of the little girl with the red cap and mittens, and it made her sad with longing for her, for she felt that she might never see her again.

Thus began a new life for Snowflake, and it was not a happy one. Each time there was a fresh storm, or the rain fell and turned the surface to a hard crust of ice, it grew deeper and darker where she lay.

Soon even the sounds barely came through to her, and when they did, they were muffled so that she could hardly make them out. Often it was difficult to tell whether it was the church bells calling to mass, or the hammer of the metal-smith, whether it was the merry cries and shouts of the school children or the gabble of the chickens, whether it was the lowing of the grey cow or the whistle of the railway train running along the river far away in the valley below.

But what made Snowflake the saddest, sadder even than missing the gay children, or the sight of the sunrise and the sunset and the feel of the crisp cool air against her cheek, or losing her beautiful shape and having to lie there in the dark, muddied and soiled, was the thought that she had been abandoned by the One who had created her and whose love had made her feel so happy and secure in the cradle of the wind when first she was born.

Buried there, Snowflake thought that surely this could not be the end, that she had been born only to see a sunrise, hear a little girl laugh, and become the nose on a snowman.

When she remembered the care with which she had been made and the love she had felt she knew that it could not be so but only perhaps that she had been forgotten. One who could create so many stars in the sky, who could think of a church with a steeple like an onion, who could put together a grey cow with soft eyes and people a whole village, must be very busy.

And so she decided that she would speak to Him and ask Him to help her. And when she had thought this it seemed to her as if He were there, close to her and listening.

She said: "Dear One who made me, have you forgotten me? I am lonely and afraid. Please help me. Take me out of the darkness and let me see the light once more."

And having asked that, she added timidly, "I love you."

As soon as she had said that she no longer felt so lonely but happy and excited instead as though perhaps something wonderful

might be about to happen to her.

It began first with a strange drumming that sounded from overhead and seemed to go on endlessly. Snowflake had never before heard anything like it, for it was the noise made by rain when first it falls in the early spring upon the hard crust of the winter's snow.

Yet, somehow, Snowflake had the feeling that whatever was happening above was welcome and might be in answer to her prayer. Her fears were quieted and she listened to the new sound with a sense of comfort and hope.

The drumming softened to a plashing to which was added now a gentle murmuring. The long rains at last had filtered down from above and the waters were moving restlessly beneath the layers of frozen snow and ice that still covered the earth.

Then one day the rain ceased and it began to grow lighter. At first Snowflake could not believe it was true. But the darkness in which she had lived so long turned to deep blue, then emerald green, changing to yellow as though a strong light were shining through a heavy veil.

The next moment, as though by magic, the veil was lifted. Overhead the sun, warm and strong, burned from a cloudless sky. Snowflake was free once again. Her heart gave a great shout:

"The sun! The sun! Dearly beloved sun! How glad I am to see you."

TO COMFORT ALL THAT MOURN

Catherine Marshall

Most people accept intellectually a belief in some kind of life after death. But usually it remains a theoretical belief until death invades one's immediate family circle.

Then at the time of the funeral, we are handed the victory. The working through of the specific problems that sorrow brings

must come later.

Many know that initial victory. As with all God's gifts, we do nothing to earn or to deserve it. Undoubtedly a loving Father knows that without this kind of help, many of us could never withstand the emotional shock, would never even be able to get through the funeral.

At that time, the first need of the bereaved person is for comfort—just plain comfort. In sorrow, we are all like little children, hurt children who yearn to creep into a mother's arms and rest there; have her stroke our foreheads and speak softly to us as she used to do. But, of course, that is impossible; we are grown men and women. Yet the need for comfort remains.

Our God has promised precisely that . . . "Comfort ye, comfort ye my people, saith your God . . ." "For thus saith the Lord . . . As one whom his mother comforteth, so will I comfort you. . . ."

Strangely in my case I was given the beginning of that experience of comfort a few hours prior to my husband's death. That morning Peter had wakened about three-thirty with severe pains in his arms and chest. The doctor had come as quickly as he could. He had insisted that Dr. Marshall be taken immediately to the hospital.

As we had waited for the ambulance, Peter had looked up at me through his pain and said, "Catherine, don't try to come with me. We mustn't leave Wee Peter alone in this big house. You can come to the hospital in the morning."

Reluctantly I had agreed. I knew that he was right, though I wanted so much to be with him.

After the ambulance had come and gone, I went back upstairs and sank to my knees beside the bed. There was the need for prayer, for this was an emergency indeed. It could mean only one thing—another massive heart attack. But how was I to pray?

Swirling emotions had plunged my mind into utter confusion.

Suddenly the unexpected happened. Over the turbulent emotions there crept a strange all-pervading peace. And through and around me flowed love as I had never before experienced it. It was as if body and spirit were floating on a cloud, resting—as if Someone who loved me very much were wrapping me round and round with His love.

I knelt there marveling at what was happening. I had done nothing, said nothing, to bring it about. Through my mind trooped a quick procession of thoughts . . . the Three Persons of the Godhead . . . Father, Son and Holy Spirit. . . . Sometimes I've known the spirit within as a nudge, as direction, or reminder, or conscience. . . . Once that was the turning point in my long illness. . . . But this is different . . . this must be the Father. . . . Maybe this is what the Bible means by that lovely statement— "underneath are the everlasting arms." That describes exactly what I'm feeling. . . .

But what did this mean in relation to Peter, his ailing heart, and the emergency that threatened us? I thought it meant that everything was going to be all right, that Peter would be healed. There seemed to be nothing for which to ask God. Surely there was no need of asking for His Presence; that Presence was all around me. So my prayer took the form of simply thanking Him for the miracle that His love could be such a personal love; for His tender care of Peter and Wee Peter and me.

At 8:15 the same morning, Peter stepped across the boundary that divides this life from the next. Then I knew that the experience of the night before had meant something far different. I had been granted it so that when the blow fell I might have the certainty that a loving Father had not deserted me.

If we put our problems in God's hand,
There is nothing we need understand—
It is enough to just believe
That what we need we will receive.

Helen Steiner Rice

HE THAT LOVETH ME . . .
John 14: 1-27

"Let not your heart be troubled: ye believe in God, believe also in me. In my Father's house are many mansions: if it were not so, I would have told you. I go to prepare a place for you. And if I go and prepare a place for you, I will come again, and receive you unto myself; that where I am, there ye may be also. And whither I go ye know, and the way ye know."

Thomas saith unto him, "Lord, we know not whither thou goest; and how can we know the way?"

Jesus saith unto him, "I am the way, the truth, and the life: no man cometh unto the Father, but by me. If ye had known me, ye should have known my Father also: and from henceforth ye know him, and have seen him."

Philip saith unto him, "Lord, shew us the Father, and it sufficeth us."

Jesus saith unto him, "Have I been so long time with you, and yet hast thou not known me, Philip? He that hath seen me hath seen the Father; and how sayest thou then, 'Shew us the Father'? Believeth thou not that I am in the Father, and the Father in me? The words that I speak unto you I speak not of myself: but the Father that dwelleth in me, he doeth the works. Believe me that I am in the Father, and the Father in me: or else believe me for the very works' sake.

"Verily, verily, I say unto you, He that believeth on me, the works that I do shall he do also; and greater works than these shall he do; because I go unto my Father. And

COMFORT

whatsoever ye shall ask in my name, that will I do, that the Father may be glorified in the Son. If ye shall ask any thing in my name, I will do it.

"If ye love me, keep my commandments. And I will pray the Father, and he shall give you another Comforter, that he may abide with you for ever; Even the Spirit of truth; whom the world cannot receive, because it seeth him not, neither knoweth him: but ye know him; for he dwelleth with you, and shall be in you. I will not leave you comfortless: I will come to you. Yet a little while, and the world seeth me no more; but ye see me: because I live, ye shall live also. At that day ye shall know that I am in my Father, and ye in me, and I in you.

"He that hath my commandments, and keepeth them, he it is that loveth me; and he that loveth me shall be loved of my Father, and I will love him, and I will manifest myself to him."

Judas saith unto him, Not Iscariot, "Lord, how is it that thou wilt manifest thyself unto us, and not unto the world?"

Jesus answered and said unto him, "If a man love me, he will keep my words: and my Father will love him, and we will come unto him, and make our abode with him. He that loveth me not, keepeth not my sayings: and the word which ye hear is not mine, but the Father's which sent me.

"These things have I spoken unto you, being yet present with you. But the Comforter, which is the Holy Ghost, whom the Father will send in my name, he shall teach you all things, and bring all things to your remembrance, whatsoever I have said unto you.

" Peace I leave with you, my peace I give unto you: not as the world giveth, give I unto you. Let not your heart be troubled, neither let it be afraid."

EVENSONG

The embers of the day are red
Beyond the murky hill.
The kitchen smokes; the bed
In the darkling house is spread:
The great sky darkens overhead,
And the great woods are shrill.
So far have I been led,
Lord, by Thy will:
So far I have followed, Lord, and
    wondered still.
The breeze from the embalmed land
Blows sudden towards the shore,
And claps my cottage door.
I hear the signal, Lord—I understand.
The night at Thy command
Comes. I will eat and sleep and will not
    question more.

Robert Louis Stevenson

WISDOM

A FRAGILE MOMENT . . .

Seven things I have tried:
Laughing at difficulties, and found them disappearing.
Attempting heavy responsibilities, and found them
　　growing lighter.
Facing a bad situation, and found it clearing up.
Telling the truth, and found it the easiest way out.
Doing an honest day's work, and found it the most
　　rewarding.
Believing men honest, and found them living up to
　　expectation.
Trusting God each day, and found Him surprising me
　　with His goodness.

D. Carl Yoder

SOLOMON ASKS FOR WISDOM

The Living Bible, I *Kings 3*

Solomon made an alliance with Pharaoh,
the king of Egypt, and married one of his
daughters. He brought her to Jerusalem to
live in the City of David until he could finish
building his palace and the Temple and the
wall around the city.

At that time, the people of Israel
sacrificed their offerings on altars in the
hills, for the Temple of the Lord hadn't yet
been built.

King Solomon loved the Lord. One night
He appeared to him in a dream and told
him to ask for anything he wanted, and it
would be given to him!

Solomon replied, "You were wonderfully
kind to my father David because he was

honest and true and faithful to You, and
obeyed Your commands. And You have
continued Your kindness to him by giving
him a son to succeed him. O Lord my God,
now You have made me the king instead of
my father David, but I am as a little child
who doesn't know his way around. And
here I am among Your own chosen people,
a nation so great that there are almost too
many people to count! Give me an
understanding mind so that I can govern
Your people well and know the difference
between what is right and what is wrong.
For who by himself is able to carry such a
heavy responsibility?"

The Lord was pleased with his reply and
was glad that Solomon had asked for
wisdom. So He replied, "Because you have
asked for wisdom in governing My people

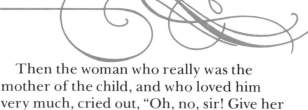

and haven't asked for a long life or riches for yourself, or the defeat of your enemies—yes, I'll give you what you asked for! I will give you a wiser mind than anyone else has ever had or ever will have! And I will also give you what you didn't ask for—riches and honor! And no one in all the world will be as rich and famous as you for the rest of your life! And I will give you a long life if you follow Me and obey My laws as your father David did.

Then Solomon woke up and realized it had been a dream. He returned to Jerusalem and went into the Tabernacle. And as he stood before the Ark of the Covenant of the Lord, he sacrificed burnt offerings and peace offerings. Then he invited all of his officials to a great banquet.

Soon afterwards, two young prostitutes came to the king to have an argument settled.

"Sir," one of them began, "we live in the same house, just the two of us, and recently I had a baby. When it was three days old, this woman's baby was born too. But her baby died during the night when she rolled over on it in her sleep and smothered it. Then she got up in the night and took my son from beside me while I was asleep, and laid her dead child in my arms and took mine to sleep beside her. And in the morning when I tried to feed my baby it was dead! But when it became light outside, I saw that it wasn't my son at all."

Then the other woman interrupted, "It certainly was her son, and the living child is mine."

"No," the first woman said, "the dead one is yours and the living one is mine." And so they argued back and forth before the king.

Then the king said, "Let's get the facts straight: both of you claim the living child, and each says that the dead child belongs to the other. All right, bring me a sword." So a sword was brought to the king. Then he said, "Divide the living child in two and give half to each of these women!"

Then the woman who really was the mother of the child, and who loved him very much, cried out, "Oh, no, sir! Give her the child—don't kill him!"

But the other woman said, "All right, it will be neither yours nor mine; divide it between us!"

Then the king said, "Give the baby to the woman who wants him to live, for she is the mother!"

Word of the king's decision spread quickly throughout the entire nation, and all the people were awed as they realized the great wisdom God had given him.

THE LEGEND OF THE SPIDER AND THE SILKEN STRAND HELD IN GOD'S HAND

There's an old Danish Legend
  with a lesson for us all
Of an ambitious spider
  and his rise and his fall,
Who wove his sheer web
  with intricate care
As it hung suspended
  somewhere in midair,
Then in soft, idle luxury
  he feasted each day
On the small, foolish insects
  he enticed as his prey,
Growing ever more arrogant
  and smug all the while
He lived like a "king"
  in self-satisfied style—
And gazing one day
  at the sheer strand suspended,
He said, "I don't need this,"
  so he recklessly rended
The strand that had held
  his web in place
And with sudden swiftness
  the web crumpled in space—
And that was the end
  of the spider who grew
So arrogantly proud

that he no longer knew
That it was the strand
   that reached down from above
Like the chord of God's grace
   and His infinite love
That links our lives
   to the great unknown,
For man cannot live
   or exist on his own—
And this old legend
   with simplicity told
Is a moral as true
   as the legend is old—
Don't sever the "lifeline"
   that links you to
THE FATHER IN HEAVEN
   WHO CARES FOR YOU.

Helen Steiner Rice

   To reach the port of heaven we must
sail, sometimes with the wind and
sometimes against it—but we must sail, not
drift or lie at anchor.

Oliver Wendell Holmes

The lowest ebb is the turn of the tide.

Henry Wadsworth Longfellow

Teach us, good Lord,
to give and not to count the cost;
to fight and not to heed the wounds;
to toil and not to seek for rest;
to labor and not to ask for any reward
save that of knowing that we do Thy will.

St. Ignatius of Loyola

   I have held many things in my hands, and
have lost them all; but whatever I have
placed in God's hands, that I still possess.

Martin Luther

I ASKED . . .

I asked God for strength,
   that I might achieve,
  I was made weak, that I might learn
    humbly to obey . . .

I asked for health,
   that I might do greater things,
  I was given infirmity,
   that I might do better things . . .

I asked for riches,
   that I might be happy,
  I was given poverty,
   that I might be wise . . .

I asked for power,
   that I might have the praise of men,
  I was given weakness,
   that I might feel the need of God . . .

I asked for all things,
   that I might enjoy life,
  I was given life,
   that I might enjoy all things . . .

I got nothing that I asked for—
   but everything that I had hoped for,
  Almost despite myself, my unspoken
   prayers were answered.

I am, among all,
   most richly blessed!

Author Unknown

THE SEARCH

Arthur Gordon

It was one of those curiously aimless
Sunday afternoons that every family knows.
I had driven the children out into the
country to look for pinecones and acorns;
any objective is better than none! Their
mother had a touch of flu; I was mainly
interested in letting her get some rest. So

we were on our own, the kids and I.

It was one of those hazy autumn days we get sometimes in the Deep South when no wind stirs and the dust motes hang like golden smoke in the soft air. It was also one of those days when I was feeling depressed. No single, overwhelming problem. Just a combination of things. A friend had done me an unkindness, or so I thought. A promising writing assignment had fallen through. There was, inside our family circle, a corrosive little problem of human relationships that stubbornly refused to yield to reason or common sense.

These things kept eddying through my mind, and just about sundown we came across a place that seemed to fit my mood perfectly; a forgotten cemetery in a quiet oak grove, lichen-covered headstones tilted fantastically under a ghostly canopy of Spanish moss. The children ran around like a pack of hounds, making a game of finding the oldest date. ("Hey, look, an 1840!" "Ha, that's young. Here's an 1812!") I stood by one of the weathered stones and watched. Disturbed by the shouts and laughter, a big brown owl drifted out of a magnolia tree and vanished on reproachful wings. *Don't be upset, old owl*, I said to him in my mind, *children's voices don't trouble the dead*.

The stone beside me marked the resting place of somebody's BELOVED WIFE who died in 1865 OF A FEVER. Beneath her name was a line of script, almost indistinguishable. I looked closer, wondering which biblical phrase her grieving children might have chosen. But it was not a quotation; it was a statement: EVER SHE SOUGHT THE BEST, EVER FOUND IT.

Eight words. I stood there with my fingers on the cool stone, feeling the present fade and the past stir behind the illusion we call time. A century ago this woman had been living through a hideous war. Perhaps it took her husband from her,

perhaps her sons. When it ended her country was beaten, broken, impoverished. She must have known humiliation, tasted despair. Yet someone who knew her had written that she always looked for the best, and always found it.

It's strange, sometimes, how a single phrase will haunt you. As we walked back to the car through the gray twilight, I could not get this one out of my mind. EVER SHE SOUGHT THE BEST. There was courage in the words, and dignity, and purpose. And a kind of triumph, too, as if they contained a secret of inestimable value. What you look for in life, they seemed to be saying, you will surely find. But the direction in which you look is up to you.

The station wagon was waiting by the side of the road. As the miles fled past, I found myself thinking of the things that had been bothering me. They were real enough, but now I saw that I had been focusing, not on the best, but on the worst. Where my friend was concerned, what was one misunderstanding compared to years of affection? The lost assignment was disappointing, but there would be others. The family difficulty was a rocky little island, but after all, it was surrounded by an ocean of love.

We were home at last. The children straggled in, tired now, ready for their supper. I looked at the house and thought of the worries I had often entertained there like honored guests, inviting them in, spreading banquets before them, giving them a preposterous preference over all the good things the same house contained. *Perhaps*, I told myself, *you've learned something today*: SEARCH FOR THE BEST.

The living room was familiar and quiet; the chair was an old friend; the fire muttered in the grate. *Search for it?* I said to myself. *You don't have to search very far. No one does. It's around us all the time, the goodness, the abundance, the wonder of living. The miracle of it all*.

The five-year-old climbed up on my lap and burrowed his porcupine head into my shoulder. I could see the firelight reflected in his dreaming eyes. "Daddy?"

"Yes?" It would be dark, now, in the old burial ground. Darkness and silence, and the old owl watching the shifting leaf patterns, and wisdom carved on an ancient stone.

"Tell me a story."

"A story?" *One generation passeth away, and another generation cometh.* "Well, once upon a time. . . ."

"GOOD EVENING, PROFESSOR"

Ruth Stafford Peale

One of the chief ingredients of fun is a sense of humor, and most good senses of humor include a sense of the ridiculous. Norman and I still laugh over an episode that happened early in our marriage. Norman was the young minister in charge of the staid and impressive University Church in Syracuse. Somewhat in awe of the dignified deans and erudite professors who were in his congregation, he took pains never to say or do anything unconventional or bizarre. He was always very proper indeed.

One summer afternoon, coming home from the church, he passed by the house of an elderly spinster named Miss Foote, who was also a member of his congregation. Miss Foote was in her front yard looking distractedly for her favorite cat, which apparently had run away.

Norman says that I was forever lecturing him on the importance of always helping his parishioners, no matter what their problem might be. So he offered to help Miss Foote find her cat. "Where did you see him last?" Norman wanted to know. "Right over there," cried Miss Foote. "I think he went through that hole in the hedge!"

The hole was a small one, but Norman

gallantly got down on his hands and knees and started crawling through it. Twigs and leaves rained down upon him, brambles pulled his glasses askew, but he kept going until suddenly his head emerged on the far side of the hedge about eighteen inches above a sidewalk. There was no sign of the cat, but on the sidewalk was a pair of feet belonging to a pedestrian who had halted in amazement. Looking up, Norman saw the austere countenance of Professor Perley O. Place, the most imperious and forbidding member of the entire faculty. The gaze of incredulity and disapproval that the professor bestowed upon his spiritual guide and counselor was so paralyzing that Norman couldn't even attempt an explanation. All he could say was, "Good evening, Professor!"

"Extraordinary!" murmured the learned pedagogue frostily, "Most extraordinary!" And he stalked away.

TODAY

Mend a quarrel. Search out a forgotten friend. Dismiss suspicion and replace it with trust. Write a letter. Share some treasure. Give a soft answer. Encourage youth. Manifest your loyalty in a word or deed.

Keep a promise. Find the time. Forego a grudge. Forgive an enemy. Listen. Apologize if you were wrong. Try to understand. Flout envy. Examine your demands on others. Think first of someone else. Appreciate, be kind, be gentle. Laugh a little more.

Deserve confidence. Take up arms against malice. Decry complacency. Express your gratitude. Worship your God. Gladden the heart of a child. Take pleasure in the beauty and wonder of the earth. Speak your love. Speak it again. Speak it still again. Speak it still once again.

Author Unknown

There is a time for everything, and a season for every activity under heaven.

Ecclesiastes 3:1 (N.I.V. Bible)

THE THREE QUESTIONS

Leo Tolstoi

It once occurred to a certain King, that if he always knew the right time to begin everything; if he knew who were the right people to listen to, and whom to avoid; and, above all, if he always knew what was the most important thing to do, he would never fail in anything he might undertake.

And this thought having occurred to him, he had it proclaimed throughout his kingdom that he would give a great reward to any one who would teach him what was the right time for every action, and who were the most necessary people, and how he might know what was the most important thing to do.

And learned men came to the King, but they all answered his questions differently.

In reply to the first question, some said that to know the right time for every action, one must draw up in advance a table of days, months and years, and must live strictly according to it. Only thus, said they, could everything be done at its proper time. Others declared that it was impossible to decide beforehand the right time for every action; but that not letting oneself be absorbed in idle pastimes, one should always attend to all that was going on, and then do what was most needful. Others, again, said that however attentive the King might be to what was going on, it was impossible for one man to decide correctly the right time for every action, but that he should have a Council of wise men, who would help him to fix the proper time for everything.

But then again others said there were some things which could not wait to be laid before a Council, but about which one had at once to decide whether to undertake them or not. But in order to decide that, one must know beforehand what was going to happen. It is only magicians who know that; and, therefore, in order to know the right time for every action, one must consult magicians.

Equally various were the answers to the second question. Some said the people the King most needed were his councillors; others, the priests; others, the doctors; while some said the warriors were the most necessary.

To the third question, as to what was the most important occupation; some replied that the most important thing in the world was science. Others said it was skill in warfare; and others, again, that it was religious worship.

All the answers being different, the King agreed with none of them, and gave the reward to none. But still wishing to find the right answers to his questions, he decided to consult a hermit, widely renowned for his wisdom.

The hermit lived in a wood which he never quitted, and he received none but common folk. So the King put on simple clothes, and before reaching the hermit's cell dismounted from his horse, and, leaving his bodyguard behind, went on alone.

When the king approached, the hermit was digging the ground in front of his hut. Seeing the King, he greeted him and went on digging. The hermit was frail and weak, and each time he stuck his spade into the ground and turned a little earth, he breathed heavily.

The King went up to him and said: "I have come to you, wise hermit, to ask you to answer three questions: How can I learn to

do the right thing at the right time? Who are the people I most need, and to whom should I, therefore, pay more attention than to the rest? And, what affairs are the most important, and need my first attention?"

The hermit listened to the King, but answered nothing. He just spat on his hand and recommenced digging.

"You are tired," said the King, "let me take the spade and work a while for you."

"Thanks!" said the hermit, and, giving the spade to the King, he sat down on the ground.

When he had dug two beds, the King stopped and repeated his questions. The hermit again gave no answer, but rose, stretched out his hand for the spade, and said:

"Now rest awhile—and let me work a bit."

But the King did not give him the spade, and continued to dig. One hour passed, and another. The sun began to sink behind the trees, and the King at last stuck the spade into the ground, and said:

"I came to you, wise man, for an answer to my questions. If you can give me none, tell me so, and I will return home."

"Here comes someone running," said the hermit, "let us see who it is."

The King turned round and saw a bearded man come running out of the wood. The man held his hands pressed against his stomach, and blood was flowing from under them. When he reached the King, he fell fainting on the ground moaning feebly. The King and the hermit unfastened the man's clothing. There was a large wound in his stomach. The King washed it as best he could, and bandaged it with his handkerchief and with a towel the hermit had. But the blood would not stop flowing, and the King again and again removed the bandage soaked with warm blood, and washed and rebandaged the wound. When at last the blood ceased flowing, the man revived and asked for something to drink. The King brought fresh water and gave it to him. Meanwhile the sun had set, and it had become cool. So the King, with the hermit's help, carried the wounded man into the hut and laid him on the bed. Lying on the bed the man closed his eyes and was quiet; but the King was so tired with his walk and with the work he had done, that he crouched down on the threshold, and also fell asleep—so soundly that he slept all through the short summer night. When he awoke in the morning, it was long before he could remember where he was, or who was the strange bearded man lying on the bed and gazing intently at him with shining eyes.

"Forgive me!" said the bearded man in a weak voice, when he saw that the King was awake and was looking at him.

"I do not know you, and have nothing to forgive you for," said the King.

"You do not know me, but I know you. I am that enemy of yours who swore to revenge himself on you, because you executed his brother and seized his property. I knew you had gone alone to see the hermit, and I resolved to kill you on your way back. But the day passed and you did not return. So I came out from my ambush to find you, and I came upon your bodyguard, and they recognized me, and wounded me. I escaped from them, but should have bled to death had you not dressed my wound. I wished to kill you, and you have saved my life. Now, if I live, and if you wish it, I will serve you as your most faithful slave and will bid my sons do the same. Forgive me!"

The King was very glad to have made peace with his enemy so easily, and to have gained him for a friend, and he not only

forgave him, but said he would send his servants and his own physician to attend him, and promised to restore his property.

Having taken leave of the wounded man, the King went out into the porch and looked around for the hermit. Before going away he wished once more to beg an answer to the questions he had put. The hermit was outside, on his knees, sowing seeds in the beds that had been dug the day before.

The King approached him, and said:

"For the last time, I pray you to answer my questions, wise man."

"You have already been answered!" said the hermit, still crouching on his thin legs, and looking up at the King, who stood before him.

"How answered? What do you mean?" asked the King.

"Do you not see," replied the hermit. "If you had not pitied my weakness yesterday, and had not dug those beds for me, but had gone your way, that man would have attacked you, and you would have repented of not having stayed with me. So the most important time was when you were digging the beds; and I was the most important man; and to do me good was your most important business. Afterwards when that man ran to us, the most important time was when you were attending to him, for if you had not bound up his wounds he would have died without having made peace with you. So he was the most important man, and what you did for him was your most important business. Remember then: there is only one time that is important—now! It is the most important time because it is the only time when we have any power. The most necessary man is he with whom you are, for no man knows whether he will ever have dealings with anyone else; and the most important affair is to do him good, because for that purpose alone was man sent into this life!"

MEET THE MASTER

Charles L. Allen

He was born in a village, of poor parents in an insignificant little country. When He was twelve years old He was conscious of the fact that God had placed Him here for a specific purpose. At the age of thirty He made public His plans and purposes and began the three short years of His public ministry.

He loved people and enjoyed being with them. He went to their parties; He was a popular dinner guest; even the little children crowded around Him. He invited twelve men to work with Him, and later He commissioned them to carry on His work. He told a ruler about an experience called the "new birth."

He offered an outcast woman water that would quench the thirst of her very soul. He healed the sick, raised the dead, opened the eyes of the blind, loosed the tongues of the dumb, brought hearing to the deaf, and caused the lame to walk. He fed those who were hungry, and brought peace to troubled minds.

He taught the people that happiness comes from the inside, that the solution to hates and prejudices is not in laws but in love. He told of the amazing power of prayer, that the treasures one lays up in heaven are more important than the treasures one accumulates on earth, that a divided heart leads to destruction.

Faith in God was to Him a matter of supreme importance. Because God so beautifully clothed the lilies of the field, and because God cared so tenderly for even the birds of the air, He concluded that humans who are to live eternally should not worry about the things of this life. Instead, one should seek God's kingdom first, and the other things of life would be taken care of.

He warned against people judging each

other. He warned that a life built on any other principles than the ones He taught would be like a house built on sand that would not stand in the face of a storm.

He said that His Kingdom was like the growth of the tiny seed that eventually becomes a tree, or like the leaven that eventually leavens the entire loaf. And that possessing Him was worth all else one had, just as the merchant sold all his possessions in order to own the one pearl of supreme worth.

When one of His disciples suggested, after a marvelous worship experience, that He just continue there, He refused. Every mountaintop experience of worship was translated by Him into acts of service and of living. He said that the way to become great was to become a servant.

Firmly He taught that one is never justified in holding an unforgiving spirit. To a crowd which was preparing to stone a sinner to death He suggested that the one without sin cast the first stone. And to the sinner He said, "Neither do I condemn thee, go and sin no more." He loved sinners and freely forgave everyone who would accept forgiveness.

Simple stories from everyday life illustrated the eternal principles He taught. The Samaritan who turned aside to help one in need, the foolish rich man who thought of his physical needs but forgot his soul, the shepherd who hunted until he found just one lost sheep, the father who welcomed his prodigal son home, are some of those stories.

He wept with friends who had lost a loved one by death. He was disappointed when some people He had healed expressed no gratitude. He pointed out that God expects every person to do his part, even though he has only one talent.

He cursed a fig tree for not producing fruit. He drove people out of the church who were misusing it. He said that we have duties to our government and duties to God. He praised a widow who gave a small gift.

He did not want to die, but He chose death rather than lower His standards. But as He died, He prayed for the forgiveness of those who were killing Him, He gave comfort to a man dying with Him, He thought of the care of His mother, and He expressed His faith in God.

Three days after He was buried, He came back to life. He spoke to a woman, He encouraged some disheartened people, He spoke peace to His disciples, and one morning He even cooked their breakfast. He told His few followers to carry on His work until it covers the world, and finally He ascended into heaven.

He is today the one hope of the world. He is Jesus Christ, the Son of God and the Saviour of man.

I believe in the light of shining stars,
　　I believe in the sun and the moon;
I believe in the flash of lightning,
　　I believe in the night-bird's croon.
I believe in the faith of the flowers,
　　I believe in the rock and sod,
For in all of these appeareth clear
　　The handiwork of God.

Author Unknown

THE STORY OF THE OTHER WISE MAN

Henry van Dyke

The Sign in the Sky

In the days when Augustus Caesar was master of many kings and Herod reigned in Jerusalem, there lived in the city of Ecbatana, among the mountains of Persia, a certain man named Artaban, the Median.

WISDOM

His house stood close to the outermost of the seven walls which encircled the royal treasury. From his roof he could look over the rising battlements of black and white and crimson and blue and red and silver and gold, to the hill where the summer palace of the Parthian emperors glittered like a jewel in a sevenfold crown.

Around the dwelling of Artaban spread a fair garden, a tangle of flowers and fruit trees, watered by a score of streams descending from the slopes of Mount Orontes, and made musical by innumerable birds. But all color was lost in the soft and odorous darkness of the late September night, and all sounds were hushed in the deep charm of its silence, save the splashing of the water, like a voice half sobbing and half laughing under the shadows. High above the trees a dim glow of light shone through the curtained arches of the upper chamber, where the master of the house was holding council with his friends.

He stood by the doorway to greet his guests—a tall, dark man of about forty years, with brilliant eyes set near together under his broad brow, and firm lines graven around his fine, thin lips; the brow of a dreamer and the mouth of a soldier, a man of sensitive feeling but inflexible will—one of those who, in whatever age they may live, are born for inward conflict and a life of quest.

His robe was of pure white wool, thrown over a tunic of silk; and a white, pointed cap, with long lapels at the sides, rested on his flowing black hair. It was the dress of the ancient priesthood of the Magi, called the fire-worshippers.

"Welcome!" he said, in his low, pleasant voice, as one after another entered the room—"welcome, Abdus; peace be with you, Rhadaspes and Tigranes, and with you, my father, Abgarus. You are all welcome, and this house grows bright with the joy of your presence."

There were nine of the men, differing widely in age, but alike in the richness of their dress of many-colored silks and in the massive golden collars around their necks, marking them as Parthian nobles, and in the winged circles of gold resting upon their breasts, the sign of the followers of Zoroaster.

They took their places around a small black altar at the end of the room, where a tiny flame was burning. Artaban, standing beside it, and waving a barsom of thin tamarisk branches above the fire, fed it with dry sticks of pine and fragrant oils. Then he began the ancient chant of the Yasna, and the voices of his companions joined in the beautiful hymn to Ahura-Mazda:

We worship the Spirit Divine,
    all wisdom and goodness possessing,
Surrounded by Holy Immortals,
    the givers of bounty and blessing,
We joy in the works of His hands,
    His truth and His power confessing.

We praise all the things that are pure,
    for these are His only Creation;
The thoughts that are true, and the words
    and deeds that have won approbation;
These are supported by Him
    and for these we make adoration.

Hear us, O Mazda! Thou livest
    in truth and in heavenly gladness;
Cleanse us from falsehood, and keep us
    from evil and bondage to badness;
Pour out the light and the joy of Thy life
    on our darkness and sadness.

Shine on our gardens and fields,
    Shine on our working and weaving;
Shine on the whole race of man,
    Believing and unbelieving;
    Shine on us now through the night,
    Shine on us now in Thy might,
The flame of our holy love
    and the song of our worship receiving.

The fire rose with the chant, throbbing as if it were made of musical flame, until it cast a bright illumination through the whole apartment, revealing its simplicity and splendor.

The floor was laid with tiles of dark blue veined with white; pilasters of twisted silver stood out against the blue walls; the clear-story of round-arched windows above them was hung with azure silk; the vaulted ceiling was a pavement of sapphires, like the body of heaven in its clearness, sown with silver stars. From the four corners of the roof hung four golden magic-wheels, called the tongues of the gods. At the eastern end, behind the altar, there were two dark-red pillars of porphyry; above them a lintel of the same stone, on which was carved the figure of a winged archer, with his arrow set to the string of his bow drawn.

The doorway between the pillars, which opened upon the terrace of the roof, was covered with a heavy curtain of the color of a ripe pomegranate, embroidered with innumerable golden rays shooting upward from the floor. In effect the room was like a quiet, starry night, all azure and silver, flushed in the east with rosy promise of the dawn. It was, as the house of a man should be, an expression of the character and spirit of the master.

He turned to his friends when the song was ended, and invited them to be seated on the divan at the western end of the room.

"You have come tonight," said he, looking around the circle, "at my call, as the faithful scholars of Zoroaster, to renew your worship and rekindle your faith in the God of Purity, even as this fire has been rekindled on the altar. We worship not the fire, but Him of whom it is the chosen symbol, because it is the purest of all created things. It speaks to us of one who is Light and Truth. Is it not so, my father?"

"It is well said, my son," answered the venerable Abgarus, "The enlightened are never idolaters. They lift the veil of the form and go in to the shrine of the reality, and new light and truth are coming to them continually through the old symbols."

"Hear me, then, my father and my friends," said Artaban, very quietly, "while I tell you of the new light and truth that have come to me through the most ancient of all signs. We have searched the secrets of nature together, and studied the healing virtues of water and fire and the plants. We have read also the books of prophecy in which the future is dimly foretold in words that are hard to understand. But the highest of all learning is the knowledge of the stars. To trace their courses is to untangle the threads of the mystery of life from the beginning to the end. If we could follow them perfectly, nothing would be hidden from us. But is not our knowledge of them still incomplete? Are there not many stars still beyond our horizon—lights that are known only to the dwellers in the far southland, among the spice-trees of Punt and the gold-mines of Ophir?"

There was a murmur of assent among the listeners.

"The stars," said Tigranes, "are the thoughts of the Eternal. They are numberless. But the thoughts of man can be counted, like the years of his life. The wisdom of the Magi is the greatest of all wisdoms on earth, because it knows its own ignorance. And that is the secret of power. We keep men always looking and waiting for a new sunrise. But we ourselves know that the darkness is equal to the light, and that the conflict between them will never be ended."

"That does not satisfy me," answered

Artaban, "for, if the waiting must be endless, if there could be no fulfillment of it, then it would not be wisdom to look and wait. We should become like those new teachers of the Greeks, who say that there is no truth, and that the only wise men are those who spend their lives in discovering and exposing the lies that have been believed in the world. But the new sunrise will certainly dawn in the appointed time. Do not our own books tell us that this will come to pass, and that men will see the brightness of a great light?"

"That is true," said the voice of Abgarus; "every faithful disciple of Zoroaster knows the prophecy of the Avesta and carries the word in his heart. 'In that day Sosiosh the Victorious shall arise out of the number of the prophets in the east country. Around him shall shine a mighty brightness, and he shall make life everlasting, incorruptible, and immortal, and the dead shall rise again.' "

"This is a dark saying," said Tigranes, "and it may be that we shall never understand it. It is better to consider the things that are near at hand, and to increase the influence of the Magi in their own country, rather than to look for one who may be a stranger, and to whom we must resign our power."

The others seemed to approve these words. There was a silent feeling of agreement manifest among them; their looks responded with that indefinable expression which always follows when a speaker has uttered the thought that has been slumbering in the hearts of his listeners. But Artaban turned to Abgarus with a glow on his face, and said:

"My father, I have kept this prophecy in the secret place of my soul. Religion without a great hope would be like an altar without a living fire. And now the flame has burned more brightly, and by the light of it I have read other words which also have come from the fountain of Truth, and speak yet more clearly of the rising of the Victorious One in his brightness."

He drew from the breast of his tunic two small rolls of fine linen, with writing upon them, and unfolded them carefully upon his knee.

"In the years that are lost in the past, long before our fathers came into the land of Babylon, there were wise men in Chaldea, from whom the first of the Magi learned the secret of the heavens. And of these, Balaam, the son of Beor, was one of the mightiest. Hear the words of his prophecy: 'There shall come a star out of Jacob, and a sceptre shall arise out of Israel.' "

The lips of Tigranes drew downward with contempt, as he said:

"Judah was a captive by the waters of Babylon, and the sons of Jacob were in bondage to our kings. The tribes of Israel are scattered through the mountains like lost sheep, and from the remnant that dwells in Judea under the yoke of Rome neither star nor sceptre shall arise."

"And yet," answered Artaban, "it was the Hebrew Daniel, the mighty searcher of dreams, the counsellor of kings, the wise Belteshazzar, who was most honored and beloved of our great King Cyrus. A prophet of sure things and a reader of the thoughts of God, Daniel proved himself to our people. And these are the words that he wrote." (Artaban read from the second roll:) " 'Know, therefore, and understand that from the going forth of the command-ment to restore Jerusalem, unto the Anointed One, the Prince, the time shall be seven and three-score and two weeks.' "

"But, my son," said Abgarus, doubtfully, "these are mystical numbers. Who can interpret them, or who can find the key that shall unlock their meaning?"

Artaban answered: "It has been shown to me and to my three companions among the Magi—Caspar, Melchior, and Balthazar.

We have searched the ancient tablets of
Chaldea and computed the time. It falls in
this year. We have studied the sky, and in
the spring of the year we saw two of the
greatest stars draw near together in the sign
of the Fish, which is the house of the
Hebrews. We also saw a new star there,
which shone for one night and then
vanished. Now again the two planets are
meeting. This night is their conjunction. My
three brothers are watching at the ancient
Temple of the Seven Spheres, at Borsippa,
in Babylonia, and I am watching here. If
the star shines again, they will wait ten days
for me at the temple, and then we will set
out together for Jerusalem, to see and
worship the promised one who shall be
born King of Israel. I believe the sign will
come. I have made ready for the journey. I
have sold my house and my possessions,
and brought these three jewels—a
sapphire, a ruby, and a pearl—to carry
them as tribute to the King. And I ask you
to go with me on the pilgrimage, that we
may have joy together in finding the Prince
who is worthy to be served."

While he was speaking he thrust his hand
into the inmost fold of his girdle and drew
out three great gems—one blue as a
fragment of the night sky, one redder than
a ray of sunrise, and one as pure as the peak
of a snow mountain at twilight—and laid
them on the outspread linen scrolls before
him.

But his friends looked on with strange
and alien eyes. A veil of doubt and mistrust
came over their faces, like a fog creeping up
from the marshes to hide the hills. They
glanced at each other with looks of wonder
and pity, as those who have listened to
incredible sayings, the story of a wild vision,
or the proposal of an impossible enterprise.

At last Tigranes said: "Artaban, this is a
vain dream. It comes from too much
looking upon the stars and the cherishing
of lofty thoughts. It would be wiser to
spend the time in gathering money for the
new fire-temple at Chala. No king will ever
rise from the broken race of Israel, and no
end will ever come to the eternal strife of
light and darkness. He who looks for it is a
chaser of shadows. Farewell."

And another said: "Artaban, I have no
knowledge of these things, and my office as
guardian of the royal treasure binds me
here. The quest is not for me. But may thy
steps be prospered wherever thou goest.
So, farewell."

And another said: "I am ill and unfit for
hardship, but there is a man among my
servants who I will send with thee when
thou goest, to bring me word how thou
farest."

But Abgarus, the oldest and the one who
loved Artaban the best, lingered after the
others had gone, and said, gravely: "My
son, it may be that the light of truth is in this
sign that has appeared in the skies, and
then it will surely lead to the Prince and the
mighty brightness. Or it may be that it is
only a shadow of the light, as Tigranes has
said, and then he who follows it will have
only a long pilgrimage and an empty
search. But it is better to follow even the
shadow of the best than to remain content
with the worst. And those who would see
wonderful things must often be ready to
travel alone. I am too old for this journey,
but my heart shall be a companion of the
pilgrimage day and night, and I shall know
the end of thy quest. Go in peace."

So one by one they went out of the azure
chamber with its silver stars, and Artaban
was left in solitude.

He gathered up the jewels and replaced
them in his girdle. For a long time he stood
and watched the flame that flickered and
sank upon the altar. Then he crossed the

hall, lifted the heavy curtain, and passed out between the dull red pillars of porphyry to the terrace on the roof.

The shiver that thrills through the earth ere she rouses from her night's sleep had already begun, and the cool wind that heralds the daybreak was drawing downward from the lofty, snow-traced ravines of Mount Orontes. Birds, half-awakened, crept and chirped among the rustling leaves, and the smell of ripened grapes came in brief wafts from the arbors.

Far over the eastern plain a white mist stretched like a lake. But where the distant peak of Zagros serrated the western horizon the sky was clear. Jupiter and Saturn rolled together like drops of lambent flame about to blend in one.

As Artaban watched them, behold, an azure spark was born out of the darkness beneath, rounding itself with purple splendors to a crimson sphere, and spiring upward through rays of saffron and orange into a point of white radiance. Tiny and infinitely remote, yet perfect in every part, it pulsated in the enormous vault as if the three jewels in the Magian's breast had mingled and been transformed into a living heart of light.

He bowed his head. He covered his brow with his hands.

"It is the sign," he said, "The King is coming, and I will go to meet him."

By the Waters of Babylon

All night long Vasda, the swiftest of Artaban's horses, had been waiting, saddled and bridled, in her stall, pawing the ground impatiently, and shaking her bit as if she shared the eagerness of her master's purpose, though she knew not its meaning.

Before the birds had fully roused to their strong, high, joyful chant of morning song, before the white mist had begun to lift lazily from the plain, the other wise man was in the saddle, riding swiftly along the high-road, which skirted the base of Mount Orontes, westward.

How close, how intimate is the comradeship between a man and his favorite horse on a long journey. It is a silent, comprehensive friendship, an intercourse beyond the need of words.

They drink at the same wayside springs, and sleep under the same guardian stars. They are conscious together of the subduing spell of nightfall and the quickening joy of daybreak. The master shares his evening meal with his hungry companion, and feels the soft, moist lips caressing the palm of his hand as they close over the morsel of bread. In the gray dawn he is roused from his bivouac by the gentle stir of a warm, sweet breath over his sleeping face, and looks up into the eyes of his faithful fellow-traveler, ready and waiting for the toil of the day. Surely, unless he is a pagan and an unbeliever, by whatever name he calls upon his God, he will thank Him for this voiceless sympathy, this dumb affection, and his morning prayer will embrace a double blessing— God bless us both, and keep our feet from falling and our souls from death!

And then, through the keen morning air, the swift hoofs beat their spirited music along the road, keeping time to the pulsing of two hearts that are moved with the same eager desire—to conquer space, to devour the distance, to attain the goal of the journey.

Artaban must indeed ride wisely and well if he would keep the appointed hour with the other Magi: for the route was a hundred and fifty parasangs, and fifteen was the utmost that he could travel in a day. But he knew Vasda's strength, and pushed forward without anxiety, making the fixed distance every day, though he must travel late into the night, and in the morning long before sunrise.

He passed along the brown slopes of Mount Orontes, furrowed by the rocky

courses of a hundred torrents.

He crossed the level plains of the Nisaeans, where the famous herds of horses, feeding in the wide pastures, tossed their heads at Vasda's approach, and galloped away with a thunder of many hoofs, and flocks of wild birds rose suddenly from the swampy meadows, wheeling in great circles with a shining flutter of innumerable wings and shrill cries of surprise.

He traversed the fertile fields of Conca-bar, where the dust from the threshing-floors filled the air with a golden mist, half hiding the huge temple of Astarte with its four-hundred pillars.

At Baghistan, among the rich gardens watered by fountains from the rock, he looked up at the mountain thrusting its immense rugged brow out over the road, and saw the figure of King Darius trampling upon his fallen foes, and the proud list of his wars and conquests graven high upon the face of the eternal cliff.

Over many a cold and desolate pass, crawling painfully across the windswept shoulders of the hills; down many a black mountain-gorge, where the river roared and raced before him like a savage guide; across many a smiling vale, with terraces of yellow limestone full of vines and fruit trees; through the oak groves of Carine and the dark Gates of Zagros, walled in by precipices; into the ancient city of Chala, where the people of Samaria had been kept in captivity long ago; and out again by the mighty portal, riven through the encircling hills, where he saw the image of the High Priest of the Magi sculptured on the wall of rock, with hand uplifted as if to bless the centuries of pilgrims; past the entrance of the narrow defile, filled from end to end with orchards of peaches and figs, through which the river Gyndes foamed down to

meet him; over the broad rice-fields, where the autumnal vapors spread their deathly mists; following along the course of the river, under tremulous shadows of poplar and tamarind, among the lower hills; and out upon the flat plain, where the road ran straight as an arrow through the stubble-fields and parched meadows; past the city of Ctesiphon, where the Parthian emperors reigned and the vast metropolis of Seleucia which Alexander built; across the swirling floods of Tigris and the many channels of Euphrates, flowing yellow through the corn-lands—Artaban pressed onward until he arrived at nightfall of the tenth day, beneath the shattered walls of populous Babylon.

Vasda was almost spent, and he would gladly have turned into the city to find rest and refreshment for himself and for her. But he knew that it was three hours' journey yet to the Temple of the Seven Spheres, and he must reach the place by midnight if he would find his comrades waiting. So he did not halt, but rode steadily across the stubble-fields.

A grove of date-palms made an island of gloom in the pale yellow sea. As she passed into the shadow Vasda slackened her pace, and began to pick her way more carefully.

Near the farther end of the darkness an access of caution seemed to fall upon her. She scented some danger or difficulty; it was not in her heart to fly from it—only to be prepared for it, and to meet it wisely, as a good horse should do. The grove was close and silent as the tomb; not a leaf rustled, not a bird sang.

She felt her steps before her delicately, carrying her head low, and sighing now and then with apprehension. At last she gave a quick breath of anxiety and dismay, and stood stockstill, quivering in every muscle, before a dark object in the shadow of the last palm-tree.

Artaban dismounted. The dim star-light revealed the form of a man lying across the

road. His humble dress and the outline of his haggard face showed that he was probably one of the poor Hebrew exiles who still dwelt in great numbers in the vicinity. His pallid skin, dry and yellow as parchment, bore the mark of the deadly fever which ravaged the marshlands in autumn. The chill of death was in his lean hand, and as Artaban released it the arm fell back inertly upon the motionless breast.

He turned away with a thought of pity, consigning the body to that strange funeral which the Magians deemed most fitting—the burial of the desert, from which the kites and vultures rise on dark wings, and the beasts of prey slink furtively away, leaving only a heap of white bones in the sand.

But, as he turned, a long, faint, ghostly sigh came from the man's lips. The brown, bony fingers closed convulsively on the hem of the Magian's robe and held him fast.

Artaban's heart leaped to his throat, not with fear, but with a dumb resentment at the importunity of this blind delay.

How could he stay here in the darkness to minister to a dying stranger? What claim had this unknown fragment of human life upon his compassion or his service? If he lingered but for an hour he could hardly reach Borsippa at the appointed time. His companions would think he had given up the journey. They would go without him. He would lose his quest.

But if he went on now, the man would surely die. If he stayed, life might be restored. His spirit throbbed and fluttered with the urgency of the crisis. Should he risk the great reward of his divine faith for the sake of a single deed of human love? Should he turn aside, if only for a moment, from the following of the star, to give a cup of cold water to a poor, perishing Hebrew?

"God of truth and purity," he prayed, "direct me in the holy path, the way of wisdom which Thou only knowest."

Then he turned back to the sick man. Loosening the grasp of his hand, he carried him to a little mound at the foot of the palm-tree.

He unbound the thick folds of the turban and opened the garment above the sunken breast. He brought water from one of the small canals near by, and moistened the sufferer's brow and mouth. He mingled a draught of one of those simple but potent remedies which he carried always in his girdle—for the Magians were physicians as well as astrologers—and poured it slowly between the colorless lips. Hour after hour he labored as only a skillful healer of disease can do; and at last the man's strength returned; he sat up and looked about him.

"Who are thou?" he said in the rude dialect of the country, "and why hast thou sought me here to bring back my life?"

"I am Artaban the Magian, of the city of Ecbatana, and I am going to Jerusalem in search of one who is to be born King of the Jews, a great Prince and Deliverer of all men. I dare not delay any longer upon my journey, for the caravan that has waited for me may depart without me. But see, here is all that I have left of bread and wine, and here is a potion of healing herbs. When thy strength is restored thou canst find the dwellings of the Hebrews among the houses of Babylon."

The Jew raised his trembling hand solemnly to heaven.

"Now may the God of Abraham and Isaac and Jacob bless and prosper the journey of the merciful, and bring him in peace to his desired haven. But stay; I have nothing to give thee in return—only this: that I can tell thee where the Messiah must be sought. For our prophets have said that he should be born not in Jerusalem, but in Bethlehem of Judah. May the Lord bring thee in safety to that place, because thou hast had pity upon the sick."

It was already long past midnight. Artaban rode in haste, and Vasda, restored by the brief rest, ran eagerly through the silent plain and swam the channels of the river. She put forth the remnant of her strength, and fled over the ground like a gazelle.

But the first beam of the sun sent her shadow before her as she entered upon the final stadium of the journey, and the eyes of Artaban, anxiously scanning the great mound of Nimrod and the Temple of the Seven Spheres, could discern no trace of his friends.

The many-colored terraces of black and orange and red and yellow and green and blue and white, shattered by the convulsions of nature, and crumbling under the repeated blows of human violence, still glittered like a ruined rainbow in the morning light.

Artaban rode swiftly around the hill. He dismounted and climbed to the highest terrace, looking out toward the west.

The huge desolation of the marshes stretched away to the horizon and the border of the desert. Bitterns stood by the stagnant pools and jackals skulked through the low bushes; but there was no sign of the caravan of the wise men, far or near.

At the edge of the terrace he saw a little cairn of broken bricks, and under them a piece of parchment. He caught it up and read: "We have waited past midnight, and can delay no longer. We go to find the King. Follow us across the desert."

Artaban sat down upon the ground and covered his head in despair.

"How can I cross the desert," said he, "with no food and with a spent horse? I must return to Babylon, sell my sapphire, and buy a train of camels, and provisions for the journey. I may never overtake my friends. Only God the merciful knows whether I shall not lose the sight of the King because I tarried to show mercy.

For the Sake of a Little Child

There was a silence in the Hall of Dreams, where I was listening to the story of the Other Wise Man. And through this silence I saw, but very dimly, his figure passing over the dreary undulations of the desert, high upon the back of his camel, rocking steadily onward like a ship over the waves.

The land of death spread its cruel net around him. The stony wastes bore no fruit but briers and thorns. The dark ledges of rock thrust themselves above the surface here and there, like the bones of perished monsters. Arid and inhospitable mountain ranges rose before him, furrowed with dry channels of ancient torrents, white and ghastly as scars on the face of nature. Shifting hills of treacherous sand were heaped like tombs along the horizon. By day, the fierce heat pressed its intolerable burden on the quivering air; and no living creature moved on the dumb, swooning earth, but tiny jerboas scuttling through the parched bushes, or lizards vanishing in the clefts of the rock. By night the jackals prowled and barked in the distance, and the lion made the black ravines echo with his hollow roaring, while a bitter, blighting chill followed the fever of the day. Through heat and cold, the Magian moved steadily onward.

Then I saw the gardens and orchards of Damascus, watered by the streams of Abana and Pharpar with their sloping swards inlaid with bloom, and their thickets of myrrh and roses. I saw also the long, snowy ridge of Hermon, and the dark groves of cedars, and the valley of the Jordan, and the blue waters of the Lake of Galilee, and the fertile plain of Esdraelon, and the hills of Ephraim, and the highlands of Judah. Through all these I followed the figure of Artaban moving steadily onward, until he arrived at Bethlehem. And it was

the third day after the three wise men had come to that place and had found Mary and Joseph, with the young child, Jesus, and had laid their gifts of gold and frankincense and myrrh at his feet.

Then the other wise man drew near, weary, but full of hope, bearing his ruby and his pearl to offer to the King. "For now at last," he said, "I shall surely find him, though it be alone, and later than my brethren. This is the place of which the Hebrew exile told me that the prophets had spoken, and here I shall behold the rising of the great light. But I must inquire about the visit of my brethren, and to what house the star directed them, and to whom they presented their tribute."

The streets of the village seemed to be deserted, and Artaban wondered whether the men had all gone up to the hill-pastures to bring down their sheep. From the open door of a low stone cottage he heard the sound of a woman's voice singing softly. He entered and found a young mother hushing her baby to rest. She told him of the strangers from the far East who had appeared in the village three days ago, and how they said that a star had guided them to the place where Joseph of Nazareth was lodging with his wife and her new-born child, and how they had paid reverence to the child and given him many rich gifts.

"But the travelers disappeared again," she continued, "as suddenly as they had come. We were afraid at the strangeness of their visit. We could not understand it. The man of Nazareth took the babe and his mother and fled away that same night secretly, and it was whispered that they were going far away to Egypt. Ever since, there has been a spell upon the village; something evil hangs over it. They say that the Roman soldiers are coming from

Jerusalem to force a new tax from us, and the men have driven the flocks and herds far back among the hills, and hidden themselves to escape it."

Artaban listened to her gentle, timid speech, and the child in her arms looked up in his face and smiled, stretching out its rosy hands to grasp at the winged circle of gold on his breast. His heart warmed to the touch. It seemed like a greeting of love and trust to one who had journeyed long in loneliness and perplexity, fighting with his own doubts and fears, and following a light that was veiled in clouds.

"Might not this child have been the promised Prince?" he asked within himself, as he touched its soft cheek. "Kings have been born ere now in lowlier houses than this, and the favorite of the stars may rise even from a cottage. But it has not seemed good to the God of Wisdom to reward my search so soon and so easily, The one whom I seek has gone before me; and now I must follow the King to Egypt."

The young mother laid the babe in its cradle, and rose to minister to the wants of the strange guest that fate had brought into her house. She set food before him, the plain fare of peasants, but willingly offered, and therefore full of refreshment for the soul as well as for the body. Artaban accepted it gratefully; and, as he ate, the child fell into a happy slumber, and murmured sweetly in its dreams, and a great peace filled the quiet room.

But suddenly there came the noise of a wild confusion and uproar in the streets of the village, a shrieking and wailing of women's voices, a clangor of brazen trumpets and a clashing of swords, and a desperate cry: "The soldiers! The soldiers of Herod! They are killing our children."

The young mother's face grew white with terror. She clasped her child to her bosom and crouched motionless in the darkest corner of the room, covering him with the

folds of her robe, lest he should wake and cry.

But Artaban went quickly and stood in the doorway of the house. His broad shoulders filled the portal from side to side, and the peak of his white cap all but touched the lintel.

The soldiers came hurrying down the street with bloody hands and dripping swords. At the sight of the stranger in his imposing dress they hesitated with surprise. The captain of the band approached the threshold to thrust him aside. But Artaban did not stir. His face was as calm as though he were watching the stars, and in his eyes there burned that steady radiance before which even the half-tamed hunting leopard shrinks and the fierce bloodhound pauses in his leap. He held the soldier silently for an instant, and then said in a low voice:

"I am all alone in this place, and I am waiting to give this jewel to the prudent captain who will leave me in peace."

He showed the ruby, glistening in the hollow of his hand like a great drop of blood.

The captain was amazed at the splendor of the gem. The pupils of his eyes expanded with desire, and the hard lines of greed wrinkled around his lips. He stretched out his hand and took the ruby.

"March on!" he cried to his men, "there is no child here. The house is still."

The clamor and the clang of arms passed down the street as the headlong fury of the chase sweeps by the secret covert where the trembling deer is hidden. Artaban re-entered the cottage. He turned his face to the east and prayed:

"God of truth, forgive my sin! I have said the thing that is not, to save the life of a child. And two of my gifts are gone. I have spent for man that which was meant for God. Shall I ever be worthy to see the face of the King?"

But the voice of the woman, weeping for joy in the shadow behind him, said very gently:

"Because thou hast saved the life of my little one, may the Lord bless thee and keep thee; the Lord make His face to shine upon thee and be gracious unto thee; the Lord lift up His countenance upon thee and give thee peace."

In the Hidden Way of Sorrow

Then again there was a silence in the Hall of Dreams, deeper and more mysterious than the first interval, and I understood that the years of Artaban were flowing very swiftly under the stillness of that clinging fog, and I caught only a glimpse, here and there, of the river of his life shining through the shadows that concealed its course.

I saw him moving among the throngs of men in populous Egypt, seeking everywhere for traces of the household that had come down from Bethlehem, and finding them under the spreading sycamore-trees of Heliopolis, and beneath the walls of the Roman fortress of New Babylon beside the Nile—traces so faint and dim that they vanished before him continually, as footprints on the hard river-sand glisten for a moment with moisture and then disappear.

I saw him again at the foot of the pyramids, which lifted their sharp points into the intense saffron glow of the sunset sky, changeless monuments of the perishable glory and the imperishable hope of man. He looked up into the vast countenance of the crouching Sphinx, and vainly tried to read the meaning of the calm eyes and smiling mouth. Was it, indeed, the mockery of all effort and all aspiration, as Tigranes had said—the cruel jest of a

riddle that has no answer, a search that never can succeed? Or was there a touch of pity and encouragement in that inscrutable smile—a promise that even the defeated should attain a victory, and the disappointed should discover a prize, and the ignorant should be made wise, and the blind should see, and the wandering should come into the haven at last?

I saw him again in an obscure house of Alexandria, taking counsel with a Hebrew rabbi. The venerable man, bending over the rolls of parchment on which the prophecies of Israel were written, read aloud the pathetic words which foretold the sufferings of the promised Messiah—the despised and rejected of men, the man of sorrows and the acquaintance of grief.

"And remember, my son," said he, fixing his deep-set eyes upon the face of Artaban, "the King whom you are seeking is not to be found in a palace, nor among the rich and powerful. If the light of the world and the glory of Israel had been appointed to come with the greatness of earthly splendor, it must have appeared long ago. For no son of Abraham will ever again rival the power which Joseph had in the palaces of Egypt, or the magnificence of Solomon throned between the lions in Jerusalem. But the light for which the world is waiting is a new light, the glory that shall rise out of patient and triumphant suffering. And the kingdom which is to be established forever is a new kingdom, the royalty of perfect and unconquerable love.

"I do not know how this shall come to pass, nor how the turbulent kings and peoples of earth shall be brought to acknowledge the Messiah and pay homage to Him. But this I know. Those who seek Him will do well to look among the poor and the lowly, the sorrowful and the oppressed."

So I saw the Other Wise Man again and again, traveling from place to place, and searching among the people of the dispersion, with whom the little family from Bethlehem might, perhaps, have found a refuge. He passed through countries where famine lay heavy upon the land and the poor were crying for bread. He made his dwelling in plague-stricken cities where the sick were languishing in the bitter companionship of helpless misery. He visited the oppressed and the afflicted in the gloom of subterranean prisons, and the crowded wretchedness of slave-markets, and the weary toil of galley ships. In all this populous and intricate world of anguish, though he found none to worship, he found many to help. He fed the hungry, and clothed the naked, and healed the sick, and comforted the captive; and his years went by more swiftly than the weaver's shuttle that flashes back and forth through the loom while the web grows and the invisible pattern is completed.

It seemed almost as if he had forgotten his quest. But once I saw him for a moment as he stood alone at sunrise, waiting at the gate of a Roman prison. He had taken from a secret resting-place in his bosom the pearl, the last of his jewels. As he looked at it, a mellower lustre, a soft and iridescent light, full of shifting gleams of azure and rose, trembled upon its surface. It seemed to have absorbed some reflection of the lost sapphire and ruby. So the profound, secret purpose of a noble life draws itself the memories of past joy and past sorrow. All that has helped it, all that has hindered it, is transfused by a subtle magic into its very essence. It becomes more luminous and precious the longer it is carried close to the warmth of the beating heart.

Then, at last, while I was thinking of this pearl, and of its meaning, I heard the end of the story of the Other Wise Man.

A Pearl of Great Price

Three and thirty years of the life of Artaban had passed away, and he was still a pilgrim, and a seeker after light. His hair,

once darker than the cliffs of Zagros, was now white as the wintry snow that covered them. His eyes, that once flashed like flames of fire, were dull as embers smouldering among the ashes.

Worn and weary and ready to die, but still looking for the King, he had come for the last time to Jerusalem. He had often visited the old city before, and had searched through all its lanes and crowded hovels and black prisons without finding any trace of the family of Nazarenes who had fled from Bethlehem long ago. But now it seemed as if he must make one more effort, and something whispered in his heart that, at last, he might succeed.

It was the season of the Passover. The city was thronged with strangers. The children of Israel, scattered in far lands all over the world, had returned to the Temple for the great feast, and there had been a confusion of tongues in the narrow streets for many days.

But on this day there was a singular agitation visible in the multitude. The sky was veiled with a portentous gloom, and currents of excitement seemed to flash through the crowd like the thrill which shakes the forest on the eve of a storm. A secret tide was sweeping them all one way. The clatter of sandals, and the soft, thick sound of thousands of bare feet shuffling over the stones, flowed unceasingly along the street that leads to the Damascus gate.

Artaban joined company with a group of people from his own country, Parthian Jews who had come up to keep the Passover, and inquired of them the cause of the tumult, and where they were going.

"We are going," they answered, "to the place called Golgotha, outside the city walls, where there is to be an execution. Have you not heard what has happened? Two famous robbers are to be crucified, and with them another, called Jesus of Nazareth, a man who had done many wonderful works among the people, so that they love him

greatly. But the priests and elders have said that he must die, because he gave himself out to be the Son of God. And Pilate has sent him to the cross because he said that he was the 'King of the Jews.' "

How strangely these familiar words fell upon the tired heart of Artaban! They had led him for a lifetime over land and sea. And now they came to him darkly and mysteriously like a message of despair. The King had arisen, but He had been denied and cast out. He was about to perish. Perhaps He was already dying. Could it be the same who had been born in Bethlehem thirty-three years ago, at whose birth the star had appeared in heaven, and of whose coming the prophets had spoken?

Artaban's heart beat unsteadily with that troubled, doubtful apprehension which is the excitement of old age. But he said within himself: "The ways of God are stranger than the thought of men, and it may be that I shall find the King, at last, in the hands of His enemies, and shall come in time to offer my pearl for his ransom before He dies."

So the old man followed the multitude with slow and painful steps toward the Damascus gate of the city. Just beyond the entrance of the guardhouse a troop of Macedonian soldiers came down the street, dragging a young girl with torn dress and dishevelled hair. As the Magian paused to look at her with compassion, she broke suddenly from the hands of her tormentors and threw herself at his feet, clasping him around the knees. She had seen his white cap and the winged circle on his breast.

"Have pity on me," she cried, "and save me, for the sake of the God of purity! I also am a daughter of the true religion which is taught by the Magi. My father was a merchant of Parthia, but he is dead, and I

am seized for his debts to be sold as a slave. Save me from worse than death."

Artaban trembled.

It was the old conflict in his soul, which had come to him in the palm grove of Babylon and in the cottage at Bethlehem— the conflict between the expectation of faith and the impulse of love. Twice the gift which he had consecrated to the worship of religion had been drawn from his hand to the service of humanity. This was the third trial, the ultimate probation, the final and irrevocable choice.

Was it his great opportunity or his last temptation? He could not tell. One thing only was clear in the darkness of his mind—it was inevitable. And does not the inevitable come from God?

One thing only was sure to his divided heart—to rescue this helpless girl would be a true deed of love. And is not love the light of the soul?

He took the pearl from his bosom. Never had it seemed so luminous, so radiant, so full of tender, living lustre. He laid it in the hand of the slave.

"This is thy ransom, daughter! It is the last of my treasures which I kept for the King."

While he spoke the darkness of the sky thickened, and shuddering tremors ran through the earth, heaving convulsively like the breast of one who struggles with mighty grief.

The walls of the houses rocked to and fro. Stones were loosened and crashed into the street. Dust clouds filled the air. The soldiers fled in terror, reeling like drunken men. But Artaban and the girl whom he had ransomed crouched helpless beneath the wall of the Praetorium.

What had he to fear? What had he to live for? He had given away the last remnant of his tribute for the King. He had parted with the last hope of finding Him. The quest was over, and it had failed. But even in that

thought, accepted and embraced, there was peace. It was not resignation. It was not submission. It was something more profound and searching. He knew that all was well, because he had done the best that he could, from day to day. He had been true to the light that had been given to him. He had looked for more. And if he had not found it, if a failure was all that came out of his life, doubtless that was the best that was possible. He had not seen the revelation of "life everlasting, incorruptible and immortal." But he knew that even if he could live his earthly life over again, it could not be otherwise than it had been.

One more lingering pulsation of the earthquake quivered through the ground. A heavy tile, shaken from the roof, fell and struck the old man on the temple. He lay breathless and pale, with his gray head resting on the young girl's shoulder, and the blood trickling from the wound. As she bent over him, fearing that he was dead, there came a voice through the twilight, very small and still, like music sounding from a distance, in which the notes are clear but the words are lost. The girl turned to see if someone had spoken from the window above them, but she saw no one.

Then the old man's lips began to move, as if in answer, and she heard him say in the Parthian tongue:

"Not so, my Lord: For when saw I thee and hungered and fed thee? Or thirsty, and gave thee drink? When saw I thee a stranger, and took thee in? Or naked, and clothed thee? When saw I thee sick or in prison, and came unto thee? Three- and-thirty years have I looked for thee; but I have never seen thy face, nor ministered to thee, my King."

He ceased, and the sweet voice came again. And again the maid heard it, very

faintly and far away. But now it seemed as though she understood the words:

"Verily I say unto thee, Inasmuch as thou hast done it unto one of the least of these my brethren, thou hast done it unto me."

A calm radiance of wonder and joy lighted the pale face of Artaban like the first ray of dawn on a snowy mountain-peak. One long, last breath of relief exhaled gently from his lips.

His journey was ended. His treasures were accepted. The Other Wise Man had found the King.

He spreads a table before me with all kinds of food. He puts His hand upon my head and all the tired is gone. My cup He fills till it runs over.

What I tell you is true, I lie not. These roads that are away ahead will stay with me through this life, and afterward I will go to live in the Big Tepee and sit down with the Shepherd Chief forever.

Apache version of Psalm 23

Trust in the Lord with all your heart
　　and lean not on your own understanding;
in all your ways acknowledge him,
　　and he will make your paths straight.

Proverbs 3:5, 6 , N.I.V. Bible

The Great Father above is a Shepherd Chief. I am His, and with Him I want not. He throws out to me a rope and the name of the rope is Love, and He draws me to where the grass is green and the water not dangerous, and I eat and lie down satisfied.

Sometimes my heart is very weak and falls down, but He lifts it up again and draws me into a good road. His name is Wonderful.

Sometime—it may be very soon, it may be longer, it may be a long, long time— He will draw me into a place between mountains. It is dark there, but I'll not draw back. I'll not be afraid, for it is there between the mountains that the Shepherd Chief will meet me, and the hunger I have felt in my heart all through this life will be satisfied. Sometimes He makes the love rope into a whip.

GOLDEN YEARS

A FRAGILE MOMENT . . .

Running to me through the warm spring sunshine, my daughter, Ann, held out a feather in her dirty little hand. It was a soft, beautiful blue—*unmistakably a bluebird's feather*.

"Mama, which bird does this belong to?" she asked.

I took it in my hand and we looked at it together. Then I explained that while we couldn't tell which individual bird had dropped it, we surely knew his kind.

Ann was satisfied. But I thought about it a long time after she had gone back to her play. Even if a bluebird flew over that very moment and dropped a feather, he would be so high and so fleeting I couldn't know what he was like. But the part of himself he'd left, still belonging to him, named him.

Our lives are like that, I thought. The part of ourselves that we leave behind—an act of compassion, a difficult job well done, a thoughtless word spoken in anger—these are the things that the world sees and measures. The days that drop behind are always part of us—our fallen feathers. How important to live each one of them with love and faith if we are to have no regrets.

Mildred Brown Duncan

ANNA

Eugenia Price

Bracing herself with one arm against the marble column of Solomon's porch on the eastern side of the Temple in Jerusalem, the aging prophetess, Anna, turned to greet her elderly friend, Simeon, who was slowly climbing the steps from the street. Anna did not walk toward him, and Simeon did not hurry. Neither of them had ever hurried through the years of their lives. Too much of eternity had invaded their days for haste. They geared their comings and goings to the Lord God, depending, as children depend, upon His guidance—so abandoned to the divine will, so sensitive to the divine whisper that each lived hourly within the quiet order of holy rhythm.

Slowly, Simeon shuffled toward his devout friend, a smile crinkling the thin skin around his faded eyes. "Shalom, Anna," he said. "There will be a fine sunset for us to enjoy—just enough clouds to make the light glow."

"Yes, Simeon. Clouds are needed in order to make a sunset beautiful. Thanks be to the Lord our God for clouds, I say."

Simeon chuckled. "You've earned the right to say that, Anna. You've allowed the Lord God to make your life beautiful—and heaven knows it's been full of clouds."

She sighed. "There has been nothing about which to fuss, old man. I had seven years of happiness with my husband and all the other years between his death and my eighty-fourth birthday last week to enjoy the Lord God."

"You've been in the Temple most of the day, I suppose," Simeon said, pulling his cloak around his thin throat against the chill evening breeze.

"All day," she replied. "And all day my joy has grown. Oh, Simeon, old man—the Messiah comes soon! The Spirit of our God has assured me now, even as He has assured you, that I, too, will not die until I have seen Him." Her thin, veined hands were clasped and her face glowed.

"We are old enough, both of us, Anna, for the people to call us childish for our faith in the swift coming of the Messiah, but it is not we who are loose in the head—it is they. He comes, *very* soon now, He comes. I grow weaker daily. My time to leave draws closer. And as it does, so does the coming of our Messiah. God has promised I will not die until I have seen Him, and I am going soon."

Anna turned to look at her friend. "It is all joy, Simeon, going or staying because of the Lord our God."

Day after day, the old friends met somewhere in the Temple to speak of the coming of the promised Messiah. And on one certain day, as Anna prayed in the Court of the Women, the partitioned east portion of the inner court where both men and women could pray, she felt a gentle hand on her shoulder and turned to see her friend, Simeon, standing beside her.

"My old heart pounds this day, Anna," he whispered. "Could this be the day He will come? Do you have any word from the Lord God for me, my friend?"

Anna smiled. "Only the same assurance that it will be soon, Simeon."

"Then I will go to my own prayers and let you return to yours."

Anna watched him hobble away and tried to go back to her prayers, but her mind would not focus. A great excitement seemed to grip her so that her bent old body shook. Suddenly she turned to look in the direction of the wide stair that led from the Court of the Women to the Court of the Gentiles, fully expecting to see a heavenly sign. All she saw was a simple Hebrew couple crossing the lower court, slowly, almost shyly, as though awed by the size and splendor of the Temple. In her arms, the young mother carried her baby. They have come for the purification, Anna thought, and was glad in her heart that one more man child would be the Lord's own. Anna had borne no children, and through the years, some of her happiest experiences had been to watch the young couples bring their sons to be dedicated to the Lord God.

She watched this humble, plainly dressed man and woman as they started up the stair to the Court of the Women, and then from the other side of the high partition she saw Simeon staring at the same two parents with their babe.

Anna watched Simeon cross the upper court and hurry dangerously close to the top of the stair as though he had expected this very man and woman at this very moment. He's going to fall! Anna caught her breath as Simeon lost his balance, then relaxed when the father of the child put his strong arm around Simeon to steady him. Unmindful of his narrow escape, Simeon raised both hands in the air and began to praise God in a loud voice, and Anna found herself hurrying toward the little group of people at the top of the stair—hurrying, with almost no pain in her still old legs.

When she reached them, the young mother was smiling as though for a deeper reason than that she held a new son in her arms, and Simeon was crying out: "Lord, now lettest thou thy servant depart in peace, according to thy word; for mine eyes have seen thy salvation which thou has prepared in the presence of all peoples!"

Anna gasped as she saw her friend reach for the child, take him in his arms, and lift his radiant old face to God.

"For mine eyes have *seen* thy salvation . . . a light for revelation to the Gentiles, and for glory to thy people Israel!"

The young mother stood wide-eyed, marveling at what Simeon had said of her son.

"He knows, Mary!" her kind-faced husband said. "This old man is a man of God; he knows the child is no ordinary child."

Anna stood transfixed, her eyes drinking in the beauty of the baby's face, as Simeon gently handed the child back to his mother, saying: "Behold, this child is set for the fall and rising of many in Israel, and for a sign that is spoken against—" And he stopped speaking and looked deeply into the young mother's eyes. ". . . and a sword will pierce through your own soul also, that thoughts out of many hearts may be revealed."

Anna saw the young woman frown slightly and look for some explanation from her husband. There was none. For a long moment, no one spoke, and then Anna, as though the very joy of heaven had been released within her, turned and hurried down the stair, across the Court of the Gentiles, and onto the porch, giving thanks to God and telling everyone she saw that the redemption of Israel had come to live among them!

Truly my soul waiteth upon God.

Psalm 62:1

My crown is in my heart, not on my head;
Not deck'd with diamonds, and Indian
    stones,
Nor to be seen: my crown is called Content;
A crown it is that seldom Kings enjoy.

William Shakespeare

I WISH YOU

I wish you
some new love
of lovely things,
and some new forgetfulness
of the teasing things,
and some higher pride
in the praising things,
and some sweeter peace
from the hurrying things,
and some closer fence
from the worrying things.

John Ruskin

GOD BE WITH YOU

May His Counsels Sweet uphold you,
    And His Loving Arms enfold you,
        As you journey on your way.

May His Sheltering Wings protect you,
    And His Light Divine direct you,
        Turning darkness into day.

May His Potent Peace surround you,
    And His Presence linger with you,
        As your inner, golden ray.

Author Unknown

O Lord, support us all the day long, until the shadows lengthen and the evening comes, and the busy world is hushed, and the fever of life is over, and our work is done. Then in Thy mercy grant us a safe lodging, and a holy rest, and peace at last. Amen.

John Henry Newman

THE TABLE

John V. A. Weaver

No, it isn't much of a table to look at. Just an old yellow oak thing, I suppose you'd call it. It isn't that we couldn't have had mahogany or walnut, of course. Only—well, thirty-eight years sort of turns anything into a treasure.

It was Sam's father's wedding present to us. It and the six chairs—four plain-bottomed, two with leather seats.

I recollect as well as yesterday the first supper we ate at it. We came back from our honeymoon in Canada on a Monday afternoon. Sam had made the lease for the little five-room house on Locust Street the week before we got married.

All the month we were up there lazying around and fishing and getting used to each other I was worried about what we were going to do for furnishing the dining room. I had a good deal of furniture from Mother's house, and Sam had some from his flat, but neither of us had a dining room table. We had talked a lot about it. But that trouble was settled the minute we went into the room and saw the yellow oak, bright and shiny, with a note from Father Graham on it.

I scrambled around and got some sort of a meal together. What it was doesn't matter.

Pretty soon we were sitting in the chairs opposite each other, so close we could touch hands.

Sam didn't pay much attention to the food.

He kept looking at me. You know the way newlyweds will go on. After a while Sam didn't say anything for most a minute. Then he looked and looked at me, and said, "I guess you're about the prettiest girl anywhere. Mary. I'm glad this table is so short. It lets me see you all the better."

I had to laugh. "Why, silly," I answered, "it opens in the middle. There's extra leaves in the china closet. We can make it as long as we want!"

He looked a little sheepish, and glanced around at the four other chairs. Then he grinned.

"Well," he said, "we'll have use for those leaves before we get through, I reckon."

I couldn't half eat for laughing. Yes, and blushing, too.

See that whole row of round dents up next to my place? That's what Sallie did with her spoon. She was the only one that always hammered. She was the first.

Over there, right by the opening—that's where Sam Jr. tried to carve his initials one time when he was about five. Sam caught him just as he was finishing the "S." It was a warm night for one young man, I can tell you.

Of course we'd put in one of the extra leaves a good many times before Ben came. The children were forever having friends over. Ben made the extra leaf permanent.

Then we commenced adding the second leaf. More friends, you see. Sam kept moving farther and farther away from me, I used to tell him. He'd always answer the same thing. "My eyesight's all right," he'd say. "I can see just as well how pretty you are." And he said it as if he meant it.

So the children grew up and the table came to its longest. Sallie married Tom Thorpe when she was nineteen, and they both lived with us for three years.

The boys were in high school then, and I tell you we made a big family. All three extra leaves hardly did. Sam at one end and me at the other, Ben and Sam Jr. and Sallie and Tom—and my first granddaughter, Irene, in her high chair.

But she had her place, too. By that time we were in the big house on Maple, and the noise—and the life—and the happiness! The table was certainly getting battle-scarred. Look at that brown burnt place. That's where Senator Berkeley put down

his cigar the night he stopped with us.

Well, then, Sam Jr. went off to college, and a little while after that Tom and Sallie set up housekeeping in their own home up on the Heights. So one of the leaves came out for good, and we didn't have so much use for the second, except for company once in a while. Except vacations, of course.

It was quite a shock when Sam Jr. left college at the end of his third year, and went out west to California. He didn't run off, you understand. We said he could go, although we were very disappointed he didn't stay and finish his education. But he was right. He's made a heap of money in real estate out there.

He comes back once a year for a week or so with Myra, that's his wife, and their two youngsters. Then the old table gets swollen back to its biggest. It seems mighty quiet when they go.

Ben came back and stayed with us two years after he graduated. We hoped he'd be content to settle down in town here for good, he was doing so well in life insurance. But that was just the trouble. The New York office wanted him, at twice the money, so he went. And the last leaf went out of the table with him.

That's been a year now. Sometimes I think of taking a roomer. Not just any ragtag and bobtail; some nice young fellow who needs a good home. It's so quiet—

I said so to Sam the other night. "My goodness," I said, "the table's so little again. Why, you're right on top of me. You can see all my wrinkles."

Sam laughed, and then he put his hand out and squeezed mine. "My eyes have grown dim to correspond," he answered. "You look as beautiful to me as ever. I guess you're about the prettiest girl anywhere."

But, still . . .

JENNY KISSED ME

Jenny kissed me when we met,
   Jumping from the chair she sat in:
Time, you thief, who loves to get
   Sweets into your list, put that in!
Say I'm weary, say I'm sad,
   Say that health and wealth have
      missed me,
Say I'm growing old, but add,
   Jenny kissed me.

Leigh Hunt

Day is done, gone the sun
From the lake, from the hills, from the sky.
Safely rest, all is well! God is nigh.

Author Unknown

REPENTANCE
Leo Tolstoi

Once upon a time a man lived in the world for seventy years, and lived all his life in sin. Then this man fell sick, but did not repent—except that, when death came to him in the last hour of all, he burst into tears and cried: "O Lord, pardon me as Thou didst the thief upon the cross." That was all he had time to say before his soul departed. Yet the soul of that sinner loved God, and trusted in His mercy, and thus it came to the doors of Paradise.

And the sinner began to knock thereat and beseech admittance to the Kingdom of Heaven. Then he heard a voice from within the doors saying: "What manner of man is this who is knocking at the doors of Paradise, and what deeds hath he performed during his lifetime?"

Then the voice of the Accuser answered, and recounted all the sinful deeds of the man, and named no good ones at all.

Thereupon the voice from within the doors spoke again. "Sinners," it said, "may not enter into the Kingdom of Heaven. Depart thou hence."

And the man cried: "O Judge, thy voice I hear, but thy face I cannot see, and thy name I do not know."

And the voice answered: "I am Peter the Apostle."

Then said the sinner: "Have compassion upon me, O Peter the Apostle, and remember the weakness of men and the mercy of God. Wert thou not a disciple of Christ, and didst thou not hear from His own lips His teaching, and didst thou not behold the example of His life? Dost thou not remember also the time when He was in agony of soul and did thrice ask of thee why thou didst sleep and not pray, and yet thou didst sleep, for thine eyes were heavy, and thrice He found thee sleeping?

"Dost thou not remember also how thou didst promise Him that thou wouldst not deny Him unto death, and yet how thou didst thrice deny Him when He was brought before Caiaphas? Thus hath it been with me.

"Dost thou not remember also how the cock did crow, and thou didst go out and weep bitterly? Thus hath it been with me. Thou canst not deny me admittance."

But the voice from within the doors of Paradise was silent.

Then, after waiting a little while, the sinner began once more to beseech admittance to the Kingdom of Heaven. Thereupon a second voice was heard from within the doors and said: "Who is this man, and in what manner hath he lived in the world?"

The voice of the Accuser answered, and once more recited all the evil deeds of the sinner, and named no good ones.

Thereupon the voice answered from within the doors: "Depart thou hence. Sinners such as thou may not live with us in Paradise."

But the sinner cried: "O Judge, thy voice I hear, but thy face I cannot see, and thy name I do not know."

Then the voice said to him: "I am King David the Prophet." Yet the sinner would not desist nor leave the doors, but cried again:

"Have compassion on me, O King David, and remember the weakness of men and the mercy of God. God loved thee and exalted thee above thy fellows. Thou hadst all things—a kingdom, glory, riches, wives, and children—yet didst thou look from thy roof upon the wife of a poor man, and sin did enter into thee, and thou didst take the wife of Uriah, and didst slay Uriah himself with the sword of the Ammonites. Thou, rich man, didst take from the poor man his one ewe lamb, and didst put the man himself to death. Thus also hath it been with me.

"But dost thou not remember also how thou didst repent and say—'I acknowledge my transgressions, and my sins are ever before me'? Thus is it with me now. Thou canst not deny me admittance."

But the voice from within the doors of Paradise was silent.

Then, after waiting a little while, the sinner began once more to knock and beseech admittance to the Kingdom of Heaven.

Thereupon a third voice was heard from within the doors and said: "Who is this man, and in what manner hath he lived in the world?"

And the voice of the Accuser answered, and for the third time recited the evil deeds of the man, and named no good ones.

Then the voice spoke again from within the doors. "Depart thou hence," it said. "Sinners may not enter into the Kingdom of Heaven."

But the sinner cried: "O Judge, thy voice I hear, but thy face I cannot see, and thy

name I do not know."

And the voice answered: "I am John the Divine, the disciple whom Jesus loved."

Then the sinner rejoiced and said: "Now canst thou not deny me admittance. Peter and David might have let me in because they know the weakness of men and the mercy of God; but thou wilt let me in because in thee there is abounding love. Didst not thou, O John the Divine, write in thy book that God is Love, and that who loveth not, the same knoweth not God? Didst not thou in thy old age give to men this saying—'Brethren, love one another'? How, therefore, canst thou hate me or drive me hence? Either must thou love me and yeild me admittance to the Kingdom of Heaven, or thou must deny what thou thyself has said."

Then the doors of Paradise were opened, and John received the penitent sinner, and admitted him to the Kingdom of Heaven.

Give us grace, O Lord, to work while it is day, fulfilling diligently and patiently whatever duty Thou appointest us; doing small things in the day of small things, and great labours if Thou summonest us to any; rising and working, sitting still and suffering according to Thy word.

Christina Rossetti

A CHILD FOR ABRAHAM AND SARAH

The Living Bible, Genesis 17, 18, 21, 22

When Abram was ninety-nine years old, God appeared to him and told him, "I am the Almighty; obey me and live as you should. I will prepare a contract between us, guaranteeing to make you into a mighty nation. In fact you shall be the father of not only one nation, but a multitude of nations!" Abram fell face downward in the dust as God talked with him.

"What's more," God told him, "I am changing your name. It is no longer 'Abram' ('Exalted Father'), but 'Abraham' ('Father of Nations')—for that is what you will be. I have declared it. I will give you millions of descendants who will form many nations! Kings shall be among your descendants! And I will continue this agreement between us generation after generation, forever, for it shall be between me and your children as well. It is a contract that I shall be your God and the God of your posterity. And I will give all this land of Canaan to you and them, forever. And I will be your God."

Then God added, "Regarding Sarai your wife—her name is no longer 'Sarai' but 'Sarah' ('Princess'). And I will bless her and give you a son from her! Yes, I will bless her richly, and make her the mother of nations! Many kings shall be among your posterity."

Then Abraham threw himself down in worship before the Lord, but inside he was laughing in disbelief! "Me, be a father?" he said in amusement. "Me—100 years old? And Sarah, to have a baby at 90?"

God replied, "Sarah shall bear you a son; and you are to name him Isaac, and I will sign my covenant with him forever, and with his descendants. My contract is with Isaac, who will be born to you and Sarah next year about this time."

That ended the conversation and God left.

The Lord appeared again to Abraham while he was living in the oak grove at Mamre. This is the way it happened: One hot summer afternoon as he was sitting in the opening of his tent, he suddenly noticed three men coming toward him. He sprang up and ran to meet them and welcomed them.

"Sirs," he said, "please don't go any further. Stop awhile and rest here in the shade of this tree while I get water to refresh your feet, and a bite to eat to strengthen you. Do stay awhile before

continuing your journey."

"All right," they said, "do as you have said."

Then Abraham ran back to the tent and said to Sarah, "Quick! Mix up some pancakes! Use your best flour, and make enough for the three of them!" Then he ran out to the herd and selected a fat calf and told a servant to hurry and butcher it. Soon, taking them cheese and milk and the roast veal, he set it before the men and stood beneath the trees beside them as they ate.

"Where is Sarah, your wife" they asked him.

"In the tent," Abraham replied.

Then the Lord said, "Next year I will give you and Sarah a son!" (Sarah was listening from the tent door behind him.)

Sarah laughed silently. "A woman my age have a baby?" she scoffed to herself. "And with a husband as old as mine?"

Then God said to Abraham, "Why did Sarah laugh? Why did she say 'Can an old woman like me have a baby?' Is anything too hard for God? Next year, just as I told you, I will certainly see to it that Sarah has a son."

But Sarah denied it. "I didn't laugh," she lied, for she was afraid.

"Should I hide my plan from Abraham?" God asked. "For Abraham shall become a mighty nation, and he will be a source of blessing for all the nations of the earth. And I have picked him out to have godly descendants and a godly household—men who are just and good—so that I can do for him all I have promised."

Then God did as he had promised, and Sarah became pregnant and gave Abraham a baby son in his old age, at the time God had said; and Abraham named him "Isaac" (meaning "Laughter!").

And Sarah declared, "God has brought me laughter! All who hear about this shall rejoice with me. For who would have dreamed that I would ever have a baby? Yet I have given Abraham a child in his old age!"

Time went by and the child grew and was weaned; and Abraham gave a party to celebrate the happy occasion.

Later on, God tested Abraham's faith and obedience.

"Abraham!" God called.

"Yes, Lord?" he replied.

"Take with you your only son—yes, Isaac whom you love so much—and go to the land of Moriah and sacrifice him there as a burnt offering upon one of the mountains which I'll point out to you!"

The next morning Abraham got up early, chopped wood for a fire upon the altar, saddled his donkey, and took with him his son Isaac and two young men who were his servants, and started off to the place where God had told him to go. On the third day of the journey Abraham saw the place in the distance.

"Stay here with the donkey," Abraham told the young men, "and the lad and I will travel yonder and worship, and then come right back."

Abraham placed the wood for the burnt offering upon Isaac's shoulders, while he himself carried the knife and the flint for striking a fire. So the two of them went on together.

"Father," Isaac asked, "we have the wood and the flint to make the fire, but where is the lamb for the sacrifice?"

"God will see to it, my son," Abraham replied. And they went on.

When they arrived at the place where God had told Abraham to go, he built an altar and placed the wood in order, ready for the fire, and then tied Isaac and laid him on the altar over the wood. And Abraham took the knife and lifted it up to plunge it into his son, to slay him.

At that moment the Angel of God shouted to him from heaven, "Abraham! Abraham!"

"Yes, Lord!" he answered.

GOLDEN YEARS

"Lay down the knife; don't hurt the lad in any way," the Angel said, "for I know that God is first in your life—you have not withheld even your beloved son from me."

Then Abraham noticed a ram caught by its horns in a bush. So he took the ram and sacrificed it, instead of his son, as a burnt offering on the altar. Abraham named the place "Jehovah provides"—and it still goes by that name to this day.

Then the Angel of God called again to Abraham from heaven. "I, the Lord, have sworn by myself that because you have obeyed me and have not withheld even your beloved son from me, I will bless you with incredible blessings and multiply your descendants into countless thousands and millions, like the stars above you in the sky, and like the sands along the seashore. These descendants of yours will conquer their enemies, and be a blessing to all the nations of the earth—all because you have obeyed me."

I have lived, Sir, a long time, and the longer I live the more convincing proof I see of this truth—that God governs the affairs of men.

Benjamin Franklin

THE END OF THE ROAD IS BUT A BEND IN THE ROAD

When we feel we have nothing left to give
And we are sure that the "song has ended"—
When our day seems over and the shadows fall
And the darkness of night has descended,
Where can we go to find the strength
To valiantly keep on trying,
Where can we find the hand that will dry
The tears that the heart is crying—

There's but one place to go and that is to God
And, dropping all pretense and pride,
We can pour out our problems without restraint
And gain strength with Him at our side—

And together we stand at life's crossroads
And view what we think is the end,
But God has a much bigger vision
And He tells us it's ONLY A BEND—
For the road goes on and is smoother,
And the "pause in the song" is a "rest"
And the part that's unsung and unfinished
Is the sweetest and richest and best—
So rest and relax and grow stronger,
LET GO and LET GOD share your load,
Your work is not finished or ended,
You've just come to "A BEND IN THE ROAD."

Helen Steiner Rice

Do we carry about with us a sense of God? Do we carry the thought of Him with us wherever we go? If not, we have missed the greatest part of life. Do we have that feeling and conviction of God's abiding presence wherever we go?

Henry Drummond

HEAVEN

Think of—
Stepping on shore, and finding it Heaven!
Of taking hold of a hand, and finding it God's hand.
Of breathing a new air, and finding it celestial air.
Of feeling invigorated, and finding it immortality.
Of passing from storm to tempest to an unbroken calm.
Of waking up, and finding it Home.

Author Unknown

INNER JOY

A FRAGILE MOMENT . . .

When Leonardo da Vinci was working on his painting "The Last Supper," he became angry with a certain man. Losing his temper he lashed the other fellow with bitter words and threats. Returning to his canvas he attempted to work on the face of Jesus, but was unable to do so. He was so upset he could not compose himself for the painstaking work. Finally he put down his tools and sought out the man and asked his forgiveness. The man accepted his apology and Leonardo was able to return to his workshop and finish painting the face of Jesus.

Author Unknown

MY PILOT

Dale Evans Rogers

Ships coming into port slow down to "pick up the pilot"—to take aboard a man who knows every rock and sandbar in the harbor and who can steer the ship safely through them to the dock. When the ship leaves the harbor, the same pilot comes aboard to take her out to deep water and the open sea, and then they "drop the pilot."

"Dropping the pilot" has always made me sad, whether it happens on a ship or in a human life, but "picking up the pilot" always thrills me. "Jesus, Saviour, pilot me," I sang as a child, and it means more to me now that I have put away childish things. I suppose I picked up and dropped a dozen pilots for my life's voyage, before He came

to guide me. Don't we all? When the boy is six he wants to be a fireman; at ten he would be either a cowpuncher or president; at fifteen an astronaut, then a lawyer, doctor or minister. We all pick out our heroes and worship and imitate them—dream that we may be like them when we grow up. We'd save a lot of trouble and frustration if we would pick up Christ as our Pilot while we are still young. Why must we wait half a lifetime before taking Him aboard?

I say there is no better pilot, for He has been at it longer. He was here with the first of men and even before that; He said, "Before Abraham was, I am." He was here before Abraham was here. "For by him were all things created, that are in heaven, and that are in earth, visible and invisible, whether they be thrones, or dominions, or

principalities, or powers: all things were created by him, and for him: And he is before all things, and by him all things consist." (Colossians 1:16-17) God in Christ *created* us; could you think of one better able to guide us?

One of the Russian astronauts said he looked out of the window of his little spaceship, up there in space, and he didn't see any angel, or any heaven, or any God. Poor little man! He was looking the wrong way in the wrong place. You can't see an atom either, but you know it's there, because we've put it to work. God made the atom and He made us, and He has made them work together, and if the atheist in the space capsule had looked a little more intelligently at man he'd have seen God at work, and heaven in the human heart. He can still find plenty of Christ-guided men, if he wants to look. . . .

We belong to this God in Christ, for He created us. Without Him, we are nothing. He is our next heartbeat. Before the earth was formed and after it shall have disappeared, Jesus *is*. He has always been and always will be, even after we stupid "scientists" have used His atom to blow our earth to bits. Only when we realize this and turn to Him and put *all* our trust in Him can we live life to its fullest. The most interesting and inspiring people I have met, the most *alive* people, have been dedicated Christians. I've known some outstanding Christian doctors, musicians, athletes, teachers, scientists (yes, scientists!), writers and businessmen who have taken Christ into their lives and they vibrate with His loving and dynamic power. If that's what you are looking for—power to live—I suggest you reach out and touch Him. . . .

Look at this Christ! Born in a stable when He might have been born in a palace, He was a King in a carpenter's house, in the home of obscure Joseph and Mary. He was not educated in the schools as our children are, yet at twelve He had a wisdom so

profound that He was an amazement to the teachers in the temple of Jerusalem. He was implicitly obedient to Joseph and Mary though He had power from His Father in heaven to still the waves and the storms of the human heart. He fed thousands with five loaves and two fishes; He healed with the mere touch of His hand and He raised more than one from the dead.

He was no weakling, this Christ. He was strong. In the carpenter shop at Nazareth He lifted long heavy beams of wood and did hard labor without benefit of machinery and electric tools. He walked long miles in the hot and dusty roads of Judea and Galilee, on errands of healing and pity, asking no pay but the following of His way and truth. Strong Himself, He knew well that most of us would be too weak to win His everlasting life by any efforts of our own, so in the end, He paid the price for our weakness and selfishness as He offered His blood to wash it all away, at the cross. He died there for multitudes of us whom He had never seen, yet loved.

Some thought it was all over when He died; they smiled, "Well, that's the last of *Him*!" It wasn't. The third day He rose and walked out of the tomb where they had laid Him, God in the flesh of man, proving that there was a life beyond the tomb for other men, bought for them on that cross. Then He went to sit at the right hand of His Father, to intercede for us with Him. . . .

This then is Jesus called the Christ. This is what He was, and what He did. This is the brief account of His brief, matchless life; even His worst enemies wonder at it and admit the glory and the power in it. I believe in Him, I believe all this about Him, not so much because I want to but because I have to. The evidence that He is all this and did all this is too strong for me to doubt. I believe that He is the Word, that it is He of whom John speaks when he tells of the Word being made flesh. I believe He is the Lamb without spot whom the prophet

predicted would come; I believe He is God's only Begotten, come to save. I believe it because He has saved me.

Often I am overwhelmed with the immensity of it all, and I feel completely inadequate and unworthy of such a Saviour, and unable to explain any of it. So much of the story of Jesus—the incarnation, the works of wonder, the resurrection—is too much for my small heart. I cannot grasp their full meaning, cannot begin to explain the mysteries involved. I am no trained theologian, but this I do know: Though the mystery remains, Jesus Christ has led me as a shepherd leads his uncomprehending sheep. He leads me in not just great moments of blazing crisis, at the great crucial moments of decision in my life, but—which may be more important—He leads me every day, every hour, in every little moment on the road I walk.

I have now disposed of all my property to my family. There is one thing more I wish I could give them, and that is the Christian religion. If they had that, and I had not given them one shilling, they would have been rich, and if they had not that, and I had given them all the world, they would be poor.

Patrick Henry

Blessed is the man that walketh not in the counsel of the ungodly, nor standeth in the way of sinners, nor sitteth in the seat of the scornful.

But his delight is in the law of the Lord; and in his law doth he meditate day and night.

And he shall be like a tree planted by the rivers of water, that bringeth forth his fruit in his season; his leaf also shall not wither; and whatsoever he doeth shall prosper.

Psalm 1:1-3

A VIGOROUS DISCIPLE

Norman Vincent Peale

He was a no-fooling sort of person. Anything could be accomplished if you had faith enough, so he believed. Indeed, this was the principle that motivated Fred R., one of the most enthusiastic and vigorous Christians of my experience. When he was changed by a Christian conversion he *really* changed.

But before his change he was a kind of wandering son of a good church family; not all that bad, perhaps, but neither was he in the kingdom of righteousness. He attended my church in New York occasionally, although he lived in Connecticut. I was not personally acquainted with him at the time. It seems that he was somewhat of a scoffer and had a particular dislike for the pastor of his church at home—called him a "stuffed shirt" and various other uncomplimentary designations.

One afternoon a friend telephoned him. "Hey, Fred, what are you doing tonight?" Fred fell into what turned out to be the Lord's trap. "Nothing. What's up?"

"The famous missionary Dr. E. Stanley Jones is preaching at a big meeting tonight in Hartford. Some of us are going. This man is one of the world's great preachers. Come along with us, since you have nothing scheduled."

"Are you kidding?" stormed Fred. "Me—go to hear a missionary? Come off it! Count me out. Nothing doing."

"Now look, Fred," said his friend, "I've done some things for you. You have nothing to do tonight. So humor me and come along." Fred, always genial, a good fellow ever desiring to oblige, capitulated. "Oh, O.K., if you can stand it, guess I can, too. I'll go with you."

So Fred went to Hartford and sat in the seat of the scornful. But not for long. Soon he sat upright from his slumped position, then leaned forward. Jones was getting to

him—or was it the Christ, whom Jones represented so well, who was getting to him? With irrefutable logic and undeniable persuasion the great missionary put forward the claims of Christ that had won so many thousands during his epoch-making ministry in India.

Fred was enthralled, captivated, convinced. And when Dr. Jones announced that he was about to dismiss the huge crowd and invite those who were ready to accept Christ to remain, Fred said to the others, "I'm sticking around. This guy Jones is terrific." The others also stayed, and in that after-meeting Fred made the decision, as he put it, "to go the rest of the way with Jesus Christ."

When Fred was convinced, he was really convinced. When he was sold, he was really sold. Now that he was converted he wanted to "get going." When the group got back to their Connecticut town, even though it was after one o'clock in the morning, Fred insisted on going to the minister's house. He pounded on the door. "Hey, Reverend, wake up!" he cried. The tousled head of the minister appeared at the window. "What's going on down there? Who wants me, and what about?"

"It's Fred R.," said our spiritually reborn friend. "I've just been converted and you are the first person I want to see."

"Well," said the startled pastor, "O.K., but why couldn't you be converted at a more convenient hour? Hold on and I'll come down."

Soon Fred was excitedly telling the minister about the events of the evening; how he had gone to the meeting in Hartford, heard Stanley Jones, and accepted Christ, and now his life was changed. "And since I've never liked you and have said all kinds of mean things about you, I wanted you to be the first one I saw after my conversion, to tell you that I've been wrong about you. I want to tell you

that now I love you and want to help you in the church in any way you want me to serve." The minister naturally was dumbfounded by the change in this young man, about whom he had an opinion that could not be considered the most favorable. But he responded in kind to the honest, enthusiastic outgoingness of the new convert and joined him in a prayer of thanksgiving for the great change which had come about in his life.

So they talked until night gave way to daybreak. "How about it if I rustle up some bacon and eggs, some toast and hot coffee?" said the pastor.

"I'm for that," agreed Fred, and soon the two men were consuming a man-sized breakfast. "Now," said Fred, "how can I help in the church? I want to get going in the Lord's work to make up for a lot of lost time." The pastor, still wary, parried the question by suggesting that they wait awhile to see what might develop. But Fred would brook no delay. "No, sir, I want to get at it. Let's turn the church and the town upside down for Jesus Christ."

"Well," said the pastor, bewildered by the vigorous new convert, "tell you what: I'll make you a member of the official board of the church. The board is meeting tonight. You be on hand and we will give you some kind of job in the church. What do you say to that?"

"O.K.," declared Fred, "that sounds pretty good. I'll be there tonight and let's get some action going." The exhausted pastor ushered his superenthusiastic nocturnal visitor out of the door and collapsed into a chair. "Brother," he asked himself, "what do I do with this guy now?"

That night at the board meeting Fred, not previously very interested in the church but now a board member, found his welcome a bit short of cordial. While the members were pleased to learn of his spiritual rebirth, they were still hesitant to

accept him in church leadership. When the treasurer's report was given, it indicated an $11,000 deficit in the current expense budget of the church. Fred heard this news with disbelief and excited concern. "Why," he asked, "should the church of God operate at a deficit? It's incredible, disgusting. Something must be done about this at once. I will start by giving $1,000 to wipe out that deficit. Come on, now, you fellows, pony up like I'm doing." The response was negligible, the atmosphere cool.

But Fred was not daunted. "I'll raise that budget deficit in a few days," he said confidently, and proceeded to do just that by vigorous and positive calling throughout the community. Despite his perhaps overly-enthusiastic and ill-advised aggressiveness, his sincerity and changed life became apparent and respected. He took hold of a sleepy and ineffective Sunday school class for teen-agers. By his dynamic attitude, his zeal, and his with-it program dealing with matters of interest to young people, he soon built it into the largest and best-conducted class of its kind in the state.

Regularly he would bring his class down to New York to our Marble Collegiate Church to attend the service in a body. His manner of doing this was characteristic. He would get me on the telephone and announce, "Hey, Norman, I'm bringing a big gang of kids down Sunday night to hear you talk. So for heaven's sake have something on the ball, will you?" Thus prompted, I would indeed try to come up with something of a vital spiritual nature to match the powerful spiritual vitality of this tremendous person.

So the years passed and Fred creatively touched the lives of boys and girls in a manner quite unequaled. Once, on an airplane en route to Chicago, a young businessman sitting beside me apparently recognized me. "I owe everything that I am," he told me in a choked-up voice, "to

dear old Fred R. What a guy! I love him, as do hundreds of other kids whom he saved. He certainly got me on the right track." Fred knew the joy and he had the power— the positive power of Jesus Christ. And others got it from him, and they got it good.

It all came about because someone cared enough to take him to a vital meeting and expose him to Christ. A preacher had a message that made sense, and he knew how to reach a mixed-up young man. And the man became a vigorous disciple, a memorable layman, a great teacher, a powerful motivator for Christ. He had the power and the joy.

No frown ever made a heart glad; no complaint ever made a dark day bright; no bitter word ever lightened a burden or made a rough road smooth; no grumbling ever made the sun shine in a home. The day needs the resolute step, the look of cheer, the smiling countenance, the kindly word.

Author Unknown

A CHILD'S KISS

A child's kiss
Set on thy sighing lips shall make thee glad;
A poor man served by thee shall make thee
  rich;
A sick man helped by thee shall make thee
  strong;
Thou shalt be served thyself by every sense
Of service which thou renderest.

Elizabeth Barrett Browning

Do the very best you can and leave the outcome to God.

Author Unknown

OUR LADY'S JUGGLER

Anatole France

In the days of King Louis there was a poor juggler in France, a native of Compiegne, Barnaby by name, who went about from town to town, performing feats of skill and strength. On fair days he would unfold an old worn-out carpet in the public square, and when by means of a jovial address, which he had learned of a very ancient juggler, and which he never varied in the least, he had drawn together the children and loafers, he assumed extraordinary attitudes, and balanced a tin plate on the tip of his nose. At first the crowd would feign indifference.

But when, supporting himself on his hands face downwards, he threw into the air six copper balls, which glittered in the sunshine, and caught them again with his feet; or when, throwing himself backwards until his heels and the nape of the neck met, giving his body the form of a perfect wheel, he would juggle in this posture with a dozen knives, a murmur of admiration would escape the spectators, and pieces of money rain down upon the carpet.

Nevertheless, like the majority of those who live by their wits, Barnaby of Compiegne had a great struggle to make a living.

Earning his bread by the sweat of his brow, he bore rather more than his share of the penalties consequent upon the misdoings of our father Adam.

Again, he was unable to work as constantly as he would have been willing to do. The warmth of the sun and the broad daylight were as necessary to enable him to display his brilliant parts as to the trees if flower and fruit should be expected of them. In wintertime he was nothing more than a tree stripped of its leaves, as if it were dead. The frozen ground was hard to the juggler, and, like the grasshopper of which Marie de France tells us, the inclement season caused him to suffer both cold

and hunger. But as he was simple-natured he bore his ills patiently.

He had never meditated on the origin of wealth, nor upon the inequality of human conditions. He believed firmly that if this life should prove hard, the life to come could not fail to redress the balance, and this hope upheld him. He did not resemble those thievish and miscreant Merry Andrews who sell their souls to the devil. He never blasphemed God's name; he lived uprightly, and although he had no wife of his own, he did not covet his neighbor's . . . . He was a worthy man who feared God, and was very devoted to the Blessed Virgin.

Never did he fail, on entering a church, to fall upon his knees before the image of the Mother of God, and offer up this prayer to her:

"Blessed Lady, keep watch over my life until it shall please God that I die, and when I am dead, ensure to me the possession of the joys of paradise."

Now, on a certain evening after a dreary wet day, as Barnaby pursued his road, sad and bent, carrying under his arm his balls and knives wrapped up in his old carpet, on the watch for some barn where, though he might not sup, he might sleep, he perceived on the road, going in the same direction as himself, a monk, whom he saluted courteously. And as they walked at the same rate they fell into conversation with one another.

"Fellow traveler," said the monk, "how comes it about that you are clothed all in green? Is it perhaps in order to take the part of a jester in some mystery play?"

"Not at all, good father," replied Barnaby. "Such as you see me, I am called Barnaby, and for my calling I am a juggler. There would be no pleasanter calling in the world if it would always provide one with daily bread."

"Friend Barnaby," returned the monk, "be careful what you say. There is no calling more pleasant than the monastic life. Those

who lead it are occupied with the praises of God, the Blessed Virgin, and the saints; and, indeed, the religious life is one ceaseless hymn to the Lord."

Barnaby replied, "Good father, I own that I spoke like an ignorant man. Your calling cannot be in any respect compared to mine, and although there may be some merit in dancing with a penny balanced on a stick on the tip of one's nose, it is not a merit which comes within hail of your own. Gladly would I, like you, good father, sing my office day by day, and especially the office of the most Holy Virgin, to whom I have vowed a singular devotion. In order to embrace the monastic life I would willingly abandon the art by which from Soissons to Beauvais I am well known in upwards of six hundred towns and villages."

The monk was touched by the juggler's simplicity, and as he was not lacking in discernment, he at once recognized in Barnaby one of those men of whom it is said in the Scriptures: Peace on earth to men of good will. And for this reason he replied, "Friend Barnaby, come with me, and I will have you admitted into the monastery of which I am prior. He who guided Saint Mary of Egypt in the desert set me upon your path to lead you into the way of salvation."

It was in this manner, then, that Barnaby became a monk. In the monastery into which he was received the religious vied with one another in the worship of the Blessed Virgin, and in her honor each employed all the knowledge and all the skill which God had given him.

The prior on his part wrote books dealing according to the rules of scholarship with the virtues of the Mother of God.

Brother Maurice, with a deft hand, copied out these treatises upon sheets of vellum.

Brother Alexander adorned the leaves with delicate miniature painting. . . .

Brother Marbode was likewise one of the most loving children of Mary.

He spent all his days carving images in stone, so that his beard, his eyebrows, and his hair were white with dust, and his eyes continually swollen and weeping; but his strength and cheerfulness were not diminished, although he was now well gone in years.

. . . In the priory, moreover, were poets who composed hymns in Latin, both in prose and verse, in honor of the Blessed Virgin Mary, and amongst the company was even a brother from Picardy who sang the miracles of Our Lady in rhymed verse and in the vulgar tongue.

Being a witness of this emulation in praise and the glorious harvest of their labors, Barnaby mourned his own ignorance and simplicity.

"Alas!" he sighed, as he took his solitary walk in the little shelterless garden of the monastery, "wretched wight that I am, to be unable, like my brothers, worthily to praise the Holy Mother of God, to whom I have vowed my whole heart's affection. Alas! alas! I am but a rough man and unskilled in the arts, and I can render you in service, Blessed Lady, neither edifying sermons, nor ingenious paintings, nor statues truthfully sculptured, nor verses whose march is measured to the beat of feet. No gift have I, alas!"

After this fashion he groaned and gave himself up to sorrow. But one evening, when the monks were spending their hour of liberty in conversation, he heard one of them tell the tale of a religious man who could repeat nothing other than the Ave Maria. This poor man was despised for his ignorance; but after his death there issued forth from his mouth five roses in honor of the five letters of the name Mary (Marie), and thus his sanctity was made manifest.

Whilst he listened to this narrative, Barnaby marveled yet once again at the loving-kindness of the Virgin; but the

lesson of that blessed death did not avail to console him, for his heart overflowed with zeal, and he longed to advance the glory of his Lady, who is in heaven.

How to compass this he sought, but could find no way, and day by day he became the more cast down, when one morning he awakened filled full with joy, hastened to the chapel, and remained there alone for more than an hour. After dinner he returned to the chapel once more.

And, starting from that moment, he repaired daily to the chapel at such hours as it was deserted, and spent within it a good part of the time which the other monks devoted to the liberal and mechanical arts. His sadness vanished, nor did he any longer groan.

A demeanor so strange awakened the curiosity of the monks.

These began to ask one another for what purpose Brother Barnaby could be indulging so persistently in retreat.

The prior, whose duty it is to let nothing escape him in the behavior of his children in religion, resolved to keep a watch over Barnaby during his withdrawals to the chapel. One day, then, when he was shut up there after his custom, the prior, accompanied by two of the older monks, went to discover through the chinks in the door what was going on within the chapel.

They saw Barnaby before the altar of the Blessed Virgin, head downwards, with his feet in the air, and he was juggling with six balls of copper and a dozen knives. In honor of the Holy Mother of God he was performing those feats, which aforetime had won him most renown. Not recognizing that the simple fellow was thus placing at the service of the Blessed Virgin his knowledge and skill, the two old monks exclaimed against the sacrilege.

The prior was aware how stainless was Barnaby's soul, but he concluded that he had been seized with madness. They were all three preparing to lead him swiftly from the chapel, when they saw the Blessed Virgin descend the steps of the altar and advance to wipe away with a fold of her azure robe the sweat which was dropping from her juggler's forehead.

Then the prior, falling upon his face upon the pavement, uttered these words, "Blessed are the simple-hearted, for they shall see God."

"Amen!" responded the old brethren, and kissed the ground.

THANKSGIVING

For each new morning, with its light,
    Father, we thank Thee,
For rest and shelter of the night,
    Father, we thank Thee,
For health and food, for love and friends,
For everything Thy goodness sends,
    Father, in heaven, we thank Thee.

Ralph Waldo Emerson

ENOUGH STARS TO GO AROUND

Marjorie Holmes

It's good to be a woman when . . .

Your husband suggests, "Let's sit on the patio and watch the stars. They look different tonight."

As they do. Instead of peppering the sky in their usual profusion, they climb its infinite reaches like ladders of light. The very constellations have assumed a new position, leading the eye up and up these diamond-studded stairs. The Milky Way is a plume of silver smoke.

The children, bound for bed, come spilling down to join you, trailing blankets, and you all huddle and cuddle together, remarking the thrilling mystery of the heavens.

"Just think, maybe the people on Mars are looking down at us right now wondering what we're like."

"Not down, stupid, they'd be looking up too. Besides, you can't tell from the pictures whether there's life there yet."

"There will be when we get there. Only I'm heading for the moon first, man. It's closer to home, easier to get back."

"What makes you think you're going?" . . . "Oh, I'm going, all right." They speak of space travel with the excited confidence with which people once watched ships set forth across uncharted seas, or the first airplane wing daringly off from a pasture.

"I think I'll visit that big green star over there first," the little one announces. "What's its name? It's my star, it winked at me."

"That's Jupiter," an older one advises importantly. "And it's not green and it didn't wink at you, you just think so. Besides, it's not yours."

"It is too my star if I want it, isn't it, Daddy?"

"Okay, sure, take any star you want."

"I choose that one!" another voice pipes up. "That big white one."

"No, no, that's my star, I saw it first!"

"For heaven's sake, don't fight," you laugh. "There are plenty of stars to go around."

HELP YOURSELF TO HAPPINESS

Everybody, everywhere seeks happiness, it's
 true
But finding it and keeping it seems difficult
 to do,
Difficult because we think that happiness is
 found
Only in the places where wealth and fame
 abound—

And so we go on searching in "palaces of
 pleasure"
Seeking recognition and monetary
 treasure,
Unaware that happiness is just a "state of
 mind"

Within the reach of everyone who takes
 time to be kind—

For in making Others Happy we will be
 happy, too,
For happiness you give away returns to
 "shine on you."
For Happiness is something we create in
 our mind,
It's not something you search for and so
 seldom find—

It's just waking up and beginning the day
By counting our blessings and kneeling
 to pray—
It's giving up thoughts that breed
 discontent
And accepting what comes as a "gift
 heaven-sent"—

It's giving up wishing for things we
 have not
And making the best of whatever we've
 got—
It's knowing that life is determined for us,
And pursuing our tasks without fret, fume
 or fuss—
For it's by completing what God gives us
 to do
That we find real contentment and
 happiness, too.

Helen Steiner Rice

Let the heavens rejoice, and let the earth be glad; let the sea roar, and the fulness thereof. Let the field be joyful, and all that is therein: then shall all the trees of the wood rejoice before the Lord.

Psalm 96: 11, 12, 13

"He that is of a merry heart hath a continual feast."

Proverbs 15:15

Index of Authors

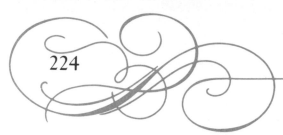

224